THE
GOLDEN
AGE OF
FENDER

1946-1970

THE GOLDEN AGE OF FENDER

1946-1970

martin kelly
terry foster
paul kelly

This book is dedicated
to Judy Kelly and Bob Trick

The Golden Age of Fender
by Martin Kelly, Terry Foster, Paul Kelly

First published in Great Britain in 2010 by Cassell Illustrated,
an imprint of Octopus Publishing Group Limited
Endeavour House, 189 Shaftesbury Avenue
London, WC2H 8JY
www.octopusbooks.co.uk

An Hachette UK Company
www.hachette.co.uk

Distributed in the US and Canada by Octopus Books USA
c/o Hachette Book Group USA
237 Park Avenue South, New York, NY 10017

ISBN: 978 1 84403 666 0

A CIP record for this book is available from the British Library and the
Library of Congress.

Commissioning Editor – Matthew Clayton
Project Editors – Georgina Atsiaris and Laura Price
Text – Martin Kelly
Design and Photography – Paul Kelly
Foreword – Terry Foster
Copy-editor – Louise Chandler
Proofreader – Jo Richardson
Production – Caroline Alberti
Indexer – John Noble
Typesetting – Lora Findlay

Set in Franklin Gothic LT and Century LT

Colour reproduction Hong Kong
Printed and bound in China

If you have any photographs, guitars or ephemera that you feel would make
a worthy addition to any future editions of this book please contact the
authors via www.vintageguitarbooks.com

foreword

Leo Fender was a simple man who loved music and musicians, but who had no real musical aptitude himself. He was a methodical thinker with a passion for perfection and an ear for tone. A workaholic who, by his own admission, "…never had any time to do anything but to build guitars and listen to 'em," his genius was in his ability to take his own ideas and refine them, incorporating the suggestions of musicians, and surround himself with people who were able to fill the gaps in his skill set. Quite simply, Leo Fender was one of the greatest industrial designers of the 20th century. His inventions were revolutionary, versatile, practical and emotionally engaging.

Fender guitars and amplifiers are the pinnacle of contemporary musical instrument design. They are the essence of the governing design ideology of the 20th century, the Modern Movement, and its guiding principle of 'form follows function.' It is unusual for an industrial design to remain in production without alteration for several decades, as Fender's have. Most manufactured goods are transitory in nature, evolving as public tastes change or made obsolete by advances in technology. Leo's designs, however, had an emotional impact and have remained unchanged for over 50 years, as perfect today as the day they were released.

Leo's greatest achievement was, without question, the Stratocaster. Its design was the perfect marriage of form and function with its organic, feminine, body-hugging curves. At the same time, it was incredibly futuristic and its name was perfect for the 'Jet Age'. When Buddy Holly appeared for the first time on *The Ed Sullivan Show* in December 1957 with his Stratocaster, you could forgive the audience for thinking that he was wielding a ray gun instead of a guitar. Its shape, and the sounds he made with it, seemed to be from another world. The success of the Fender Stratocaster and the Telecaster reinvigorated original design within the guitar industry, and many other iconic 1950s designs, such as Gibson's Les Paul, Flying V and Explorer, would not have come about without them.

The best of Fender's designs aren't simply tools with which to make music. They are part of the cultural landscape of the 20th century and meaningful to each successive generation that experiences them. So pervasive were Fender's designs in the latter half of the last century that the pop culture iconography would not be complete without the inclusion of the Stratocaster.

Leo Fender's influence on the course of popular music is immeasurable. Many of the sounds heard in recorded and live music have been created using his instruments. However, he seemed largely unaffected by his role in popular music. He barely acknowledged the most famous and influential artists who used his gear, such as Buddy Holly, Jimi Hendrix, Eric Clapton, Jeff Beck and Jimmy Page. When asked about his accomplishments, he recalled the western swing bandleaders and musicians he loved when he started the company, such as Hank Thompson, Wade Ray, Bob Wills and

Spade Cooley. Leo was always proud of what he had achieved and, although he created some wonderful instruments after Fender at Music Man and G&L, he was never able to better himself, always returning to the essence of his original designs. Nonetheless, his quest for perfection never stopped and, despite his declining physical health in later years, he worked every day until the day before he died in 1991, aged 81. He was, as Richard Smith, the author of *Fender: The Sound Heard 'Round The World*, noted, 'the personification of the American spirit of invention'.

The success of Fender during the golden age was not dependent upon the genius of Leo alone. His business partner, Don Randall, who is often forgotten when Fender is written about, was an integral part of the organization during that period. Don, as President of Fender Sales, was responsible for all sales and marketing activities; he named almost all Fender products and advised Leo on what was needed in the company's product range. Don was the public face of the company at trade shows and to the dealers and as such he built up a huge dealer network and created innovative sales promotions and marketing strategies that were revolutionary in the 1950s. Don even negotiated the $13.2 million sale of the company to CBS in 1965, a record price for a musical instrument manufacturer at the time.

Don's work at Fender Sales did much to shape the company's aesthetic, contextualizing Leo's creations and making them relevant to the buying public. Much of this was done through print advertising in major music trade magazines such as *Downbeat*, *Musical Merchandise* and *Country And Western Jamboree*. The musical instrument business in the late 1940s and early 1950s was conservative and staid and the supporting sales material reflected that. Unexciting, matter-of-fact advertisements were the norm. Fender's efforts were no exception, until 1957 when Don hired the Los Angeles-based Perine/Jacoby advertising agency. Within months of being retained, Fender's ads began to reflect the creative, youthful and progressive nature of their product line. This differentiated Fender from the competition in exactly the way the instruments had already done. Bob Perine instantly understood the product and the target audience. His design style was clean, with great use of white space, and featured wonderful photography that instantly drew the reader in. Bob's creative campaigns, like the long-running 'You won't part with yours either' series, set a new standard and his design style was reflected in Fender's catalogs and price lists. Fender marketed their instruments as consumer products rather than just tools for musicians. This was an industry first, and Don and Leo made sure there was a Fender at every price point to take advantage of the postwar boom in America.

Neither Don nor Leo fully appreciated one another's contribution to their collective success. Leo told Richard Smith in the 1980s that Don's head was 'lost in a golf bag,' and Don was known to have called Leo a 'weirdo' when asked if he thought him a genius. As uneasy as the relationship may have seemed, given the playful jabs at one another in later years, they continued to invest together, even after the sale of the company. As late as 1981, they still jointly owned a parcel of land in Riverside, California. It was the alchemy of their differences that made the partnership work and left us with a legacy that has a broad cultural impact.

The evolution of Fender's designs – from planks of wood to pop culture icons – is outlined here. Just as Leo toiled away every day on something he loved, so too is this book a labour of love. It was born of a chance meeting in The Angel pub in London's West End on a chilly Sunday afternoon in December 2000. Nearly ten years and thousands of hours in the making, the best Fender guitars, amplifiers and ephemera from the finest collections in the world grace these pages. The photography, layout and overall design represent our collective vision of a holistic celebration of the Fender aesthetic. This is the culmination of our passion and obsession with all things Fender that began with our abiding love of music. The beautiful sounds we heard growing up led us first to discover the instruments that made them and then, ultimately, to the source – the man who changed the way music was created and heard forever: Leo Fender.

early history

"You never change things by fighting the existing reality. To change something, build a new model that makes the existing model obsolete." This quote from acclaimed 20th-century architect, inventor and futurist Buckminster Fuller perfectly describes the Fender ethos during the company's golden age. Leo Fender would change the conventional rules for producing electrified musical instruments and, in turn, alter the path of popular music and culture forever. His contribution to electrified music, rock'n'roll, country'n'western, rhythm'n'blues, rock and pop during the second half of the 20th century is immense. Without his incredible innovations, popular music, as we know it, would not have been possible.

Born in a barn in a small suburb of Los Angeles on 10 August 1909, Clarence Leonadis Fender was the first child of Clarence 'Monte' and Harriet Fender, two newlyweds setting up to farm on land that lay just outside the small town of Fullerton in Southern California. The family home was not yet built and the Fenders divided a barn on Lone Oak Ranch into two halves, sharing its roof with farm equipment and livestock. When the house was completed a year or so later, the farm was beginning to flourish. From an early age, Leo had an inquisitive mind and was always looking for solutions to problems; ways of fixing things that didn't work as they should or could. Although he would become a proficient saxophone player during his teenage years, he never learned to play the guitar, the instrument with which his name is so closely associated.

During the early part of the 1900s, Fullerton, California was a small town that had grown up around the Santa Fe Railroad. It was the main stopping point between Los Angeles and San Diego, and because of its rich, fertile soil and sunny climate, it had become a major producer of citrus fruits – in particular oranges, from which the area became known as Orange County. Fender's parents had set up growing vegetables, melons and, later, oranges on the outskirts of Fullerton where it bordered with Anaheim. Leo's father did well selling his produce from a truck in Long Beach and Leo's upbringing could be described as comfortable by the time he attended Orangethorpe School in Fullerton. Tragedy befell the young Leo when he lost his right eye as a result of a cancerous tumour. He would spend the rest of his life with one glass eye, an obstacle that would not deter him.

During his early teens, Leo developed a keen interest in electronics. Radio was still new and exciting, and he loved listening to the music broadcast by local stations. Before long, Leo was able to build his own simple radios and would take on repairs for friends. Graduating from high school in 1928, Leo spent the next ten years in various jobs, mainly accountancy based, while repairing radios by night. During the early 1930s, he began to build and supply public address systems for local dances and functions, which strengthened his knowledge of electronics. Leo found himself out of work in 1938 and decided it was time to take to the radio repair business – his real love – full time. He borrowed $600 and set up the Fender Radio Service in Fullerton. Business was good. Leo quickly earned himself a reputation for reliable, quality workmanship, and by

1940, he'd moved to larger premises at 112 South Spadra, Fullerton, and taken on staff. The shop soon became a retail outlet for all sorts of electrical goods of the day, including radios, record players, amplifiers and television sets. It also sold records and sheet music. Leo was always keen to examine the items he sold and repaired at the shop to figure out exactly how they worked and why they would sometimes fail. His knowledge and expertise in electronics was rapidly growing.

Over the coming months and years, Fender's little shop was a magnet for local musicians and music lovers alike. When Leo was asked to repair lap steel guitars and their matching amplifiers by local musicians, he would often spend time chatting with them, gaining valuable insight into their world and their needs as working professionals.

The lap steel, or Hawaiian guitar, had become extremely popular during the 1920s and 1930s. Usually featuring six strings, the instrument rests flat on the player's lap, one hand picking the strings while the other slides a metal bar over the strings to produce the notes and melody. The instrument's history stretches back to Hawaii in the late 1800s where players adapted their acoustic Spanish guitars for this style of playing. It produces an exotic, romantic sound reminiscent of faraway places, which quickly caught on and swept through America and Europe in the early 1900s. During the 1920s, Hawaiian guitar was adopted by a new breed of musician who played a fresh style of music that fused rural cowboy and folk music with New Orleans jazz and swing. The new music was called western swing and the bands that played it were often

large in number, featuring drums, double bass, guitars, fiddles and a horn section. In order for the Hawaiian guitar to be heard among all this instrumentation, players began experimenting with primitive pickups and amplifiers during the late '20s and early '30s. In response, the California-based Rickenbacker company debuted the first commercially available electric lap steel guitar in 1931. It was made from solid aluminium and is recognized by many as the first solid-body electric guitar design. Nicknamed the frying pan because of its circular body, long neck and metal construction, the guitar went on to be not only successful but very influential. A solid-body design, instead of hollow, meant that an instrument could be turned up to much greater volume before it would cause the amplifier to feed back or distort. This was just what the new players wanted: loud, clear amplified music that could keep up with the drums, fiddles and horns of the bandstand. Western swing flourished in the southwestern states of Texas and Southern California, and would play a big part in Fender's early success long before the term rock'n'roll had been coined.

Of the many visitors to the Fender Radio Service shop during the early '40s, two people in particular would go on to play a huge role: Donald D. Randall and Clayton Kauffman. Don Randall was working as a salesman for a local radio parts supplier that Leo used and would often visit the store. He shared Leo's interest in radio and, as well as his own homemade radios, he too had built PA systems for local functions. As the pair got to know each other, they often discussed the idea of working together. Leo, ever the inventor,

suggested various hair-brained schemes – often nothing to do with musical instruments – but nothing reached fruition. As America entered World War Two in 1941, Don was conscripted and the pair lost touch.

At around the same time, a local musician by the name of Clayton Orr Kauffman (known simply as 'Doc' to friends) stopped by the shop to have his amplifier repaired. Doc was a respected player and, like Leo, fancied himself as an inventor. Indeed, he had two patents to his name already: the first was for a vibrato unit – the Vibrola – he had designed for guitar; another was for a mechanical version of the same device. Both designs had been successfully put into production and marketed by Rickenbacker. Doc had a small workshop at home where he would tinker for hours on a variety of projects. Leo, who was becoming more interested in the guitar and amplifiers, was impressed by Doc's inventions and the pair got on well.

Following the attack on Pearl Harbour in December 1941, Doc began work at the Douglas aircraft factory in LA making jigs. Leo was not eligible for conscription, because of the eye he had lost as a child, so continued work as normal at the radio shop. Because new electrical goods were in short supply, the repair work mounted up and Fender was busier than ever. He approached Doc and asked if he could help out with repairs during the evenings. It was during these times that Leo discussed an idea he'd had for a new type of pickup for a guitar, one where the strings passed through the center of the magnetic coil, not over the top as on standard pickups.

(preceding page) Leo Fender at Orangethorpe School, Fullerton, 1924

(this page, top) Leo mans the Fender mobile PA system in 1941

(above, left to right) Clayton 'Doc' Kauffman, Don Randall and Leo Fender

Leo showed his ideas to Doc, and in 1943, they built a crude instrument that featured the new pickup. It was a Spanish guitar with a fretted fingerboard that the pair had ordered in, pre-made, from a catalog. Due to the wartime shortage of materials, the solid wooden body was incredibly small and the instrument looked more like a lap steel than a conventional Spanish. That said, it was a huge leap forward for Leo – not only his first guitar but his first solid-body design. The new instrument was placed in the shop for rental, and although it didn't receive much attention at the time, it has become a milestone piece and currently resides at the Acuff Museum in Nashville, Tennessee. Doc and Leo quickly realized that the new pickup (dubbed by Fender the 'Direct String Pickup') suited lap steel playing more than Spanish guitar. They hatched a plan to start up a new company, the K&F (Kauffman and Fender) Manufacturing Corporation, to produce a range of lap steels and matching amplifiers, and during the spring of 1945, the pair built six sets of their new design. These first sets, probably the only ones produced during wartime, differed from later models in that the guitar featured a square-shaped headstock with three tuning keys on each side. The speaker grille on the amplifier carried a logo with the letters K&F and a lightning bolt through the middle.

At around the same time the first K&F sets were being produced, Leo, Doc and another employee of the radio shop, Clifton Abbot, were working on a novel design for a device that changed records on a record player. It was a simpler, more effective design than those on the market at the time and a patent was filed by all three men in May 1945. The invention was licensed to the Voice Of Music (VM) company in October of that year for an initial advance of $5000, a lot of money back in 1945. Leo accidentally allowed the patent to lapse later, a mistake he would subsequently estimate cost him over $1 million in lost revenue. The pioneering days for Leo proved to be a steep learning curve.

World War Two ended in September 1945 and Leo and Doc set themselves a goal to get the K&F business up and running as soon as possible. Other musical instrument manufacturers had had production suspended by wartime activities and Leo and Doc wanted to seize the opportunity to get their new product into the marketplace as soon as possible. With the income from the record changer, new manufacturing equipment was purchased, along with war-surplus vacuum tubes, capacitors, wire and speakers to be used in the manufacture of the K&F sets. Full production was underway by November 1945.

The new K&F steels featured an improved design with an angled three-a-side headstock that gave each string a straighter path towards the tuning keys and, ultimately, better tuning stability. The bodies were of pine construction, finished in a gray crinkle paint that required baking on, and many of the early instruments were finished in Doc's kitchen oven. The pair worked hard and enlisted the skills of Ray Massie from the radio shop in amplifier design and assembly, and Dale Hyatt for guitar and amp cabinet assembly. By early 1946, this small team was producing 30 – 40 guitars a week from Leo's shop. K&F could best be described as a cottage industry at this point, selling directly to the customer and local music schools via the radio shop outlet. However, all this was about to change.

Don Randall was discharged from the army in February 1946. Filled with dreams of starting a new life and a new career, he was quickly approached by an old business colleague named Francis Hall who ran a large electronic parts distributor called the Radio & Television Equipment Company – Radio-Tel for short. Francis offered Don the job of general manager, and although it wasn't exactly what he'd had in mind, he accepted the position and began working for Hall only days after leaving the services. It wasn't long before Don looked Leo up again and he was impressed by the new K&F steel guitar sets he'd started producing. No hair-brained schemes this time. These were, in Don's own words, "something you could sell that every Tom, Dick and Harry wasn't selling." Ambitious and driven, Don was quick to make Leo an offer he couldn't refuse. Radio-Tel would guarantee 5000 orders if Leo would give them exclusive rights to distribute K&F products, so a deal was signed between the two companies on 1 March 1946.

The future looked bright. But, as Leo started to gear towards larger-scale production, Doc hit him with the news that he no longer wanted to continue with K&F. He didn't share Leo's optimism for the venture and was worried that he would lose money he had recently inherited. The two parted company amicably in mid-1946, with Doc taking back several of the tools they had bought together, and it was agreed that Leo would carry on alone. In his characteristic penny-pinching way, Leo continued to make K&F steels until all the existing nameplates had been used up. This would have been around September 1946, only nine months after full-scale production began. Today, K&F lap steels are rare finds; the matching amplifiers rarer still. Doc and Leo remained the best of friends right up until Doc's death in June 1990. He never begrudged his friend's success or the chance he missed out on.

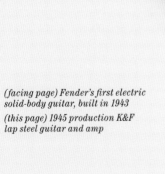

(facing page) Fender's first electric solid-body guitar, built in 1943

(this page) 1945 production K&F lap steel guitar and amp

lap steels

Long before Leo Fender began mass production of electric guitars and basses, lap steel guitars would provide the bread and butter of his business as it slowly grew during the late '40s. His interest in these small, basic instruments, and the amplifiers that accompanied them, would unlock the doors to all his future creations. Many features that became standard on his electric Spanish and bass guitars were pioneered on his student-model lap steels. Such was the popularity of Hawaiian and western swing music in the late '40s and early '50s that many towns and cities across America had a music school or retail outlet that offered lessons in playing the lap steel. Student sets were affordable and often offered by music retailers, keen to sell an accompanying course of lessons, on hire purchase terms. This enabled even those on a modest budget to get on the bandwagon.

K&F launched at the perfect moment, just as World War Two ended and people turned to music as a form of escape. Production between K&F lap steels and the first badged as Fender was seamless. "We had the same employees; it grew out of it. I just continued and changed the name," Leo told guitar historian Tom Wheeler in the 1980s. Early K&F and Fender steels show a gradual evolution in design from 1945 to 1949. All feature variations of the Direct String Pickup that Leo and Doc developed in 1943, mounted to a chromed control plate with simple volume and tone controls. Early

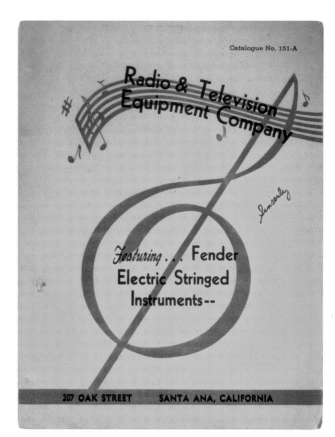

(above) Radio Tel's 1947 Fender catalog (below) The first Fender factory, Fullerton 1950

K&Fs were made from pine and featured straight body sides. These were finished in a gray crinkle paint with fret markers added in white. A smart enamel badge with the lightning bolt K&F logo in black, gold and red was fixed to the face of the headstock and a basic bone nut elevated the strings. Within a few months, K&F steels incorporated an improved design with a combination chrome headstock plate and nut. Soon afterwards, bodies were produced from selected hardwoods, such as maple or walnut, and finished in clear lacquer. The last of the K&Fs, produced during the spring and summer months of 1946, featured a more elegant body design with curved sides and a chrome metal fingerboard with black-painted position markers. This model was carried over by Leo and became the first Fender lap steel, the De Luxe, debuting in late summer 1946. The only differences between the K&F and the Fender De Luxe were a restyled body shape, control panel and a new logo – still featuring the lightning bolt design – impressed into the headstock plate, proclaiming: "Fender Electric Instrument Co – Fullerton, California." Leo was on his own now, but had already found the perfect ally in Don Randall at Radio-Tel. Don knew Leo was on to something good, something he could sell, and the pair were about to embark on an incredible journey together.

In December 1946, Fender set up his first factory in two steel buildings on Santa Fe Avenue, just across the street from Fullerton railroad station. Although the buildings were small, just 60ft by 30ft each, they marked a huge step for Leo. The expansion had drained his limited finances and

he soon needed an influx of cash to keep his business afloat. In January 1947, Fender reluctantly mortgaged his factory to Radio-Tel owner Francis Hall for $14,000. It was a move he had to make, but it didn't rest easy with Leo, who felt that it gave Hall the upper hand in their business dealings. Fender was eager to repay the debt as fast as possible, while claiming Hall was slow paying through sums owed to him via the distribution agreement. Although the loan – a generous offer and a big risk on F.C. Hall's part – had saved Fender, it created an atmosphere of mistrust between the two men that would only deepen as the years passed. Hall would send letters to Fender, badgering him to increase the production at his small factory, and the two men often fell out while Randall was left to mediate.

With a vested interest in the new business, Radio-Tel wasted no time in promoting the new Fender brand and by mid-1947 had both a small fold-out catalog and a dealer version worked up that featured a whole range of new Fender instruments. Leo was now producing three amplifiers, three lap steels and a big twin-neck table steel, 'The Professional,' which was aimed squarely at working musicians. The K&Fs had sold well but these products were superior and Fender was quickly gaining a reputation for quality workmanship. The three lap steels produced between 1946 and 1949 were all variations on a basic theme to suit budget requirements. Bottom of the range in 1947 was the Princeton, with a single volume control, priced at just $36.50. Next came the De Luxe, with volume and tone controls, priced at $54.50, proving that

(facing page, left to right) 1945 K&F lap steel – Gray Crinkle finish, 1946 K&F – Mahogany, 1946 K&F – Maple, 1947 Fender De Luxe – Walnut

(below) 1953 Fender Deluxe – Blond

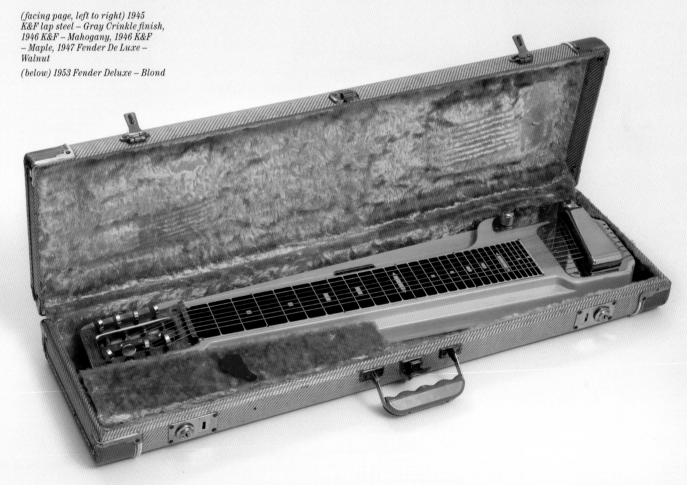

tone didn't come cheap in the late '40s. At the top of the range sat the Organ Button model. This was, essentially, a De Luxe with an added tone circuit that enabled muted bass sounds via a small red button mounted to the control panel. This extra feature would set the buyer back a grand total of $64.50, and for protection, hard cases covered in striped luggage linen were available for an additional $21.00.

Fender experimented with pickup designs during the late 1940s, and in 1949, he redesigned his Direct String Pickup with a coil that fanned out at one end to aid bass frequencies. The new pickup looked smarter and more upmarket than the earlier types, and the De Luxe was completely redesigned to accommodate it. A heavier body design, with cutaways that ran down each side and a new tuning gear assembly recessed into the head of the guitar was offered in either six- or eight-string combinations. The De Luxe, now named Deluxe, had evolved into a decidedly more professional model, leaving room for a new Fender lap steel to fill the gap

(facing page, left to right) 1951 Champion – Blue, 1950 Champion – Gray, 1954 Champion – Yellow

(this page, left to right) 1952 Champion – Green, 1950 Champion – Copper

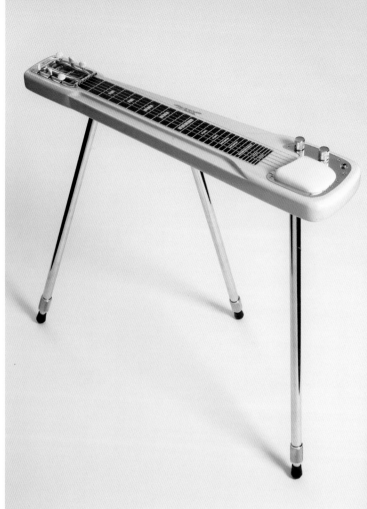

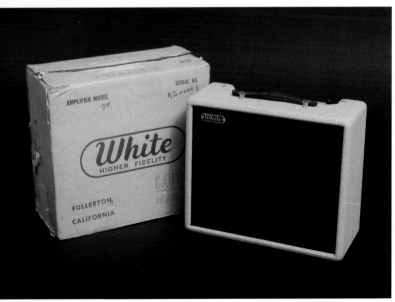

*(top left, left to right) 1956 Champ
– Desert Sand, 1960 Studio Deluxe –
Desert Sand, 1955 White – Pale Blue*

(top right) 1956 White – Pale Blue

*(above) 1955 White amp with its
original packing box*

in the student market. The Champion, also launched in 1949, has become a classic and sold in huge numbers throughout the 1950s and early '60s. The key to its success lay in a brand-new pickup design, an efficient yet compact unit that sat under the strings. It featured six individual magnets, one for each string, and a single coil of wire that wrapped around these to produce a bright, crisp tone ideally suited to Hawaiian lap steel playing. To partner the new student steel, Leo had also designed a small Champion 4-watt amp. Thousands of 'Champ' sets would be sold during the golden age, giving many budding musicians their first Fender experience.

Early Champion steels were simple, solid-body designs – not unlike Fender's early student guitars – with machine keys mounted in strips of three on each side to the back of the headstock. Bodies were now covered in a layer of imitation pearl-effect plastic usually referred to as 'pearloid' or 'mother of toilet seat.' Pearloid, usually yellow in color, was heated and stretched over the front and sides of Champion steels, while backs were painted a matching shade to cover the wood beneath. Though most Champ steels from the early '50s were produced in yellow pearloid, blue examples were occasionally manufactured and rare instruments, perhaps experiments or trade show pieces, have surfaced in gray, green and copper shades.

In mid-1955, the Champion was completely overhauled and renamed the Champ. Pearloid was done away with in favour of a new painted finish called Desert Sand and the body design

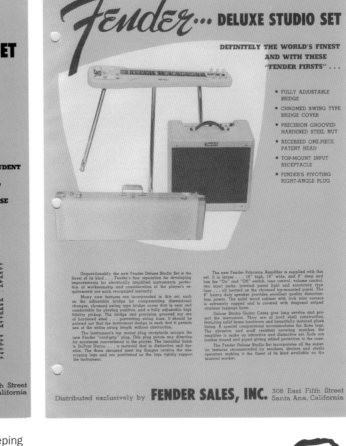

was brought in line with the Deluxe, featuring wide, sweeping cutaways running down both sides, upon one of which a Fender decal was placed. Machine keys were now housed in a recessed chrome unit and plastic tuner buttons and control knobs were black to distinguish the Champ from a new sister model, the Studio Deluxe. While essentially the same as the Champ, the Studio Deluxe featured a thicker, heavier body with detachable chrome legs, white tuner buttons and chromed volume and tone knobs. The Deluxe also saw changes to its layout in 1955 as the old Direct String Pickup was replaced with a pair of single coils that sat under the strings, and detachable legs were included. These three remained in production virtually unchanged throughout Fender's golden age. The year 1955 also saw the introduction of Fender-made lap steels manufactured under the White brand name. In a sly move to circumvent distribution arrangements that gave certain retailers exclusivity over Fender products, Leo produced a lap steel named in honour of factory manager Forrest White. These were essentially redesigned Studio Deluxe guitars finished in an off-white, almost blue, color with white plastic bridge covers and matching amplifier. Leo and Don neglected to inform their factory manager of the new instrument and he was understandably surprised upon seeing one. Although the heyday of lap steel playing has long since passed, these little guitars have stood the test of time and bear witness to the birth of the Fender operation before Leo would refine his ideas in an electric Spanish design.

woodie amplifiers 1946 – 1948

The first generation of amplifiers to carry the Fender name are affectionately known as 'Woodies.' Almost Art Deco in design, they are instantly recognisable with their natural wood cabinets, large wooden handles and brightly colored red, blue or gold grille cloths that feature two or three chrome-plated strips running from top to bottom. The amplifier cabinets were constructed from hand-rubbed, 'lustrously finished' hardwoods including dark mahogany, black walnut, blond maple and oak. Woodie amps were intended as companions to the lap steel and double-neck steel guitars that Fender was producing at the time and were often sold as sets. Lap steel players usually play seated with the amplifier placed at their feet. This meant that the controls for adjusting volume and tone were best positioned at the rear of the cabinet within easy reach of the player, a feature that remained a constant on Fender amplifiers until 1959.

There were three models in the original range: The Princeton, aimed at the student and beginners market; the Deluxe/Model 26 for players who required more volume and a better tonal range; and the Professional, which, as its name suggests, was for the working musician who needed enough volume to be heard in ballrooms, clubs or bars. At 18 watts, and carrying an enormous 15" Jensen speaker, this amplifier – the partner to Fender's double-neck steel – was a serious piece of equipment in 1946 and soon earned Leo Fender a reputation in and around Southern California for reliable, quality workmanship.

Leo developed the Woodie amps with Ray Massie, who assembled them with factory foreman Dale Hyatt alongside a small team of three or four workers producing amp cabinets and steel guitars. Fender soon realized that he needed to devote all his energy to the new business and sold his radio shop to Dale Hyatt during early 1948. Dale's departure meant that a new foreman was required and Leo offered the position to a new factory employee he had befriended during the last days of the radio shop, George Fullerton. George had a keen interest in electronics and played guitar in a local band called the Gold Coast Rangers. Though his name suggested otherwise, he was not a native of Fullerton. As the company quickly grew, George became a close and loyal friend to Fender and a valuable asset to the company.

In early 1947, Fender introduced a new style of amplifier to sit at the top of the range. The rustic charm of the early wooden cabinets gave way to a smarter, more refined-looking unit that featured a 16-watt amplifier and two 10" speakers housed in an elegant cabinet covered in an off-white luggage linen tweed, with a dark brown mohair grille cloth. The front panel was angled so that the speakers faced slightly outwards, giving a greater spread of sound. A chromed metal strip that ran down the center section completed the look. The new amplifier, the Dual Professional, featured many 'Fender firsts' and gave more than a hint of what was to come.

Princeton: 4.5 watt; 1 x 8" speaker
Deluxe – Model 26: 10 watt; 1 x 10" speaker
Professional: 18 watt; 1 x 15" speaker
Dual Professional (V-front): 16 watt; 2 x 10" speakers

introducing FENDER
ELECTRIC INSTRUMENTS

NOW YOU CAN PROCURE THE FINEST ELECTRIC GUITARS & AMPLIFIERS

GUITAR FEATURES: Fashioned from choicest quality light and dark lustrously finished hard woods. Not affected by temperature or climatic changes will stay tuned longer. The exact weight and conformity for ease of playing. Exclusive new patented pick-up unit completely shielded against hum pick-up and affording greater brilliance and presence. Equal volume output from all strings without compensating adjustments. Nut plate, fret board and bass plate all heavily chrome plated. Beautiful new heavily chrome plated solid brass "Roll Easy" knobs.

Deluxe Guitar

Three Guitar Models.

Deluxe

Deluxe Organ Button Princeton Student

STUDENT AMPLIFIER FEATURES: 6 Watts Output. Heavy 8" Speaker. Two instrument inputs. Beautiful hand-rubbed, chrome trimmed, solid hardwood cabinet to match guitar.

DELUXE AMPLIFIER FEATURES: 14 Watts Output. Heavy duty 10" PM Speaker. Two instrument and one microphone input. Separate microphone and instrument volume controls. Electronic mixing of instrument and microphone inputs.

Mail Coupon Now

RADIO & TELEVISION EQUIPMENT CO.
207 Oak Street, Santa Ana, Calif.
Send me, without obligation, complete descriptive literature on your instruments.

NAME
ADDRESS
CITY   STATE
DEALER ☐   STUDIO ☐   STUDENT ☐

DELUXE AND STUDENT AMPLIFIERS

IMMEDIATE DELIVERY on all models in either light or dark finishes.
CONSULT YOUR LOCAL MUSIC DEALER OR STUDIO.
Distributed Internationally By

RADIO AND TELEVISION EQUIPMENT CO.
207 Oak St., Santa Ana, Calif.

The Fender
Electric Guitar

Designed With Exclusive
Direct String High Fidelity Pick-Up Unit

LOCAL DEALER

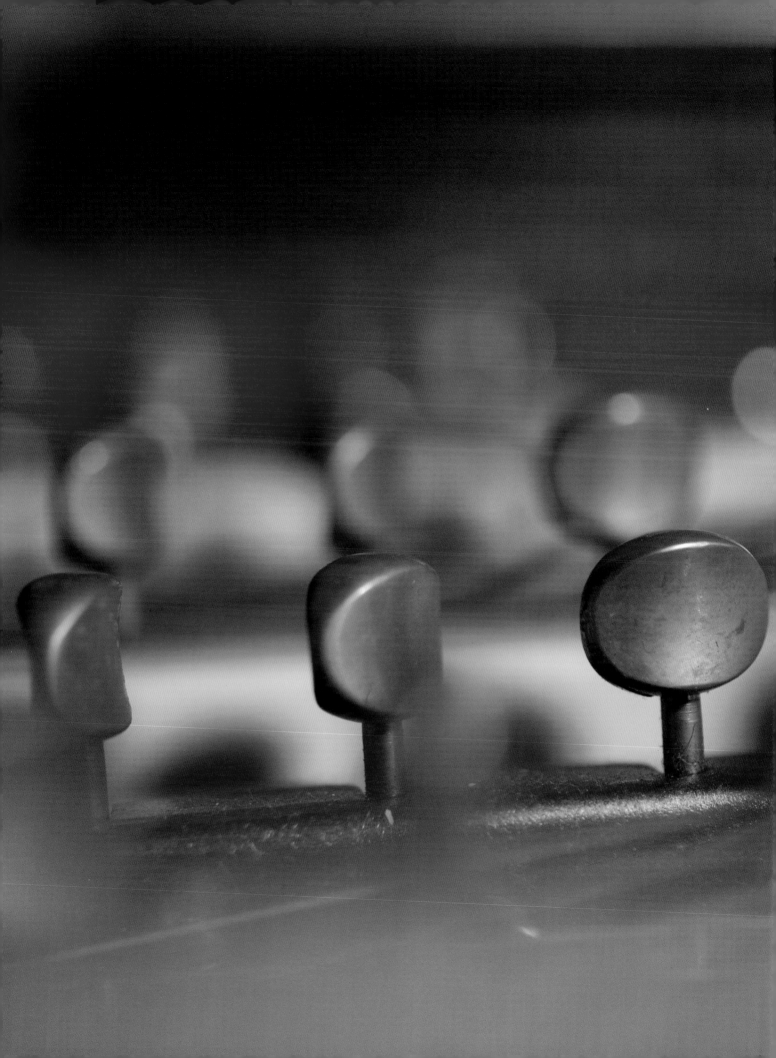

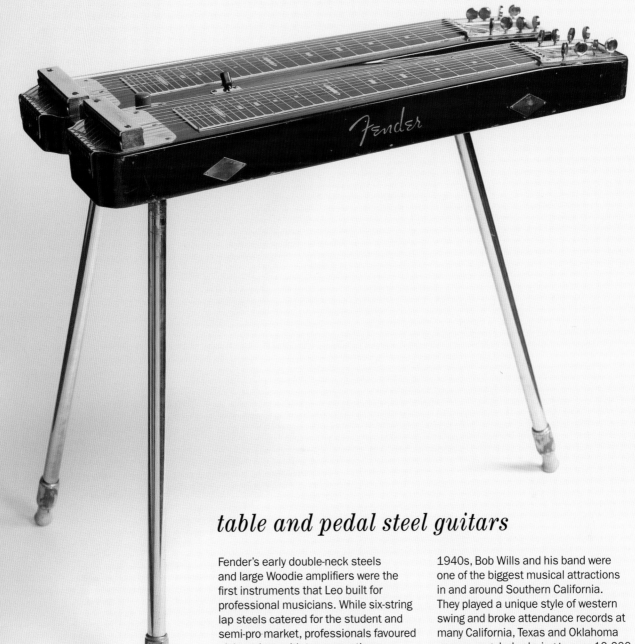

table and pedal steel guitars

Fender's early double-neck steels and large Woodie amplifiers were the first instruments that Leo built for professional musicians. While six-string lap steels catered for the student and semi-pro market, professionals favoured eight strings with two, sometimes three, necks joined together in a 'table' or 'console' format. This allowed for different tunings on each neck and a wider range of sounds. Large and far too heavy to rest on the player's lap, multi-neck steels came with detachable legs, which gave rise to the term 'table steel'. Leo had begun work on an early twin-neck design with Doc Kauffman during the K&F days, but the first double-neck steel built by Fender was made for Noel Boggs of Bob Wills' Texas Playboys in 1946. During the late

1940s, Bob Wills and his band were one of the biggest musical attractions in and around Southern California. They played a unique style of western swing and broke attendance records at many California, Texas and Oklahoma venues, regularly playing to over 10,000 people a week. For Leo to place his new Fender electric stringed instruments in the hands of such high-profile users, at such an early stage, was a key move and one that gave Don Randall and F.C. Hall at Radio-Tel something to shout about. Noel Boggs had favoured an Epiphone-made steel prior to switching to the new Fender double-neck, and before long, the Texas Playboys were fully equipped with a set of matching Woodie amplifiers, including a special 2 x 15" speaker model built especially for Wills by Leo

himself. According to Fender historian Richard Smith: "Wills carried suitcases stuffed with ballroom proceeds, expecting no favours from Fender, and always paid cash."

The new twin-neck Fender steel was aptly named the Professional and partnered the 18-watt Woodie amp of the same name. Radio-Tel's 1947 catalog announced, 'The Fender double-neck guitar introduces a new era of superior performance for the professional player,' and that it was 'ruggedly constructed to give a long and faithful service.' Leo was quickly gaining invaluable knowledge of how his equipment coped under touring conditions as more and more pros turned to the Fender brand. Road-weary amplifiers and steels were often returned for repair work or replacement by musicians who visited the small factory between gigs and Leo was learning fast as he made changes and improvements to his range of products. Others quick to endorse the Fender Professional steel included national stars Alvino Rey and Leon McAuliffe, and the sound of Fender's excellent table steels and amplifiers were soon heard on radio stations across America.

The earliest Professional steels were made from dark walnut or mahogany and featured two box-shaped direct string pickups with twin chromed fingerboards, one for each eight-string neck. Volume and tone controls, plus a switch that allowed the player to select between necks/pickups, completed these simple but highly effective steels. By 1947, lighter colored ash and maple woods were also offered and an upmarket three-neck model was made available. Also, fingerboards switched from chrome to an etched black and silver design to eliminate glare when playing. During 1949, Leo introduced a new asymmetrical Direct String Pickup designed to give better bass-end response. With this addition, the three-neck steel became known as the 'Custom', and twin-neck models – now available in either six-string or eight-string configurations – were named the 'Dual Eight' or 'Dual Six Professional'.

In 1953, Fender launched a brand-new range of table steel guitars. The Stringmaster series represented the pinnacle in table steel design and were offered in two-, three- and four-neck models, with each neck carrying eight strings and two chrome-covered single-coil pickups that sat under the strings. The Stringmaster was essentially separate units that bolted together to give the desired number of necks. The four-neck model was designed with a set of heavy bass strings that could be tuned either one or two octaves below ordinary steel guitar tuning, offering an impressive array of tunings. By 1955, the old-style, three-neck Custom and twin-neck Dual Eight and Dual Six Professional models were dropped from the table steel range, marking the end of the line for Leo Fender's original Direct String Pickup where strings passed through the coil. The Deluxe Lap Steel, 'available in six- and eight-string models,' now also featured two single-coil pickups, plus detachable legs, effectively making it the single-neck offering in the Stringmaster table steel range. To round out the line, a new twin-neck Dual Six Professional, with two single coils for each neck, was introduced. Chrome pickup covers switched to black plastic by 1955 and this range of table steels remained available in blond or dark brown finishes virtually unchanged until the early '70s.

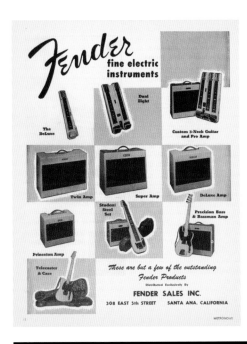

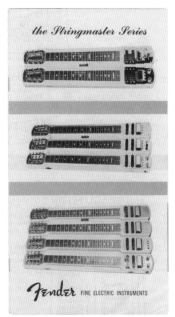

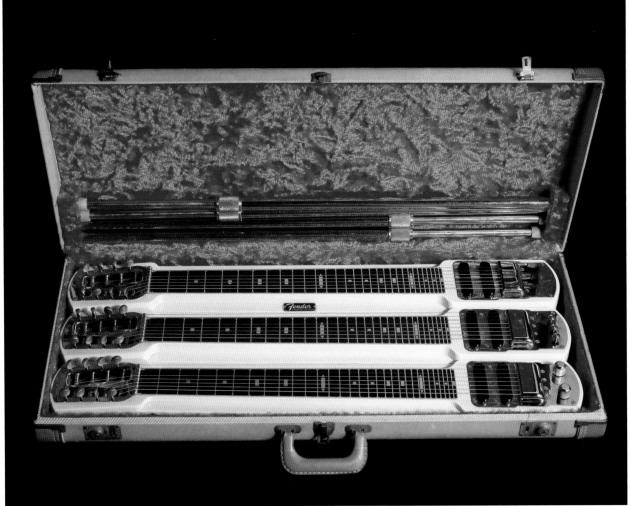

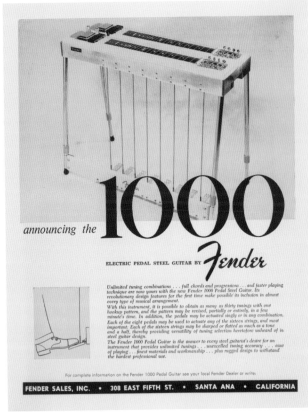

announcing the 1000

ELECTRIC PEDAL STEEL GUITAR BY *Fender*

Unlimited tuning combinations . . . full chords and progressions . . . and faster playing technique are now yours with the new Fender 1000 Pedal Steel Guitar. Its revolutionary design features for the first time make possible its inclusion in almost every type of musical arrangement.
With this instrument, it is possible to obtain as many as thirty tunings with one hookup pattern, and the pattern may be revised, partially or entirely, in a few minute's time. In addition, the pedals may be actuated singly or in any combination.
Each of the eight pedals may be used to actuate any of the sixteen strings, and most important: Each of the sixteen strings may be sharped or flatted as much as a tone and a half, thereby providing versatility of tuning selection heretofore unheard of in steel guitar design.
The Fender 1000 Pedal Guitar is the answer to every steel guitarist's desire for an instrument that provides unlimited tunings . . . unexcelled tuning accuracy . . . ease of playing . . . finest materials and workmanship . . . plus rugged design to withstand the hardest professional use.

For complete information on the Fender 1000 Pedal Guitar see your local Fender Dealer or write:

FENDER SALES, INC. • 308 EAST FIFTH ST. • SANTA ANA • CALIFORNIA

During the early 1950s, the popularity of western swing was on the wane, but a new style of country music was emerging in Nashville that would take the genre to mass audiences around the world. Producers such as Owen Bradley, Chet Atkins and, later, Billy Sherrill would popularize the Nashville Sound which relied heavily on lush arrangements featuring string sections, vocal harmonies and prominent steel guitars. A new type of table steel, played by Bud Isaacs, became instantly popular when featured on Webb Pierce's 1954 hit 'Slowly.' It employed foot pedals that adjusted the tuning on the guitar's strings. Pedal steels had been commercially available since Gibson introduced their Electraharp Steel in 1941 where six pedals attached to one of the guitar's legs were pushed down to raise or lower the pitch of certain strings. This negated the need for multi-neck steels, as several different tunings were now easily available on one neck. However, these were expensive and sold in relatively small numbers, and up until the early 1950s, steels that incorporated this feature were usually adjusted for tuning between songs. Bud Isaacs dropped and raised the pitch of strings mid-song, bending notes to produce a haunting, mournful effect that instantly caught on with country players everywhere. Bud's instrument was hand built for him by Paul Bigsby, who had made pioneering pedal steel instruments for Speedy West during 1948, Ernie Ball in 1949 and Bob Meadows in 1951, and it's likely that Isaacs saw these in action prior to placing an order with Bigsby. Pedal steel quickly became the most in-demand sound on the country music scene and Leo set to work developing his own model to augment his popular range of table steels.

The twin-neck Fender 1000 pedal steel was launched in mid-1957 and early sales literature proudly proclaimed: 'the new Fender 1000 Pedal guitar is, without a doubt, the most advanced instrument of its type on the market today.' It sat at the top of the Fender line, retailing at a whopping $1000, which was equivalent to the price of four non-tremolo Stratocasters or six Fender Esquires. Leo spent long hours developing his own system of cables, springs and pulleys that adjusted string pitch via no less than eight pedals mounted to a board that ran between the front two legs of the new instrument. A further two pedals could be added, if desired, and a brand-new pickup, with eight individual pole pieces, was developed with a flat, wide coil that produced a fuller, warmer tone. The new pickup would resurface in a redesigned format on the Fender Jazzmaster guitar the following year. Leo field-tested the new steel on several name players while perfecting the design. Speedy West, Alvino Rey, Leon McAuliffe and Jody Carver all acted as guinea pigs for the '1000,' reporting back to Leo with valuable suggestions as to how the design could be improved. Despite this outside input, the Fender pedal steel made it into production with one minor flaw: it used steel cables instead of metal rods to link the pedals to string-pull devices that sharpened or flattened the notes. With constant use, the cables had a tendency to stretch and become slack, and would require tightening up. Fender wouldn't accurately remedy this fault until the 1970s, by which time a host of pedal steel makers, such as Sho-Bud and Emmons, had become market leaders in this small but nonetheless important, niche for stringed instruments.

The earliest Fender 1000 pedal steels were finished in desert sand and sat in polished aluminium frames with matching desert sand pedal boards, which proudly displayed a large Fender decal. In early 1958, Fender introduced a single-neck, eight-string pedal steel. The 400, at $379.50 for a four-pedal model, was considerably more affordable to aspiring pedal steel players. These too were finished in desert sand, but the aluminium frames on both 400s and 1000s were now painted black, which provided a smarter, contrasting appearance. By 1961, bodies and pedal boards on the 1000 were finished in a shaded sunburst, and during 1964, a ten-string single neck, the 800, was introduced alongside a ten-string double neck, the 2000, retailing at $1250. At this time,

(preceding pages, top left)
1948 Fender catalog
(preceding pages, bottom left)
Virgillo 'Babe' Simoni making
Stringmaster bodies in October 1957
(preceding pages, bottom right)
1955 Stringmaster three-neck
model – Blond

(this page, bottom)
1959 400 pedal steel – Desert Sand

(this page) 1962 1000 pedal steel –
Sunburst

(facing page, bottom left)
1955 Stringmaster tweed case

sunburst became the standard finish on all Fender pedal steels, and during 1966, Fender offered custom finishes at no extra charge in an effort to combat dwindling sales.

Leo Fender always loved the sound of Hawaiian steel guitars and spent much of his time during Fender's early years perfecting these instruments for musicians who would become his friends. Fender steel guitars were used on countless western swing and country recordings during the period 1946 – 1970, but perhaps one of the most memorable recordings to feature a Fender steel was Santo & Johnny's 1959 chart-topping instrumental 'Sleep Walk,' recorded on a triple-neck Stringmaster. It conjured up romantic visions of paradise islands, moonlit beaches and twinkling stars above; vivid images created in sound on a Fender steel guitar.

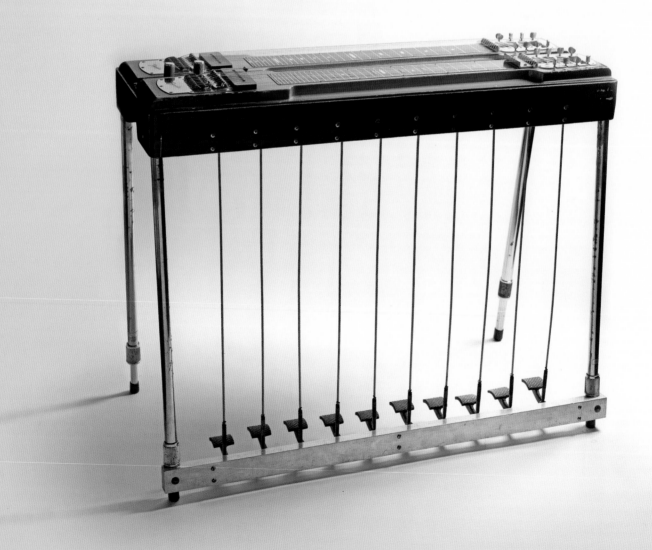

esquire and broadcaster

By the late 1940s, the Fender operation had grown steadily and gained a reputation for producing 'fine electric instruments' with its amplifiers and steel guitars. Don Randall and Francis Hall at Radio-Tel were doing great business distributing Fender products across America and were selling equipment faster than Leo's small factory could produce it. Leo had hatched the notion of building a solid-body electric guitar as far back as 1943 when he and Doc Kaufman built their small-bodied instrument to test out his Direct String Pickup. During the postwar years, the electric Spanish guitar, now given the ES moniker by Gibson, was growing in popularity and Leo decided it was time to turn his attentions to designing his own model. Radio-Tel sales rep Charlie Hayes had encouraged Leo, suggesting there would be a market for a Fender electric Spanish model, and Leo began work in earnest during early 1949. Up to this point, electric Spanish guitars were nearly always large, hollow-bodied acoustic instruments with a pickup fitted under the strings almost as an afterthought. Hollow-bodied instruments fitted with pickups have a tendency to feed back and squeal at high volumes, and Leo was already well aware of the advantages – increased volume and sustain – that his solid-body lap steels had over acoustic instruments. The concept of a solid-body electric Spanish guitar was not completely new; other makers had toyed with the idea. Rickenbacker had pioneered a Bakelite Spanish guitar in the '30s that failed to catch on and famed guitarist and producer Les Paul, an acquaintance of Leo during the late '40s, had been working on a prototype instrument, the 'Log', which featured a solid wooden block running through its center. Though several makers, including Leo, had dabbled with the idea, no manufacturer had set up to mass produce a solid-body electric Spanish guitar, and this would become Fender's goal.

One individual in particular, a California-based guitar maker, machinist and motorcycle designer called Paul Bigsby, would play a vital role in influencing Leo's new design. Bigsby had built a custom-ordered electric guitar for renowned guitarist Merle Travis during 1948. The instrument was of solid-body construction with a single cutaway that gave access to the higher frets, but its real innovation was a headstock design that featured all six tuning keys on one side of the headstock. This concept had appeared on some early European stringed instruments, and a handful of Martin-built acoustics in the 1830s, but had not been used in many years and certainly not on an electric guitar. Like Leo's lap steels, it allowed the strings a straight path towards each tuning gear and gave greater stability of tuning. Merle Travis claimed to have conceptualized the instrument but it was Bigsby who brought the ideas to life. It's known that Leo saw the guitar on several occasions during the late '40s, and undoubtedly, that played a big part in influencing and inspiring his own design. In a letter from Don Randall to Francis Hall in 1950, Don described the scene at WRVA radio station in Richmond, Virginia, where he had taken Leo's first electric

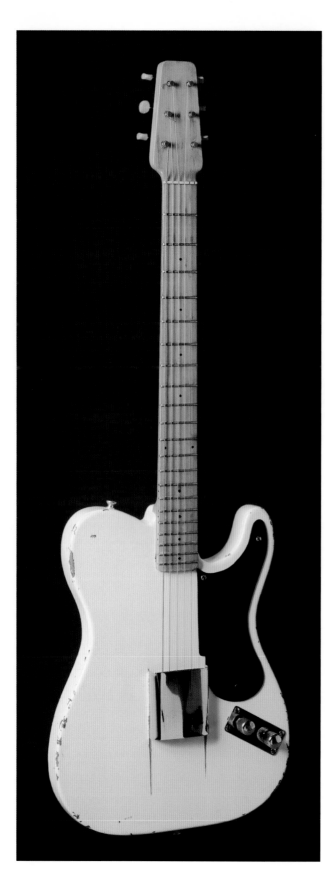

Spanish and a new Fender Pro-amp for demonstration: "Merle Travis is on the program and he is one of the country's foremost guitar stylists. He is playing the granddaddy of our Spanish guitar, built by Paul Bigsby – the one Leo copied. Merle liked our guitar very well and our Pro-Amp very much."

To describe the first Fender electric guitar as a copy of anything that went before would be unfair. Leo would throw out all convention with his design, and during 1949, he developed a guitar that would revolutionize guitar building and guitar playing forever. He knew he could not compete on the same playing field as established makers like Gibson or Epiphone, as he didn't have the tooling or skilled labour to produce lavish instruments like the ones from Kalamazoo or New York. He was, after all, still working from two tin sheds in provincial Southern California. Leo realized that he needed a design that was simple to build yet functional, like his lap steel guitars. Unlike other manufacturers who were busy converting conventional acoustic guitars into electrics, Leo's idea was to adapt his steel design, recycling ideas and incorporating lessons learned from it into the new instrument.

With the help of George Fullerton, a simple but iconic body shape was soon developed. Fender historian Richard Smith would state, "I'm fairly convinced, although this has never really been confirmed, that much of the shape of the Telecaster was George's interpretation... I don't think that it's a coincidence that George was a noted artist – he had a real visual sense and Leo didn't draw as well as George." It's unlikely George and Leo realized that they were already well on the way to developing a classic. Leo's real breakthrough came with the idea of a detachable neck held on by four screws and a mounting plate at the rear of the guitar's body. This was a common feature on certain Rickenbacker steels and banjos, but had not been used on a Spanish guitar before. As well as making for simpler construction, Leo believed that a removable neck made his guitar more like an automobile, where damaged parts could be easily replaced with new ones. If a conventional guitar neck warped or cracked, the whole instrument was deemed useless; Leo's logical thinking allowed for any part of his new instrument to be replaced by the owner with little or no prior knowledge of guitar repair. His new guitar was clearly designed for mass production and easily assembled from a set of parts. That said, it would be built, like all his other instruments, to exacting standards and a quality far superior than most of his rivals' products. A prototype was built during the summer months of 1949 and Leo and George set about field-testing the guitar on local musicians by taking it to clubs and dance halls to gauge reactions. This first guitar, which still exists today, featured a solid maple neck and a three-a-side headstock similar to those on the student lap steels Fender were producing at the time. Perhaps Leo was still unsure about using the Bigsby design. He would later claim that he drew his inspiration for a six-a-side headstock from instruments he'd seen used by Croatian musicians playing in California.

The first prototype featured a single pickup with a design that incorporated separate magnets for each string. "I think

that perhaps I was the first person to use separate magnets, one for each string. That way, I found that the notes didn't seem to run together – you could get more of an individual performance off each string," claimed Leo. He certainly had a clear idea of how he wanted his guitar to sound and had developed the new pickup for his Champion steel guitar in early 1949. Leo wanted to retain the tonal characteristics of his steel guitars and believed that a good guitar pickup should faithfully reproduce the sound of the vibrating strings. He liked bright, bell-like tone with clear, deep, bottom-end response, and the unit he designed in 1949 for the Champion and his new electric Spanish would give his guitars a trademark sound that would span decades. The pickup was adjustable for height and could be raised or lowered at either end to gain a balanced tone. This was a feature that would be a constant on all new Fender stringed instruments from this point onwards.

One thing that quickly becomes apparent when a guitar is amplified is that slight inaccuracies in the intonation between individual strings are clearly audible, making instruments sound out of tune. Acoustic instruments mask these inaccuracies by the nature of overtones produced by their hollow bodies. These overtones merge to produce a wholly musical sound, but on an electric guitar, the notes are exposed and any slight defects in intonation produce unpleasant, discordant sounds. To compensate for this, Leo realized that his guitar needed a bridge where the length and height of each string could be adjusted

(preceding page) 1950 pine-body Esquire

(facing page) first prototype Esquire/ Telecaster, 1949

(above) final assembly at the original steel factory building

(below) the new brick factory building, 1950

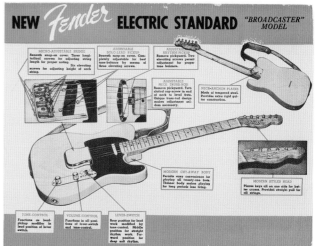

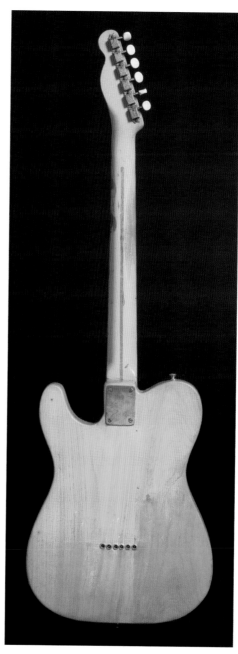

to give the guitar accurate intonation. Instead of opting for an adjustable bridge saddle for each string, Leo designed a bridge that would accommodate two strings per saddle. This didn't produce perfect intonation, but was a workable, practical solution to the inherent problem. The pickup and bridge saddles sat in a pressed-steel bridge plate that featured a simple removable cover. Like Leo's steel guitars, strings passed through the body and over the bridge saddles via holes drilled in the back of the guitar. This gave the instrument added tone as the strings resonated through the wood. Volume and tone controls were mounted to an angled metal plate and a small, black pickguard completed the design. For a first draft, Leo Fender had got

(facing page, left) second prototype Esquire/Telecaster 1949

(facing page right, top to bottom) the same guitar being played at a local show in Fullerton by Roy Watkins - wearing white hat, 1950, visitors to the Fender factory with a pine body Esquire, 1950, Broadcaster insert/flyer from Musical Merchandise magazine February 1951

(above left and center) second prototype Esquire/Telecaster front and back

(above right) Immaculate 1950 Broadcaster – Blond

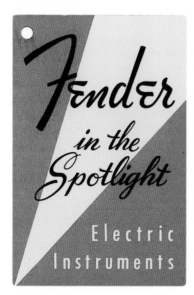

remarkably close to a design that would reach perfection during 1950.

Initial reactions to the prototype were good and soon a second, more refined version was built. This guitar featured a slightly narrower neck with a six-a-side tuner arrangement that would become standard on all Fender Spanish guitars and Leo came up with a neat, subtle design for the headstock that perfectly complemented the body. It differed from the styling of the headstock on the Bigsby guitar and has become an instantly recognizable symbol of Fender's first electric guitar ever since. Tuning keys that sat closely in a line were not available, so Leo adapted Kluson-made keys from his lap steel instruments which came three on a strip. The instrument was almost complete, but it still lacked a name. Don Randall wrote to Francis Hall in mid-1949 insisting that Leo deliver the new guitar in time for upcoming trade shows. As he and other Radio-Tel sales reps built up interest in the guitar, Leo worked at his own pace and the instrument took shape slowly during the fall of 1949 into early 1950. Although Don thought that a two-pickup model would fair better in the growing electric Spanish market, Fender's first electric Spanish model was a one-pickup guitar. Don would name it the 'Esquire,' just in time for the new Fender full-line catalog issued in spring 1950. The Esquire was priced at $139.95, plus $39.95 for a tweed-covered Bulwin hard case.

The earliest Esquires featured lightweight pine bodies that were painted black to disguise the often knotted timber beneath. Necks, like the prototypes before and all Fender guitars from this point onwards, were made from hard rock maple, an incredibly tough, durable wood that can withstand the immense pull that steel strings exert on them. Leo believed that his one-piece maple necks — which were quite unlike those of other makers who used mahogany backs topped with rosewood or ebony fingerboards — would not require truss rods, an adjustable steel bar that runs through most guitar necks to prevent them from twisting or bowing under the enormous pressure of fully tensioned strings. Frets were applied straight into the face of the

Fender neck and black dot position markers were added prior to a layer of clear lacquer being sprayed to seal the wood. A smart decal, which featured an adaptation of Leo's reverse 'F' signature in silver with a black outline and the model name 'ESQUIRE', was applied to the headstock over the lacquer. A stylish but simple new pickguard design, made from white pressed fibreboard, complemented the body shape and a chromed control plate that now ran parallel with the strings featured volume and tone controls. The bridge design was refined and a new chromed bridge cover pressed from steel completed the look. Bridge covers were usually dispensed with by players who felt that they got in the way, preferring to use them as ash trays. The overall balance and symmetry of the design was perfection itself. The Esquire looked and sounded like no other guitar that had existed before. It was completely modern and yet timeless; the perfect marriage of form and function and a masterpiece of economical design. Leo Fender had created a new breed of instrument that would free guitarists from their bulky semi-acoustics with feedback problems. Leo's design was compact, lightweight and fantastically playable. It had a bright, crisp tone that cut through in a way guitarists liked, and in 1950, it was years ahead of its time.

By May 1950, the Fender operation had outgrown the two steel factory buildings on Sante Fe Avenue. Plans were made with a local building contractor named Grady Neal for the construction of a new concrete building adjacent to the existing site in Fullerton. The new building gave much-needed space and the added luxury of staff toilets – a first for Fender employees who, up to this point, had been using the facilities across the street at Fullerton Station.

As the Esquire had only one pickup, there was no need for a pickup selector. Leo did, however, develop a tone circuit that allowed the player a choice of settings. The earliest known picture of an Esquire, from the 1950 Fender full-line catalog, shows a small button similar to those Leo used on

his Organ Button lap steels for activating the tone circuit. This was soon replaced by a conventional blade-type switch with a black plastic Dakaware tip. In different positions, the switch offered the pickup with a muted bass sound, with the tone control in line, or wired direct to the jack socket bypassing the tone control. Don's wish for a two-pickup guitar had registered with Leo and he had begun work on a second smaller unit that would sit near the neck prior to the launch of the Esquire. Several early Esquires were actually produced with two pickups during the summer months of 1950. In July of that year, Don Randall finally got the chance to exhibit the new Fender guitar at the 49th annual National Association of Music Merchants (NAMM) convention held in Chicago. The instrument certainly made an impact, but its unconventional appearance was met with derogatory comments from rival guitar makers and salesmen, who poked fun at the Esquire calling it names such as 'plank,' 'canoe paddle' or 'snow shovel'. Two years on, almost every other manufacturer would be tripping over themselves to release their own offering in the solid-body guitar field.

Leo was decidedly pleased with the two-pickup Esquire. Bodies were no longer made from pine but from quality ash with attractive grain. A translucent blond cellulose paint that highlighted the wood was applied. To complement the new finish, pickguards were now made from a black pressed fibreboard called Phenolite and instruments produced in this style up until 1954 have become known simply as

(this page, above)
B.B. King with black guard Esquire

(facing page, top to bottom)
a selection of early Fender players

(facing page, bottom left) telegram from Gretsch to Fender that would result in the Broadcaster's name change

'Blackguards.' Don decided that the two-pickup guitar should have its own name. He'd been selling the Esquire as a one-pickup instrument and now some had two pickups and a blond finish, unlike the black guitar pictured in his catalog. In a move to avoid further confusion and allow for two price levels, Don renamed the two-pickup Esquire the 'Broadcaster' during the fall of 1950. He had received several comments from dealers and musicians over the summer months suggesting that the Esquires he'd already shipped would be better equipped with a truss rod. Initially, Leo disagreed, claiming that the maple he used was strong enough not to require internal bracing. This dispute caused some friction between the two men, but Leo eventually relented in October 1950 and began fitting truss rods to all his guitars from this point onwards, including the first Broadcasters. In typically unconventional fashion, Leo developed a method of inserting the truss rod into the rear of the neck by routing a channel down the center, inserting the truss rod and plugging the channel with a piece of walnut. This left a dark stripe running down the back of the neck, referred to as the 'skunk stripe.' 'Skunk stripe' necks are also recognizable by a small walnut or, occasionally, maple plug on the face of the headstock where the rod is held in place. Adjustments are made by turning a circular nut at the base of the neck where it meets the body. Truss rod adjustment involves detaching the neck and, by tightening or loosening the nut, can cure slight bends or kinks in the neck that affect playability.

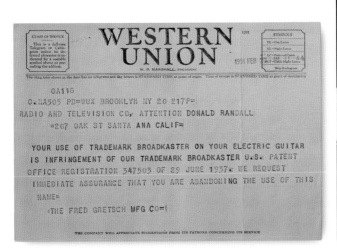

tv-front amplifiers 1947–1953

Fender's TV-Front amplifiers, produced between 1947 and 1953, are so called because of their resemblance to the television sets of the day. The earliest TV amps were covered in a new style of tweed luggage linen, yellowish in color, with fine, two-tone vertical stripes and the same dark brown grille cloth that had been employed on the earlier V- front Dual Professionals.
From this point onwards, tweed cabinets were sprayed with a coat of clear, cellulose lacquer that gave both a shine and added protection. Small metal nameplates that boldly proclaimed 'FENDER Fullerton. California' were nailed to the panel above the speaker baffle.

These new amplifiers featured chromed control panels and leather handles, and compared to the Woodies, were smarter and of far sturdier construction. Cabinets were now built from less expensive pine wood, with lock-jointed corners, which made for greater durability but left unsightly edges that necessitated the need for covering.

Fender products were steadily gaining in popularity. Don Randall at Radio-Tel was shipping to all parts of the US and customer satisfaction was high. Fender amplifiers were now aimed at the electric steel and burgeoning Spanish guitar markets, and the timing of Leo's first solid-body guitars – the Esquire and Broadcaster, introduced in 1950 – was perfect.

The basic models from the Woodie range remained in the new TV format with various upgrades. The Princeton now featured volume and tone controls, and the Deluxe switched from a 10" to a 12" speaker. The Professional, the first to receive the TV restyling, was redesigned and renamed the Pro-Amp in early 1947, while the Dual Professional was renamed the Super later the same year, but kept its split V-front look.

At the bottom of the line, a new amp was introduced during 1948, an important student model that would remain available in various guises in the Fender line for almost 50 years. The Champion 800 would be the first in

a long line of 'Champ' amps produced by Fender throughout the golden age. The 800s were manufactured in small numbers and, like the Princeton, featured an 8" speaker but a volume control only – no tone. The small Champion 800 cabinet was covered in a unique greenish tweed with a deep purple mohair grille cloth. Perhaps due to its similarity in specification to that of the TV-Front Princeton, the Champion 800 was soon downsized to a 3-watt amp with a smaller 6" speaker and renamed the Champion 600 from mid-1949. The 600s were finished in another unique covering, this time a two-tone brown and cream leatherette called Naugahyde. The brown Naugahyde would turn up again as the covering for 'thermometer' and 'poodle'-shaped cases for Fender electric Spanish guitars during the early to mid-1950s.

During 1949, a new style of tweed covering was adopted for the TV-Front amps, a harder-wearing, heavier material that had bold diagonal stripes. The grille cloths were also changed from dark brown mohair to a dark brown linen cloth less prone to attack from moths!

In 1952, Fender introduced the Bassman amplifier as a partner for his brand new creation, the Precision Bass. His was the first fretted electric bass and it would change popular music forever. The amp had to be powerful and rugged to handle the booming bottom-end notes that the new instrument could produce, and Leo did not disappoint. The new TV-style amp could propel 26 watts of pure bass tone through its specially designed 15" Jensen speaker. Music was changing fast and Leo Fender was at the forefront of those changes, giving musicians across America the tools they needed to begin a revolution.

Champion 800: 4 watt; 1 x 8" speaker
Champion 600: 3 watt; 1 x 6" speaker
Princeton: 4.5 watt; 1 x 8" speaker
Deluxe: 10 watt; 1 x 12" speaker
Super (V-Front): 16 watt; 2 x 10" speakers
Pro-amp: 18 watt; 1 x 15" speaker
Bassman: 26 watt; 1 x 15" speaker

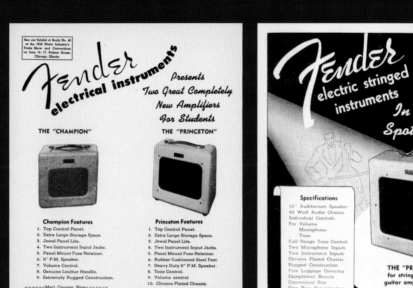

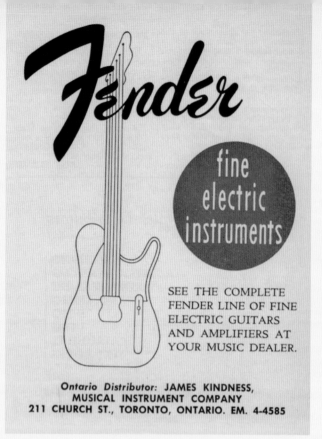
telecaster

News of Fender's revolutionary guitar spread quickly and many local musicians from western swing and country acts were quick to adopt the guitar. Bill Carson, Rex Gallion and Charlie Aldrich were among the first professional players to realize the Broadcaster's potential. National stars Alvino Rey and Jimmy Bryant were also early endorsees of the new Fender solid body. Just as things seemed to be going well for the new Broadcaster, Don Randall received a telegram in February 1951 from the mighty Fred Gretsch Manufacturing Company in Brooklyn, New York, informing him that they had a trademark in place for the name 'Broadkaster' for drums they had been marketing since the 1930s. Fender's new guitar had been brought to their attention via an insert in the February edition of *Musical Merchandise* magazine. Although the spelling differed slightly, Gretsch requested Fender abandon their use of the name immediately. Don quickly sent out a memo to salesmen informing them that the name was to be dropped, asking them to come forward if they had any suggestions for a new one. He needn't have bothered; two days later he came up with the new name himself – 'Telecaster.' Television was still new and the

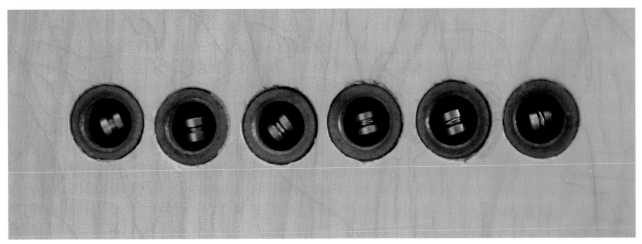

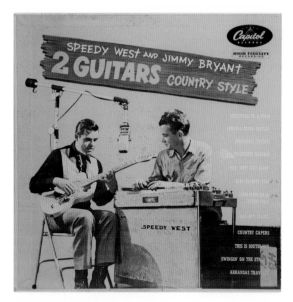

JIMMY BRYANT
prefers a
Fender GUITAR

name proved to be a stroke of genius from Don, who would go on to name most Fender stringed instruments from the golden age. Production did not halt, and while Fender waited for new Telecaster decals to arrive, guitars were shipped with decals that just read 'Fender' where the word 'Broadcaster' was clipped off. These rare instruments from early 1951 are today referred to as 'Nocasters'. It is estimated that fewer than 250 Broadcasters were built prior to switching to the Telecaster name.

By 1951, Gibson realized that the Telecaster posed a threat to their stronghold over the electric Spanish market and they began work on their own solid-body design. Launched in 1952, the Les Paul was named after and endorsed by Leo's friend who had developed the 'Log' solid-body prototype during the 1940s.

Les consulted with Gibson over the design of the new guitar, but the instrument was not strictly his own work. Rather it was that of several in-house luthiers under the guidance of Gibson president Ted McCarty. The Les Paul was a beautiful instrument in the Gibson tradition, with a body and neck constructed from solid mahogany that, like all other Gibson guitars, were glued together as one. A carved maple top and rosewood fingerboard gave the new guitar an air of class with which Fender's utilitarian Telecaster could not compete. Two effective P-90 single-coil pickups were employed and a smart gold finish helped the guitar stand out, but early Les Paul models had one major failing. This was in the form of a basic, trapeze-shaped combined tailpiece and bridge, adjustable only for height. This flaw left the Telecaster ahead of the pack for at least a further year. Gibson were playing catch-up and would be left further behind in the solid-body guitar field as Fender unveiled a new model in 1954 named the Stratocaster.

The year 1954 saw changes in the appearance of the Telecaster and Esquire to bring them in line with the new Stratocaster model. Single-ply white plastic pickguards replaced black guards and the blond cellulose finish changed from its pale butterscotch to a decidedly more creamy, translucent hue. The Telecaster had grown steadily in popularity and was now taken seriously by rival manufacturers and musicians alike. Its bright, twangy sound had become synonymous with the western swing and country players who first adopted the guitar and it would never entirely shake off its image as a basic, functional instrument suited to country playing. However, as rock'n'roll music emerged from its roots in blues, gospel and country, many up-and-coming guitarists looking to electrify their sound turned to Fender equipment to give them the tone and volume they needed. Rockabilly guitarist Paul Burlison, from the Johnny Burnette Trio, augmented Grady Martin's Bigsby lead guitar sound on his Esquire on the band's legendary 1956 recordings, creating a distorted tone by loosening the tubes in his Fender Deluxe amplifier. Blues man Muddy Waters favoured a Telecaster and B.B. King used a blackguard Esquire during his early career. Johnny Cash's ever-present sideman Luther Perkins, relied heavily

You won't part with yours either*

You won't part with yours either*

*(preceding page, right) 1957 Telecaster –
two-tone Sunburst*

(facing page) 1962 Telecaster – Blond

(above) Steve Cropper of Booker T & The MGs

(right) 1963 Telecaster – Blond

on a mid-'50s blond Esquire for his trademark 'boom-chicka' rhythmic style, while Buck Owens and Don Rich set new standards for country picking on their matching Teles during the early '60s. Fender even built Buck and Don two specially matched sets of silver sparkle Teles during the '60s as a thank you for their continued endorsement of the model. One player in particular, a young guitarist named James Burton from Shreveport, Louisiana, would make the Telecaster his signature instrument throughout the '50s, '60s and '70s on countless sessions for artists such as Ricky Nelson, Bob Luman, Elvis Presley, Merle Haggard and Gram Parsons. His raw, cutting performance on Dale Hawkins' 'Suzie Q' from 1957 shows the Telecaster at its best, and late-'60s and early-'70s recordings with Elvis Presley display some of the finest Tele playing ever.

Apart from the early Esquires finished in black, the standard finish on Telecasters and Esquires would remain blond throughout Fender's golden age. Occasional custom

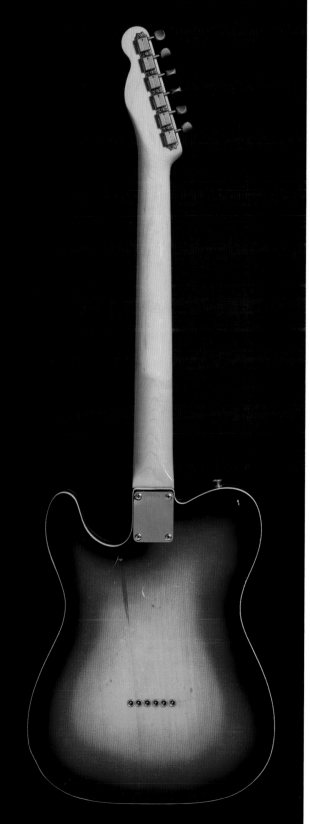

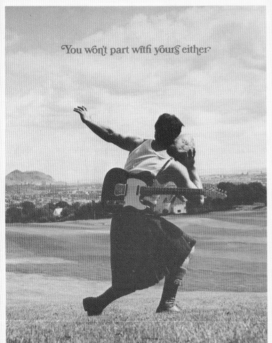

*(preceding pages, left to right) 1959
left-hand Esquire – Blond, 1963
Telecaster Custom, 1960 Telecaster
– Fiesta Red*

*(below, left to right) Telecaster
production 1957, 1966 and 1964*

ordered instruments in one-off colored finishes left the factory during the early to mid-1950s but it wasn't until 1957 that a second standardized finish would be offered. Limited numbers of Esquires and Telecasters were produced, like the Stratocaster, in attractive two-color sunbursts during '57 and '58, and rare examples of these are highly prized today. The year 1959 saw more changes to the Telecaster and Esquire. A new Fender electric six-string, the Jazzmaster, had been introduced in 1958 that featured a rosewood fingerboard glued to the face of a standard maple neck. The new look had proven popular and spread across the Fender line during 1959. Rosewood cap fingerboards did away with the need for the 'skunk stripe' and headstock plug, as truss rods now sat in a channel in the maple neck under the rosewood fretboard. Black dot position markers used on maple necks changed to an off-white color, often referred to as 'clay dots,' on Rosewood boards. In late '58, Fender experimented with a simpler bridge for the Telecaster where the strings passed through newly drilled holes in the rear lip of the bridge plate. This negated the need for strings passing through the body and the necessary holes to be drilled. It was almost certainly a cost-cutting exercise and 'top loader' bridges proved unpopular, as musicians quickly noticed a less resonant sound from the Telecaster. Fender quickly reverted to their tried-and-tested through-body arrangement by late 1959. As the '50s grew to a close, Fender launched one more important variation on the Telecaster and Esquire guitars, the 'Custom,' during June 1959. These were spruced-up, high-end alternatives to the

2

FENDER FAVORITES

have a startling, NEW LOOK!

the

FENDER TELECASTER CUSTOM

and

ESQUIRE CUSTOM GUITARS

Fender ⁝ FINE ELECTRIC INSTRUMENTS

Guitarists everywhere have made the Fender Telecaster and Esquire Guitars among the most popular instruments in the Spanish Guitar field. Now these two outstanding instruments are available with a NEW LOOK . . . select rosewood fingerboards, ovalled and precision fretted for the fastest playing technique. In addition, The Telecaster Custom and Esquire Custom cutaway bodies are beautifully finished in Sunburst, highly polished and with edges that are attractively bound with contrasting white binding. Not only does this new binding enhance their appearance, but it also protects the guitar body edges.

Both models incorporate all the well-known Fender developments which provide the player with the latest guitar design features. The fast action Fender neck has an adjustable reinforcing neck rod. Two-way adjustable bridges make possible low string settings for fast single string work and comfortable rhythm playing. String lengths are adjustable to achieve perfect string intonation throughout the frets.

Pickups on the Telecaster Custom and Esquire Custom are fully adjustable, allowing one to get any desired tone response, and in addition, there is a full range tone control. The three position tone change switch provided allows instantaneous changes from a sharp ringing "take off" or "lead" tone to a very soft "rhythm" tone. The new Telecaster Custom and Esquire Custom Guitars are outstanding instruments on today's market. They offer the player considering the Fender Telecaster or Esquire, new features readily appreciated by every guitarist and provide the most up-to-date developments in guitar design and performance.

Telecaster Custom and Esquire Custom Guitars may be ordered with left-hand construction at 10% additional cost.

This is **ECCO-FONIC** . . . a remarkable new instrument which for the first time makes possible full dimension sound plus variable echo, reverberation and stereophonic effects . . . a real addition if you play an electric instrument.

1 ADJUSTABLE NECK TRUSS ROD prevents warping and assures proper neck alignment and level frets. Adjustment is simple, though seldom if ever necessary.

2 MICRO-ADJUSTABLE BRIDGES used on the Telecaster Custom and Esquire Custom have six elevating screws to adjust string heights for fast, custom playing action. Three longitudinal screws adjust string length for true string intonation and fretting.

3 PICKUPS are fully adjustable for any desired tone response and balance by means of the elevating screws at the ends of the pickups.

4 MODERN HEAD DESIGN gives easier access to the tuning keys and the straight string pull makes tuning easier. Heavy duty patent heads are geared for accurate tuning and will not slip.

5 THREE POSITION tone change switch, plus the tone and volume control, provide rapid changes from lead to rhythm. Sharp take-off tone to mellow rhythm tone can be achieved by use of the selector switch in combination with the tone control.

Distributed Exclusively by *Fender* SALES INC. **Santa Ana, Calif.**

'plain Jane' blond Telecasters and Esquires, and featured three-tone sunbursts with white binding around the top and back edges of the body. This gave them the appearance of acoustic or semi-acoustic instruments (perhaps a move to compete with Gibson guitars that were always edge-bound). The earliest Tele and Esquire Customs feature black sides, but for a period around 1963, Fender switched to a maroon color for the sides before returning to black in 1964. Customs were also fitted with three-ply white/black/white nitrate pickguards, and although the changes were purely cosmetic, the retail price of the upmarket Telecaster Custom was $229.50, compared to the standard blond guitar at $199.50.

As the early '60s arrived, popular music was becoming more and more diverse. Gospel and rhythm'n'blues merged to create soulful sounds in the southern states of Louisiana, Alabama and Tennessee, and up around Chicago, Illinois, and Detroit, Michigan, where a new musical style was gathering momentum. Spearheaded by singers like Ray Charles, Sam Cooke and Jackie Wilson and recordings on Berry Gordy's Motown and VIP labels, this new style would be termed 'soul' by the mid-'60s. Electrically charged and high on emotion, soul music became a major force during the 1960s and many of the in-house backing groups creating the new sounds touted Fender instruments. One of the finest in-house bands of all time was Booker T

(facing page, left to right) 1964 Telecaster Custom, 1960 Telecaster Custom

(this page) 1963 Telecaster Custom, 1962 Esquire Custom

& the MGs, on the payroll of the Memphis-based Stax label. MGs guitarist Steve Cropper was seldom seen without his blond Telecaster and his playing went a long way towards changing the perception of the guitar. In Cropper's hands, the Telecaster sounded fresher than ever as he bent, chopped and picked the strings like no one before, creating classic guitar parts for Otis Redding, Wilson Pickett, Sam & Dave and countless others. The opening bars of Sam & Dave's 'Soul Man' or Eddie Floyd's 'Knock On Wood' are classic Cropper, but for a master class in Telecaster playing, one need only listen to Booker T & the MGs' instrumental 'Green Onions'. Aretha Franklin's soul recordings of the mid- to late '60s often featured outstanding Telecaster playing from the likes of Cornell Dupree, and the guitar has gone on to become an essential tool for many soul guitarists.

British rhythm'n'blues group The Yardbirds saw three of the finest guitarists of all time pass through their ranks during the 1960s. Eric Clapton, Jeff Beck and Jimmy Page all favoured the Telecaster or Esquire during their time with the band. Eric Clapton used an early '60s Fiesta Red Telecaster on recordings such as 'Got To Hurry' and 'Ain't Got You' but left the group as they headed towards pop territory, recommending Jimmy Page as his replacement. Page, a busy session guitarist, initially declined, offering up his friend Jeff Beck for the position. Beck would pioneer a snarling psychedelic lead sound on his 1954 Esquire fed through a Tone Bender fuzz pedal on singles including the 1966 hit 'Shapes Of Things'. Later that year, Jimmy Page did eventually join the group on bass, switching to guitar – a 1958 Telecaster – on Beck's departure, as the group slowly evolved into Led Zeppelin during the late 1960s.

No other guitar twangs quite like a Telecaster and it holds a special place in the hearts of many guitarists. It is a simple, no-frills instrument yet still regarded as one of the finest electric guitars ever produced. If Fender wondered in 1949 what the guitar of the future might look like as he designed his first solid-body, he need have looked no further than his own workbench. It's truly amazing that Leo Fender, a non-guitar player, got it so right with the Telecaster on his first attempt, and it is a testament to his talent and vision that the guitar has remained in production unchanged for over six decades. There are very few mass-produced items that can boast the same uninterrupted life span as the Telecaster. As the saying goes: "If it ain't broke, don't fix it."

(facing page top, left to right)
1950 Broadcaster, 1953 Telecaster,
1959 Esquire Custom

(facing page bottom, left to right)
1963 Telecaster Custom, 1966
Telecaster, 1970 Telecaster

wide panel amplifiers 1952–1955

By 1952, Fender had a well-earned reputation across the United States for building great-sounding, reliable and virtually indestructible amplifiers. Fender amps were the most powerful on the market and were selling in big numbers to musicians of all types across the country. Business was going well and Leo had begun work on a new electric Spanish guitar that would feature several improvements upon his original Telecaster design. He envisaged that the new instrument should come with its own amplifier and began work on a large 2 x 12" speaker model that would be named the Twin. Delay in the guitars' design meant that the amp would be launched first and it made it's debut at the National Association of Music Merchants show in August 1952, although it would not be widely available until spring the following year.

The Twin sported a new 'Wide Panel' look that featured thick borders of tweed-covered cabinet above and below the speaker baffle. It was similar to the earlier V-front design of the Dual Professional and Super amps, but with a flat front and no chromed center strip. The cabinet was covered in a diagonal-pattern lacquered tweed with a brown linen grille cloth and a leather handle. The same small Fender badges that had adorned the TV range completed the Wide Panel look. The Twin was the first Fender amp to employ bass and treble controls, which gave it a far greater tonal range than any previous Fender model. At 25 watts, it was the loudest Fender guitar amp to date and made a perfect partner to the recently introduced Bassman. By early 1953, all Fender amps had switched to the new Wide Panel look and sales were booming.

During the TV-Front and Wide Panel eras, the appeal of Fender electrical instruments had spread far and wide from its humble beginnings in Orange County. Leo no longer relied on local players and western swing acts to endorse his guitars and amplifiers. Jazz players, country pickers and bluegrass musicians all found the sounds they were looking for in Fender-branded products. A new style of music was emerging in the southern states and around the Chicago area. A fusion of rhythm'n'blues and country that drew influence from blues, gospel, jazz and African rhythms would soon emerge as rock'n'roll. This new music was very much an electrified art form that appealed to the youth, both black and white, of America and would go on to play a huge part in the ongoing success of Fender Fine Electric Instruments around the world.

Champl / 600/ Student Amp: 3 watt; 1 x 6" speaker
Princeton: 4.5 watt; 1 x 8" speaker
Deluxe: 10 watt; 1 x 12" speaker
Super: 20 watt; 2 x 10" speakers
Bassman: 26 watt; 1 x 15" speaker
Pro-amp: 15 watt; 1 x 15" speaker
Bandmaster: 15 watt; 1 x 15" speaker
Twin: 25 watt; 2 x 12" speakers

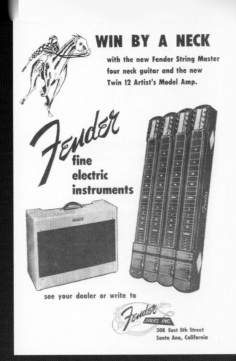

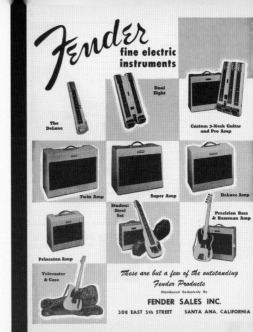

precision bass

Having created the world's first mass-produced, solid-body guitar in 1950, Leo Fender turned his attentions to another breed of musician for his next creation. Being a non-musician, Leo was able to think laterally about instrument design; he was unencumbered by preconceived ideas or perceptions of how an instrument should be manufactured. He had transformed the electric guitar from a bulky, semi-acoustic instrument into a lightweight, almost indestructible design that could be pushed to high volume levels with virtually no feedback. Why, then, could he not do the same for the bass player? This simple thought was a stroke of genius and one that would once again change the path of popular music.

Up until the early 1950s, bass players almost always used large, violin-shaped upright instruments usually referred to as 'double' or 'fiddle' basses. These 500 year-old designs featured huge hollow bodies with big f-holes, necessary to project the deep sound produced by their thick strings. Necks were fretless and strings were usually bowed to produce sound. During the early part of the 20th century, jazz musicians had begun plucking the strings to produce a more rhythmical sound, with notes that punched out in a bid to keep up with loud brass sections and drums. Makers such as Gibson, Dobro and Regal marketed large, upright acoustic basses during the

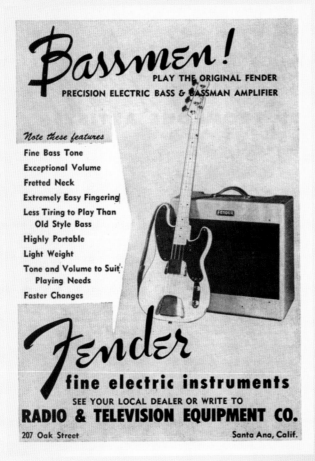

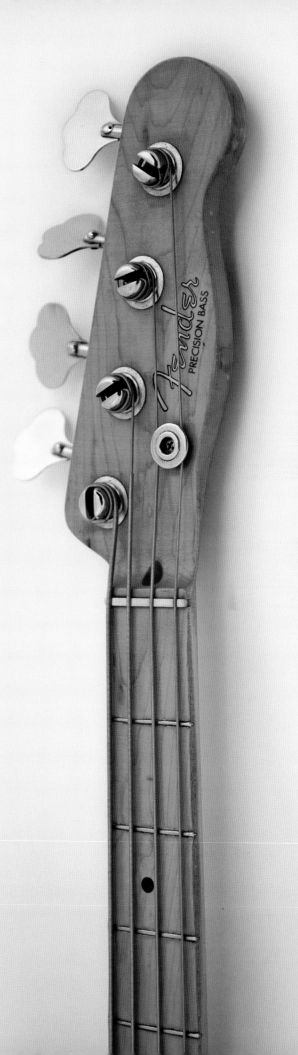

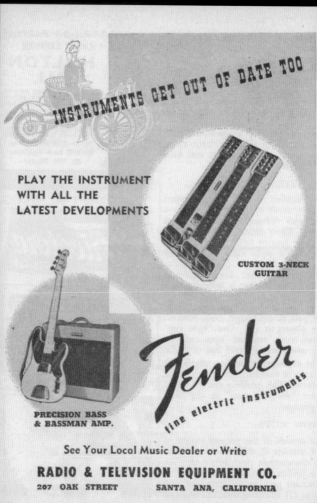

'20s and '30s, with frets and body styles that differed from the traditional violin shape, hoping to appeal to non-classical musicians. These instruments failed to overcome the inherent problem of size and sold in very small numbers. As amplified music became more popular, bass players found themselves drowned out by other band instruments. Makers including Rickenbacker and Regal offered electric basses that while cutting down on body size, still featured fretless necks playable only in an upright position.

Leo's idea was so simple that it seemed incredible no one had thought of it before: turn the electric bass on its side like a guitar, add frets to the neck and make the body smaller like the Telecaster, and from a solid piece of wood to avoid feedback. In so doing, he'd created a totally new instrument – the electric bass guitar – which he aptly named the Precision Bass during the summer of 1951. Like the Telecaster before it, the new bass required an amplifier to be heard and Leo developed a rugged 25-watt amp to partner his new invention. The Bassman utilized a huge 15" speaker and could produce enough volume to keep up with any band of the day. By the end of the decade, the Fender bass had become an industry standard and the generic term used to describe all electric basses, regardless of the manufacturer. Not only had Leo freed bassists so that they could move around the bandstand but, by allowing the instrument to be played in a horizontal position, he also gave musicians the chance to experiment in a way previously impossible. It would take bass playing to a new level where it became an essential element of the rhythm section. The bass

(facing page, left) 1951 Precision Bass

(facing page top) contestants at Santa Monica junior talent show, early 1950s

(this page, below) Fender factory, Pomona Avenue, 1952

would now partner the drums to form the backbone and groove of many new styles of electrified music. Electric bass punched through on records, jukeboxes and radio stations in a way acoustic basses had never been able to and bass players soon saw the merits of being center stage, clearly audible alongside the lead instruments.

A prototype electric bass was worked up during the summer months of 1951. Like the Esquire prototypes from '49, Leo field-tested the instrument on local musicians and friends such as the Gallion Brothers and Bill Carson. It featured a long 34"-scale length to produce the best possible bass tone, but to counterbalance the long neck, the body needed to be larger than that of his electric six-strings. The body shape

differed from the Telecaster, with two offset horns that gave it balance, but it did retain the same thickness and squared-off edges as his six-string models. A single-coil pickup with four pole pieces was developed, tuning keys were adapted from those used on upright acoustic basses and it's likely that Leo initially used piano strings.

Early production Precision Basses were finished in blond, like the Telecaster guitars, with black Phenolite plastic pickguards. Necks were solid maple with an enlarged, Telecaster-shaped headstock. Kluson now supplied specially-made tuning pegs, also similar in appearance to those seen on stand-up basses, and Leo worked with string manufacturer VC Squire to produce new steel-core, flat-wound strings especially

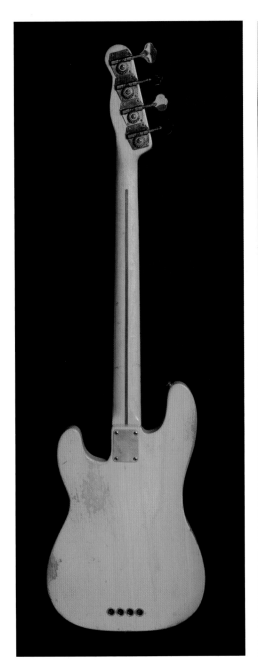

for the Precision. Volume and tone controls were mounted on a chromed metal plate, and chrome bridge and pickup covers were fitted as standard. A rubber mute (that dampened the strings to provide tones like those of a stand-up bass) was fitted to the underside of the bridge cover, but most players removed these, preferring the sound of un-muted strings. A simple bridge carried two strings per saddle for adequate – but not perfect – intonation and a thumb rest or 'tug bar' made from black painted wood was screwed just below the top G string on the front of the guitar. It was a feature added to aid stand-up bass players who often used their thumb for plucking strings and gave fingers something to hold onto. Although players soon switched to a different style of playing for the new

(facing page) Gene Vincent and The Blue Caps

(this page, left to right) 1951 Precision Bass, 1953 Precision Bass

Fender bass, the thumb rest remained standard on all Fender basses throughout the company's golden age.

Radio-Tel received its initial delivery of Precision Basses for shipment in November 1951 and the first ads, which showed the bass pictured with a TV-front Bassman, ran in April of 1952. Sales were slow to begin with, as musicians didn't know what to make of the new instrument. Jazz players Monk Montgomery, Roy Johnson and Shifti Henri were quick to endorse the new bass and all found the switch from upright to horizontal playing "no trouble at all." African American jazz players, who favored the new instrument, did a lot to help shake Fender's staunchly cowboy image projected by the Telecaster and their range of steel guitars. Don Randall wasted no time in including their pictures in sales literature of the day and these were among the first racially orientated campaigns launched by any instrument manufacturer to promote guitars. Don Randall proudly displayed the new bass with the rest of the Fender line at trade shows over the summer months of 1952, but rival manufacturers, slow to learn their lesson, mocked the new instrument.

At a cost of $199.50, plus $203.50 for the matching Bassman amp, a Precision bass represented a serious investment to any musician in 1952. Epiphone were famed for their quality stand-up 'fiddle' basses and a top-range B4-S model from the '52 catalog would set a musician back $310, almost $100 less than the Fender set. The Precision, however, boasted several important advantages. As well as the benefits of increased volume, it was incredibly lightweight and portable compared to the double bass. Even with its heavy Bassman amp, it was easily transported in a small car, thus doing away with the bass player's need for a station wagon or van. Prior to the advent of the electric bass, it was not unusual to see bands traveling around with large acoustic basses strapped to the roof of their vehicles.

Don Randall and F.C. Hall were doing a fantastic job distributing Fender Electric Instruments during the early '50s. Don's suggestion of distributing K&F and, later, Fender products was now turning a good profit for Radio-Tel. All of Leo's product lines were selling well but he had built up personal resentment towards F.C. Hall over the money loaned in 1947. Leo felt cornered by the gesture, as if it had been done to give Hall the upper hand in the manufacturing–distribution arrangement. Hall was constantly nagging Leo for more turnover – he could sell product faster than Leo could produce it – and a clash of egos was beginning to emerge. Hall complained that Leo was selling instruments directly out of the back door of his factory, circumventing the distribution arrangement. Leo had always done this and didn't see why he should stop. Both Hall and Randall were worried Leo might move to a new distributor as Hall had proposed a ten-year distribution deal in 1949 that Leo turned down. By late 1951, Leo had repaid his debt to Hall, but friction between the two men was worse than ever. Don Randall was caught in the middle of the feud and came up with the perfect solution, one that would assure the future for Fender instruments and bring an end to problems between Hall and Fender – if only in the short term. Don proposed the set-up of a designated distribution company that would handle Fender products exclusively. Fender Sales was incorporated in February 1953, with four equal partners holding 25 per cent of the

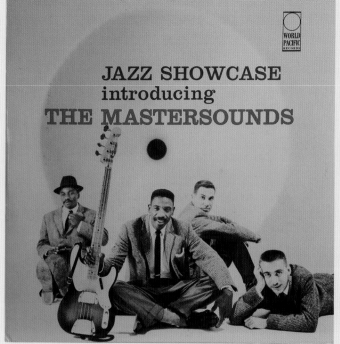

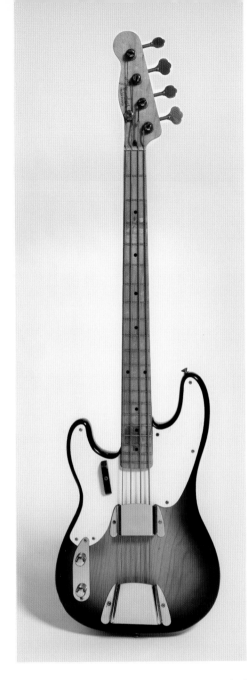

stock each. Randall stood as president, a role that freed him of his obligations at Radio-Tel and, at long last, gave him the opportunity to run a company of his own. Valued salesman and long-term friend Charlie Hayes was vice president, F.C. Hall was secretary and Leo became treasurer. This was a smart move on Don's part, as it put himself and Leo in charge of the money and left Hall on the sidelines, unable to aggravate Leo. Fender Sales was set up as a separate operation at 308 East Fifth Street in Santa Ana, ten miles from the Fender factory in Fullerton.

Perhaps as a way of getting back at Leo and Don, Francis Hall began talks with the California-based Electro String Company who produced Rickenbacker instruments. Just a few months after Fender Sales was set up, he succeeded in buying the company from Adolph Rickenbacher during late 1953. It's likely that Hall felt pushed out and wanted his own slice of the growing musical instrument industry. At that time, Rickenbacker was producing outdated steel guitars and

(preceding pages, left to right) 1954 – Blond, black guard, 1957 – Blond, white guard; 1955 – Luar Green (top left with original owner in the 1950s), 1955 – Eggshell, gold hardware and anodized guard

(facing page) 1955 – Sunburst

(this page, left to right) 1955 left-hand – Sunburst, 1955 – two-tone Sunburst, 1958 – three-tone Sunburst

(overleaf facing page, left to right) Billy Ford's Thunderbirds with a 1957–1958 Precision, 1958 – Sunburst with anodized guard

amplifiers, which were no match for Fender's modern Telecaster, Precision Bass and TV-Front amps. By 1954, however, Hall would introduce a range of electric guitars distributed by Radio-Tel in a move that would anger not only Leo but Don Randall and Charlie Hayes too. Hall was understandably the unpopular partner at Fender Sales Inc.

During 1954, Fender introduced a new, six-string model with a similar body styling to the Precision. Named the Stratocaster, it featured a new-style, contoured body with rounded-off edges, a scooped-out back section and bevelled front edge that gave greater comfort for players who had complained about the squared-off edges on slab-body Telecasters and Esquires. The new six-string also featured a smart, two-color sunburst with a white plastic pickguard and Fender were quick to apply these new features to the Precision during the course of 1954. Transitional instruments escaped the factory that year with contoured bodies finished in the old-style blond, with black Phenolite or new-style white guards. One custom-made Precision, built for Von Gallion of the Gallion Brothers, featured gold hardware, a gold anodized pickguard and an off-white finish. It was very probably the twin of the famous Stratocaster

0001, owned today by Pink Floyd's David Gilmour. By 1955, a contoured body with a two-tone sunburst and white guard was standard on the Precision. That said, '55 also saw the production of a handful of Precision Basses in custom finishes. Blue and pale pink were exhibited at 1955 trade shows and at least one metallic Luar Green instrument was produced, giving a taste of what lay ahead.

Tragedy struck the Fender organization in 1955 when Charlie Hayes was killed in a car crash while driving home to Santa Ana from meetings at the Fender plant on 9 June. The accident shocked all who worked at Fender and left Don and Leo with a problem at Fender Sales. Charlie's widow sold his shares in the company back to the remaining three partners, but the dynamic had shifted. Don and Leo urged F.C. Hall to sell out his stake in the business so that they could gain 50/50 ownership. Hall resisted, knowing all too well that his shares were gaining in value as the Fender brand florished. Eventually the issue was forced and Don and Leo took control of Fender Sales before the summer was out. Under Don's leadership, Fender Sales would grow into the most effective musical instrument sales and marketing company in the business. It was the envy of every

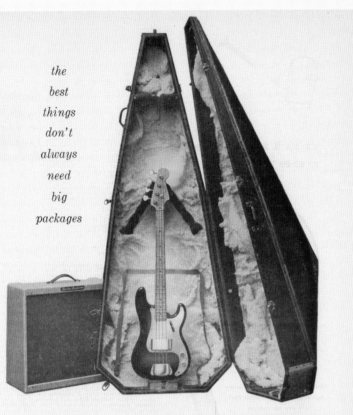

the best things don't always need big packages

Proof . . . the popular Fender precision bass. It's the instrument with the revolutionary concept . . . designed to offer the highest level of bassmanship yet possible. Conveniently smaller in size and easier to play, this sensational instrument provides the tone range and musical quality suited to every type of instrumentation, combo to full orchestra. Bassmen agree its fast-action neck improves technique and inspires a whole new concept of bass playing.

Why not visit your leading music dealer and ask to hear this remarkable instrument yourself.

Fender SALES INC.

308 E. 5th ST. • SANTA ANA, CALIF.

other manufacturer and played a vital role in the continuing success of Fender.

In 1957, a second round of changes were made to the Precision. These were mostly cosmetic and, like the changes from '54, brought the bass more in line with the design of the Stratocaster. The pickguard shape was changed to match that of the Strat and the chrome control panel, which had given electrical shielding, was dispensed with. To make up for the lost shielding, pickguards were now made from gold anodized aluminium, which Fender had introduced on its student model guitars – the Musicmaster and Duo Sonic – during 1956. The headstock was also adapted from its Telecaster shape to a decidedly more Stratocaster-style design. New bridge and

pickup covers were designed too, but the most significant changes to the Precision were hidden beneath those. A new four-saddle bridge, which allowed for perfect intonation and height adjustment on each string, was a long-overdue addition but the most important change lay in a brand-new pickup. Leo found that his early single-coil bass pickups had a tendency to thump the notes out with an attack that took its toll on bass speakers. To lessen this attack, Leo developed a new pickup design featuring two magnets for each string. In order to fit eight evenly spaced magnets under the four strings, he split the pickup into two halves, with coils wound in opposite directions to give it a hum-canceling or 'hum-bucking' effect. The new split pickup gave the Precision a rounded tone and brought bass

Fender
PRECISION
BASS
AND BASS MAN AMP

**FULL, RICH
BASS TONES**

**FASTER
PLAYING
TECHNIQUE**

**CONVENIENT
TO CARRY**

THE CHOICE OF TODAY'S LEADING BASSMEN!

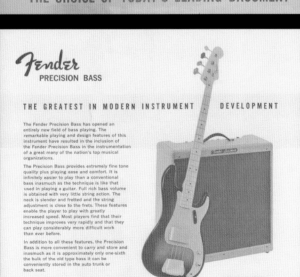

Fender
PRECISION BASS

THE GREATEST IN MODERN INSTRUMENT DEVELOPMENT

The Fender Precision Bass has opened an
entirely new field of bass playing. The
remarkable playing and design features of this
instrument have resulted in the inclusion of
the Fender Precision Bass in the instrumentation
of a great many of the nation's top musical
organizations.

The Precision Bass provides extremely fine tone
quality plus playing ease and comfort. It is
infinitely easier to play than a conventional
bass inasmuch as the technique is like that
used in playing a guitar. Full rich bass volume
is obtained with very little string action. The
neck is slender and fretted and the string
adjustment is close to the frets. These features
enable the player to play with greatly
increased speed. Most players find that their
technique improves very rapidly and that they
can play considerably more difficult work
than ever before.

In addition to all these features, the Precision
Bass is more convenient to carry and store and
inasmuch as it is approximately only one-sixth
the bulk of the old type bass it can be
conveniently stored in the auto trunk or
back seat.

BASSMAN AMP
4-10" heavy duty Jensen speaker.
Full complement tone and volume
controls. Specially designed to
handle low frequency bass tones . .
distortion-free!

players extra clarity and response from their instrument. The 1957 Precision – in two-tone sunburst with a maple neck, gold anodized guard and split pickup – is considered by many to be the finest bass Fender ever produced and is highly regarded by players and collectors alike. One young musician, who favoured a maple board, anodised guard P-Bass was Donald 'Duck' Dunn, one half of the rhythm section of Booker T & The MGs. Dunn pioneered a rhythmical, melodic style during the early '60s that set new standards for bassists everywhere.

As the 1950s drew to a close, Fender made yet more changes to the Precision Bass. Sunbursts changed in '58 from a two-color to a three-color black/red/yellow burst. The year 1959 saw rosewood fingerboards fitted as standard

to all Fender stringed instruments, dramatically changing the look and feel of the Precision. In the same year, gold guards were replaced with faux tortoiseshell, with a thin aluminium sheet placed underneath to give shielding. These final changes would remain the standard finish on Precision Basses throughout the 1960s, and while musicians had mastered the electric bass during the 1950s, they would redefine the role of the instrument during the '60s. One such musician was LA session woman Carol Kaye, a guitarist by trade who fell into bass playing accidentally during 1963. With her Precision Bass, she became the most in-demand player on countless sessions during the '60s and '70s for producers such as Phil Spector and David Axelrod. She

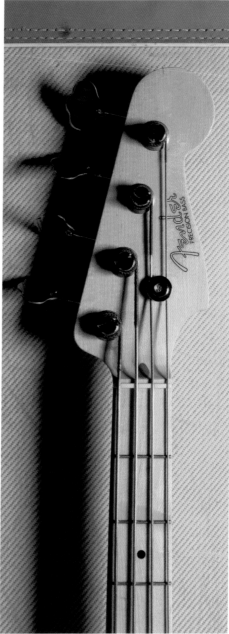

appeared on recordings with artists including Stevie Wonder, Ike & Tina Turner, Elvis Presley, The Monkees and Love, while her performance on The Beach Boys' 'Good Vibrations' ranks as one of the all-time great bass parts.

Perhaps the greatest exponent of the Precision Bass was James Jamerson, bassist with the Motown Records' in-house band, The Funk Brothers. James had started out playing upright bass in the '50s and was initially reluctant to make the switch to electric until a close friend, Horace Ruth, persuaded him to buy his black refinished '57 Precision in 1960. Jamerson would rewrite the rule book for bass playing and his driving, melodic style provided the rocket fuel that propelled the Motown hit machine throughout the

(preceding pages, left to right)
The Page Four with '57 Precision, 1957 – Blond with maple neck, 1959 – Blond with rosewood neck

(facing page, left to right) 1960 – Olympic White with gold hardware, 1963 – Fiesta Red, 1964 – Burgundy Mist

(this page, above left to right) 1955, 1957, 1963

(overleaf, left to right) 1960 – Sunburst, 1960 left-hand – Sunburst, 1960 – Black

(overleaf facing page, left to right) 1963 – Daphne Blue, 1963 – Sonic Blue

'60s. After his '57 Precision was stolen, Jamerson replaced it with another, a brand-new 1962 model in sunburst with a tortoiseshell pickguard. This instrument, through an Ampeg B-15 amplifier, was used to record more hit singles than any other bass in history. Songs like 'Get Ready,' 'Ain't Too Proud To Beg,' 'You Can't Hurry Love,' 'For Once In My Life,' 'This Old Heart Of Mine,' 'Bernadette,' 'Going To A Go-Go' and 'What's Going On' are just a few that display groundbreaking techniques employed by Jamerson on his P-Bass. He would influence Paul McCartney, Jack Bruce, Larry Graham, Bootsy Collins and a whole raft of players that followed in his wake, proving that the interplay of electric bass and drums was the key ingredient to dance-floor hits.

Today, it's almost impossible to imagine music without driving electric bass and its invention was possibly Leo's greatest single contribution to popular music. With the introduction of the Precision Bass in late 1951, Fender had begun to build a family of electric-stringed instruments, and he envisaged others that would soon follow, including a mandolin and a violin as well as further six-string models. By the close of the decade, he had built up a formidable reputation for producing some of the finest electrical instruments available. No longer would his rivals mock his new creations, and the Precision Bass would be recognized as one of the most important musical inventions of all time.

Fender . . .
the choice of
student and
professional
musicians
everywhere!

SOLD BY LEADING RETAIL MUSIC DEALERS THROUGHOUT THE WORLD

Left to right: Esquire, Telecaster Custom, Duo Sonic, Telecaster, Electric Mandolin,
Esquire Custom, Jazzmaster, Stratocaster, Musicmaster and Electric Precision Bass.
Left-hand instruments and custom finish available in most models.

Fender
SALES, INC.
SANTA ANA, CALIF.

INSTRUCTION MANUAL

Fender PRECISION BASS
BY BOB DAYTON

Fender FINE ELECTRIC INSTRUMENTS
DISTRIBUTED BY
Fender Sales, Inc.   1536 E. Chestnut
Santa Ana, California

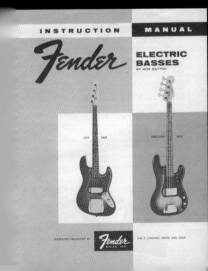

INSTRUCTION MANUAL

Fender ELECTRIC BASSES
BY BOB DAYTON

JAZZ BASS   PRECISION BASS

DISTRIBUTED EXCLUSIVELY BY Fender
SALES, INC.   1546 E. CHESTNUT, SANTA ANA, CALIF.

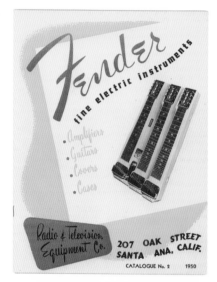

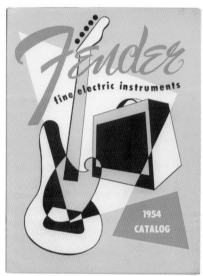

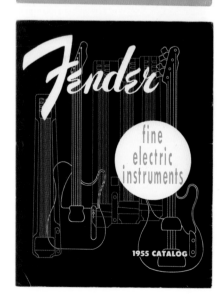

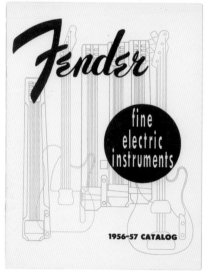

catalogs

The genius of Leo Fender's designs and technical innovations is undisputed. However, without the superb business acumen of Don Randall, head of Fender Sales, it could be argued that few people would have ever had the opportunity to see, much less buy, Fender products outside of Southern California. An extensive dealer network and a persuasive sales force, supported by stylish advertising and sales literature, all helped to establish Fender as a marque of distinction. The designs Randall chose for the company's early catalogs were, like Leo's, both bold and innovative. Early '50s catalog design from Fender's competitors was, by comparison, staid and unremarkable. Fender was a relative newcomer trying to establish its brand identity and could afford to be bolder than Gibson, Gretsch and Rickenbacker. From 1953 through to 1957, the covers of Fender full-line catalogs featured colorful illustrations rather than photographs to entice the buyer. The frugality of Leo Fender is legendary and Don Randall was not one to spend money needlessly. From 1949, as a cost-saving measure, Fender would duplicate front cover designs for two consecutive years (changing only the color), until 1956, when both the year of issue and the following year were shown on the cover to prolong shelf life. No full-line catalogs were issued in 1951 or 1952. In the light of the legal difficulties Fender experienced with Gretsch over the copyright of the Broadcaster name, perhaps Don Randall was reluctant to commit to the expense of designing and printing new promotional material.

Aside from the full line catalogs produced annually by Fender between 1949 – 1970 (excluding years 1951,1952 and 1959) shown here and on pages 206 and 271, the company also produced a two color 8 or 12 page catalog between 1955 – 1965 that was offered by dealers and given away as a free annual insert in Downbeat magazine (see page 121). Mini / foldout catalogs (shown on page 249) were also offered in the years 1952, 1953, 1954, 1959, 1960, 1961, 1965, 1966, 1967 and 1968.

stratocaster

It's difficult to imagine how futuristic the Fender Stratocaster must have looked when it was launched in April 1954. Elvis Presley had not yet recorded his first single, manned space flight was seven years away and Jimi Hendrix was still only eleven years old. Yet here it was – the most versatile, forward-thinking and beautifully designed electric guitar of all time. Inarguably the most important electric guitar in history, the 'Strat' is a true design classic and a 20th-century icon. It has been imitated by countless makers, but its original design has never been bettered. It has shown the door to its competitors for well over five decades and will doubtless be in production for many more to come.

Leo Fender was obsessed with improvement. Whether it was the record changer that he patented in 1945, his ever-growing line of amplifiers or, in this instance, his Telecaster design, he was always seeking to better what had gone before. Not content with the Tele, Leo focused on four areas that he felt could be improved upon: intonation, tone, player comfort and the addition of a vibrato unit. His idea was to make the Telecaster obsolete, to replace it with something better. Work had begun on a new guitar as early as 1951, but the exact story of how the Stratocaster would reach perfection is complex. Leo was aided by musicians who, on regular visits to the Fender factory, would bring ideas on how the Telecaster design could be improved.

Namely, contouring the guitar's body for greater comfort and an improved bridge with a saddle for each string to give better intonation and tuning. Leo was a good listener and these ideas quickly sank in. Head of Fender Sales Don Randall claimed the Stratocaster was a direct response to Gibson's Les Paul, which had appeared in mid- '52 and posed serious competition to the Telecaster: "We had a very plain-Jane Telecaster. Gibson came out with the Les Paul. It was a nice-looking instrument. It was pretty, and we needed an upgrade in our own instrument." He also suggested that the new guitar should have a vibrato and three pickups for a greater tonal range, features that would place the guitar a step ahead of the Les Paul in the marketplace.

During 1952, Leo became aware that the Fender operation was fast outgrowing the small tin and brick buildings at Pomona Avenue, so he decided to buy a large strip of land a mile due west from the existing factory in Fullerton's town center. The new site gave plenty of room for expansion and Leo made plans, once again with his friend Grady Neal, for the construction of three huge buildings that would use up around 50 per cent of the land. His thinking behind building separate units was that, if business started to wane, he could rent out one or more of the new buildings. He needn't have worried.

Since splitting with Doc Kauffman in the mid- '40s, Leo had relied on input from musicians who would drop by the factory. By the early '50s, it had become apparent that he needed a lab assistant on hand at all times, ideally a professional musician, who could work alongside him to develop his new designs. In 1953, renowned steel player and Fender endorsee Noel Boggs recommended his friend Freddie Tavares for the position. Freddie was a native of Hawaii, born in Maui in 1913, and had spent many years as a professional steel guitar player in and around Los Angeles. In order to keep his session work going, Freddie initially worked part-time at Fender – one of his more famous recordings was the swooping steel line that introduced Looney Tunes cartoons – but before long he would sacrifice his career as a musician for full-time employment at Fender. Freddie was intelligent, with a laid-back, friendly persona. Not only was he an excellent steel, Spanish and bass guitarist but he was also a dab hand in electronics and draughtsmanship. He would prove to be an invaluable asset to Leo, the perfect foil and a loyal friend. Work progressed on the new Fender guitar throughout 1953, and during that year, Don Randall would name it the 'Stratocaster.' The name was a logical, but inspired, follow-through in the Broadcaster/ Telecaster succession, aiming ever spacewards.

(this page, above) 1954 Stratocaster in its original 'poodle' case

(facing page, left) a prototype Stratocaster is road tested in late 1953, Freddie Tavares can be seen to the left backing on steel guitar in this photograph taken by Leo Fender

(facing page, right) another early Stratocaster from 1954

The instrument would indeed take guitar design into
a new stratosphere.

Local guitarists Rex Gallion and Bill Carson were
heavily involved in the initial stages of development of the
Stratocaster, especially the body design, and Leo claimed Bill
was his favourite guinea pig for the guitar. Carson had already
bevelled the front edge and scooped out the back of his
Telecaster with a saw, claiming that its squared-off edges dug
into his arm and rib cage. Leo picked up on this and rounded
off all the edges on his prototype Stratocaster. He also gave
the new body design, similar in shape to the Precision Bass,
deep contours on the front and the rear, similar to those on
Bill's customised Tele. As usual, no good idea was lost on
Leo. Carson too had suggested extra pickups for the new
instrument, as many as four or five, but Leo said they wouldn't
fit, adding just one extra in the middle position of the standard
Telecaster layout. Leo worked long and hard on the coils and
magnets, determined to get a sound that would appeal to
guitarists of all styles. Unlike the Telecaster, Leo staggered
the height of each pole piece in the new pickup design to
give a more balanced response from each string. A three-way
pickup switch allowed the player to select only one pickup at
a time, but guitarists were quick to figure out that the selector
could be jammed between settings to enable effective bridge
and middle, and middle and neck, pickup settings. The muted

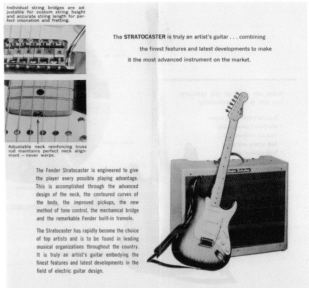

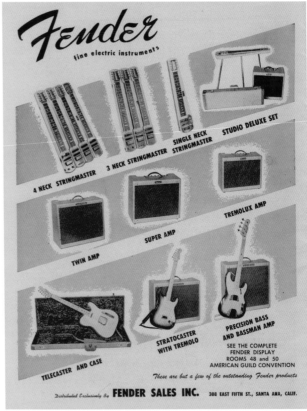

BUDDY MERRILL featured guitarist with the Lawrence Welk Orchestra uses only *Fender* Fine Electric Instruments

why Fender?

JOHN CUCCI
prefers
Fender
fine electric
instruments

CHARLEY RAYE
uses only
Fender
fine electric instruments

BILLY CARSON
uses
Fender
Fine Electric Instruments
Exclusively

twang produced by pickups paired in these positions soon became a hallmark of the Strat's tonal range – more a happy accident than an intentional feature.

Though the Stratocaster's body, pickups and pickguard design were well underway by the time Freddie Tavares began work at Fender in March 1953, it was Freddie that helped Leo perfect and refine the graceful curves. "I remember that we had a piece of paper with six lines down it: six lines for the strings, and two cross lines for the nut and the bridge. Then we drew a body on it, erasing here and there until we got the shape we liked," said Freddie in 1979, making the creation of a masterpiece sound incredibly simple. The cherry on the cake of the body design was a novel jack socket that accepted the lead into the front of the guitar at an angle. Strangely, this classic piece of design never made it onto another Fender instrument.

Like Carson's body contours, another borrowed idea was a new-style headstock design, something that would become a trademark for all Fender guitars from this point on. The neck was of all-maple construction with a 'skunk stripe' running down the back, similar to the Telecaster. The headstock was similar too, with six tuners on one side and a rounded ball shape at the end. The difference was it flared out at the bottom, giving the Fender decal room to be seen instead of being hidden under the strings. The design was remarkably similar to the one Leo had seen on the guitar Paul Bigsby built for Merle Travis in 1948 and it's fairly certain that it was adapted by Freddie and Leo from that instrument. That said, the Fender design was subtle and understated compared to Bigsby's. Although he was never set up for mass production of his guitars (he built less than 30 six-strings), Bigsby would find his own success with a vibrato design he developed. It would be adopted as the standard on all Gretsch vibrato-equipped guitars until the early '60s, and a factory-fit option on Gibson's instruments for many years to come.

For his vibrato unit, Leo was determined not to copy Bigsby. He saw inherent flaws with Paul's design and believed he could do better. True to form, Leo went back to the drawing board, designing from the ground up. Contemporary vibrato designs, including the Bigsby, utilized stationary bridges over which the strings would be pulled or loosened via a spring-loaded arm to raise or lower pitch. This abrasive action easily put guitars out of tune and Leo looked to remedy the fault. His idea was a simple one, but it would take time to perfect and would hold up the release of the Stratocaster by several months. The new unit – named a Tremolo by Leo – involved a combined bridge and vibrato where the whole unit rocked forwards and backwards as one, minimizing friction. It was simplicity itself, but designed and built to exacting standards using new tools and dies provided by Fender's trusty supply company Race & Olmstead. To keep the new design compact and neat, Leo routed into the guitar's solid body, concealing much of the workings, including the springs, inside the guitar. However, teething problems occurred on several early designs when, during testing, the string saddles proved prone to collapse under stress. Don Randall was eager to take delivery of a

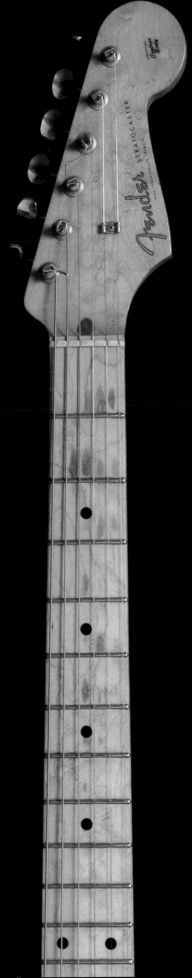

speaking
for cats
everywhere

Fender has that special sound and rare craftsmanship that makes for easy playing and enjoyable listening! Why not visit your nearest dealer . . . see and hear for yourself.

Fender SALES, INC. • 308 EAST 5th ST. • SANTA ANA, CALIF.

portrait
of success

Skilled hands take to a Fender guitar! An
instrument which combines unsurpassed
workmanship with modern electronics,
Fender offers to the serious musician the
superlative performance that spells success.
Your leading dealer will introduce you
to your new Fender guitar . . . you'll be the
proud owner of the finest electric
instrument made.

Look to Fender
for the Finest!

Fender SALES, INC.
308 East Fifth Street
Santa Ana, California

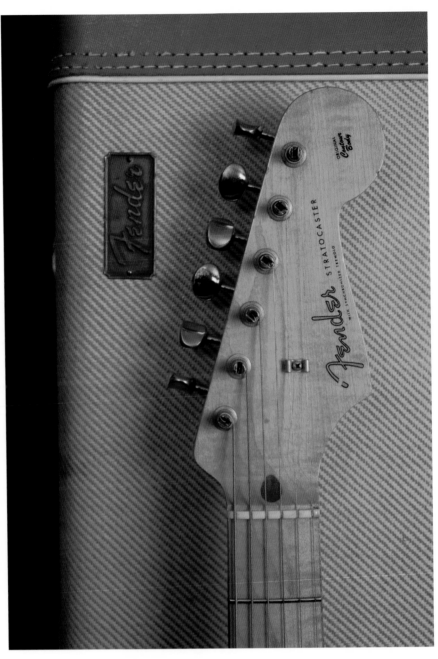

prototype instrument for the 1953 NAMM show but Leo resisted, insisting that his Tremolo unit must be perfected first. Undeterred, he forged ahead, and by late 1953, the Tremolo design was ready. It far outperformed any other device on the market and, unlike its rivals, could provide more than a gentle wobble in the guitar's pitch. Players soon learned that if they pressed down hard on the Tremolo arm, or pulled the arm out, the guitar's pitch altered dramatically, yet still returned in tune when released. By the mid- to late-'60s, the Strat Tremolo would be put to startling effect by musicians the world over.

The Stratocaster was finally ready for production. The first ads and flyers depicting the new space-age instrument,

printed during April 1954, justifiably proclaimed: 'First again in the field of amplified music... the thrilling new 'Stratocaster' by Fender! Years ahead in design – unequalled in performance... a flick of the wrist means live, Tremolo action – perfect pitch.' The new guitar featured a two-color sunburst finish, which was new to a Fender instrument in 1954. "That was another market consideration," Randall told guitar historian Tom Wheeler. "All of our competitors had one; we were the only ones who didn't. I thought a sunburst would make the guitar a little more businesslike, if you will – fancier." A single-ply white pickguard with chrome-plated hardware and nickel-plated Kluson tuning keys completed the look. The earliest Strats from '54 feature

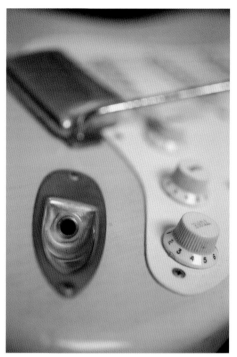

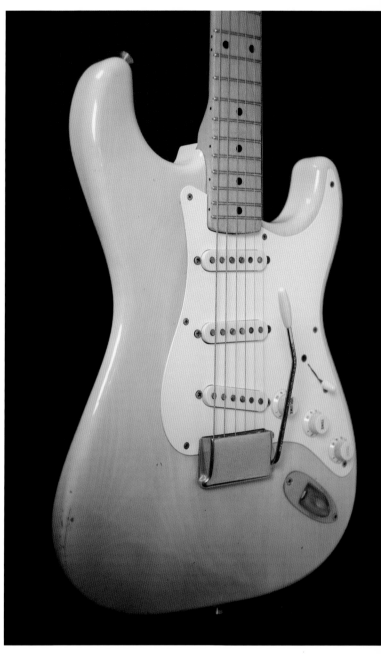

white plastic pickup covers with rounded-off top edges and unique 'short skirt' volume and tone knobs. The pearl-white plastic used for these proved fragile and prone to cracking. Sturdier materials and newly designed pickup covers, with sharp top edges and knobs with longer 'skirts' that made numbers more visible, were employed by the end of the year. Bridges were fitted with a chrome cover prior to leaving the factory, but proved impractical. Although shown on the instruments in these pages, they were usually discarded within minutes of purchase, serving only to smarten up the instrument's appearance at trade shows and in music stores. The earliest Strats were shipped in brown 'form fit' cases made by Bulwin that followed the guitar's contours on

(facing page and this page, above)
1958 – Blond with gold hardware
'Mary Kaye' Strat

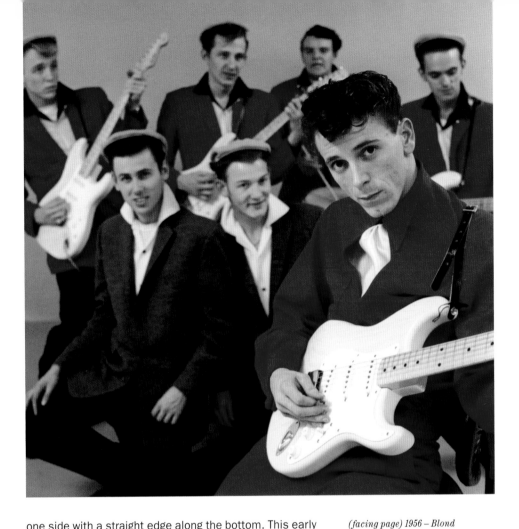

one side with a straight edge along the bottom. This early case design is often referred to as the 'poodle', so called because the outline could be mistaken for the owner taking his dog for a walk! Cases had changed by late '54 to a new rectangular design covered in striped tweed with brown leather ends. A soft, plush red lining was fitted to the interior, which added a touch of class to proceedings. The new cases, made for Fender by the Victoria Luggage Company in Los Angeles, were of far sturdier construction than the earlier 'thermometer' or 'poodle' type and did a good job of protecting instruments. This new case, in various styles of covering material, would remain a constant throughout Fender's golden age.

Only a handful of Strats left the Fender factory during the early months of 1954; full production would begin in October of that year. In the months in between, Leo Fender made the important decision to hire a factory manager. Output had grown year on year since 1946, and Leo was beginning to feel the stress of running an operation with close to 40 staff. Also, the new factory buildings were on a scale Leo simply wasn't used to. Quality control was of utmost importance and, in order to maintain the standards that the company was known for, Leo realized it was time to bring someone in to organize day-to-day operations. This would allow Leo to retreat to his lab to concentrate on developing new instruments. Forrest White was a long-term acquaintance of Leo. He'd shown an interest in Fender instruments since the late '40s and had visited the factory on a couple of occasions, showing Leo a ten-string lap steel he'd made in 1951. Born in Akron, Ohio, in 1920, Forrest had emigrated to California in 1944 to work at the Lockheed factory, producing P-38 fighters during World War Two. He would later work at the Ford plant in Riverside, California, on the production of amphibious military vehicles. He was skilled in industrial engineering and business management – just what the Fender operation needed to streamline production and to fulfil back orders on some of the more popular models. Under Forrest, the factory was more efficient than it had ever been before and productivity was on the increase, just in time to cope with the demand that lay ahead.

Sratocaster sales were slow to begin with. Richard Smith reports in his book *Fender: The Sound Heard 'Round The World* that only 268 instruments were delivered to Fender Sales during 1954, with a further 452 in 1955. Leo Fender would later state: "The Telecaster was still so new. Even when we came out with the Stratocaster, that newness hadn't really worn off." Perhaps the Strat was too big a leap for guitarists still set in their ways. Many still thought of an electric guitar as a modified acoustic with a pickup mounted to the top. The key was to get the new instrument into the hands of players. In 1954, there was simply nothing that could touch the Strat in terms of playability and tonal range. It was genuinely years ahead of its time.

Some of the first players to adopt the new guitar and put it to good use were, of course, Bill Carson and Rex Gallion, who had helped steer the design process. Both men received custom-built instruments – with special gold-anodized pickguards – as a thank you from Leo for their contribution. Carson's red Strat became his trademark during the mid- to late-'50s and another to receive a red instrument with gold guard was LA blues guitarist Pee Wee Crayton. It's likely that his 1954 recordings such as 'The Telephone Is Ringing' may be some of the first to commit a Strat to vinyl. Long-term Fender associate Eldon Shamblin of Bob Wills' Texas Playboys was another to receive a custom-finished instrument in 1954. His was gold with a white pickguard and put to good use on the band's mid-'50s western swing recordings. Two more bluesmen quick to endorse the new guitar were Buddy Guy and Otis Rush, both of whom pushed the Strat to its limits and gave early displays of what it was capable of. Gene Vincent's Blue Caps were equipped with no less than three blond Strats and a matching Precision during 1956 and when guitarist Howard Reed joined the band during the spring of 1958, he brought with him his own custom-ordered 1955 Black Strat that he'd purchased through Dallas Fender dealer J Fred McCord. The guitar was almost certainly one of the earliest Strats ordered in a custom color by a non-name artist. Another artist closely associated with the Stratocaster was Mary Kaye, often referred to as the 'First Lady Of Rock'n'Roll,' who posed with a beautiful blond Strat with gold-plated hardware for Fender ads and sales literature during 1956. This rare combination is today referred to as the 'Mary Kaye' model and original examples command huge sums.

(below) the growing factory at 500 South Raymond in September 1957

(facing page) Stratocaster production in 1957

You won't part with yours either*

You won't part with yours either*

You won't part with yours either*

You won't part with yours either*

One musician in particular, a young Texan guitarist named Buddy Holly, would play a huge role in popularizing the Stratocaster. Buddy was an astonishing songwriter and performer who did a lot to change the course of popular music in a few short years. His music was a blend of country, rockabilly, rock'n'roll and pop, and his chosen instrument was a 1955 Stratocaster that he'd bought in his hometown of Lubbock, Texas. Buddy's music was well crafted and modern, and his Stratocaster suited it perfectly. He was one of the first teen idols and his many TV appearances would have been many viewers' first glimpse of Fender's futuristic guitar. It's undoubted that Buddy's early endorsement would have promoted hundreds, perhaps thousands, of Stratocaster sales, but sadly, he would die in a plane crash during February 1959 while travelling between shows. His gravestone depicts a carving of his beloved Stratocaster guitar. It's interesting to note that Buddy never became an official Fender endorsee during his lifetime and his picture would not be featured in a Fender catalog until 1982, some 23 years after his death. Perhaps down to Don Randall's conservative musical tastes, Fender never really pushed the rock'n'roll angle through their sales literature, sticking to more traditional, uncontroversial artists to promote their products. In retrospect, this could be viewed as a missed opportunity, but sales continued to boom regardless.

Since its introduction in 1952, Gibson had made several changes to their Les Paul guitar, constantly upgrading it to compete with the Telecaster and now the Strat. Initial improvements were made to the bridge, but in 1957, a new pickup was designed by a Gibson in-house technician named Seth Lover. The humbucking pickup, or 'humbucker,' was a real breakthrough for Gibson. It featured two coils for each pickup, wound in different directions that, when linked together, produced a fantastic thick, rich tone. It also cancelled out background noise and interference that could sometimes spoil the signal on single-coil pickups, like those used on most Gibson and Fender guitars. With its new humbucking pickups, the Les Paul design had reached its

(facing page, left to right) 1955 – two-tone Sunburst, Buddy Holly photographed in England in 1958 with his second Stratocaster bought the previous year

(above, left to right) 1958 – three-tone Sunburst, 1958 – three-tone Sunburst left-hand model, 1962 – three-tone Sunburst

zenith and finally looked set to take on the Stratocaster. In 1958, Gibson dropped the gold finish that Les Paul Standards had sported since their introduction in favour of a sunburst top with natural mahogany back and sides. The top, still crafted from carved maple, now displayed beautiful, flamey, book-matched wood grains. Gibson were going all out to produce the best possible instrument in an attempt to oust Fender's supremacy in the solid-body guitar field. As well as the upgraded Les Paul Standard, Gibson also sought out-of-house designers to add futuristic body shapes to their line. They were not prepared to be outdone by the Stratocaster, which was now selling in significant numbers. The Gibson Explorer and Flying V were radical attempts to place the Kalamazoo company at the front of the electric guitar field. A new range of thin-line semi-acoustics was also launched by Gibson in '58, and under the leadership of Ted McCarty, the company was making an all-guns-blazing bid to gain a stronghold in the rapidly growing market.

While the Gibson thin-line 335 and 330 guitars were an instant success, offering players familiar Gibson features in a more compact user-friendly package, the new and updated solid-body designs didn't fare so well. Gibson had produced one of the finest electric guitars of all time in the Sunburst Les Paul Standard, but no matter how good the workmanship or how good the humbuckers sounded, the Les Paul was being outsold by the Stratocaster and ever-popular Telecaster. Gibson managed to produce only 1700 Les Paul Standard guitars between 1958 and 1960 before dropping it from the line. The futuristic guitars from the 'Modern' range had fared worse, with around 100 Flying Vs and less than 30 Explorers produced before both were discontinued in 1959. Gibson went back to the drawing board and replaced the old-style Les Paul with a new SG (solid guitar) shape in 1961. Not surprisingly, the new Les Pauls were available with or without vibrato. Gibson would rise up to rival Fender in the solid-body guitar field during the 1960s as their ever-popular acoustic and semi-acoustic lines always kept them profitable. By 1968, the old-style Les Paul, already considered a lost classic, was successfully relaunched.

Back in Fullerton in 1958, Fender were experiencing boom times. The Stratocaster, and pretty well every model in the Fender range, was selling well and Forrest White made plans for an extra four buildings to be built at South

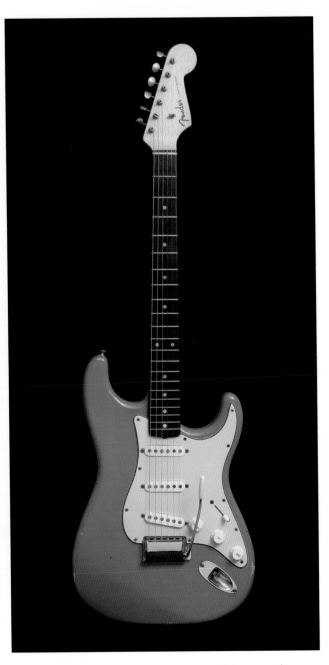

(preceding pages, left to right)
1962 – Sonic Blue, Ike Turner with
his Sonic Blue Strat

(this page, above, left to right)
'63, '62 and '61 headstocks

(this page, above right)
1962 – Foam Green

Raymond Avenue in a bid to keep pace with increased orders. Fender sales also moved in July to new, larger premises at 1536 East Chestnut, Santa Ana. In London, England, a young singer called Cliff Richard and his backing band The Shadows wrote to Fender requesting a catalog. Due to an import ban that had been in place since 1951, there had been a strict embargo on US-made musical instruments entering the UK. Cliff and The Shadows were obsessed with Buddy Holly and were desperate to get their hands on a Stratocaster like the one pictured on the first Crickets album. They also obsessed over the guitar sound of James Burton, who they also believed played a Strat – Burton actually used a Tele. When the 1958 – 1959 full-line

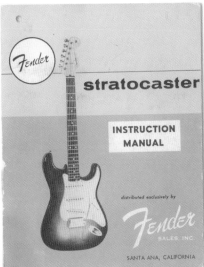

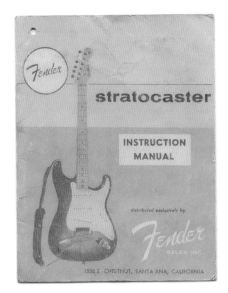

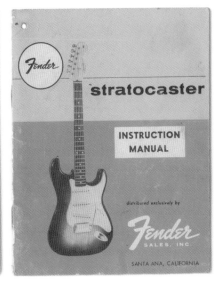

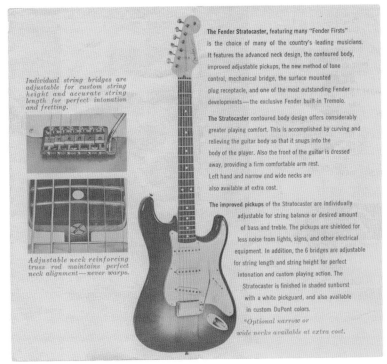

Individual string bridges are adjustable for custom string height and accurate string length for perfect intonation and fretting.

Adjustable neck reinforcing truss rod maintains perfect neck alignment—never warps.

The Fender Stratocaster, featuring many "Fender Firsts" is the choice of many of the country's leading musicians. It features the advanced neck design, the contoured body, improved adjustable pickups, the new method of tone control, mechanical bridge, the surface mounted plug receptacle, and one of the most outstanding Fender developments—the exclusive Fender built-in Tremolo.

The Stratocaster contoured body design offers considerably greater playing comfort. This is accomplished by curving and relieving the guitar body so that it snugs into the body of the player. Also the front of the guitar is dressed away, providing a firm comfortable arm rest. Left hand and narrow and wide necks are also available at extra cost.

The improved pickups of the Stratocaster are individually adjustable for string balance or desired amount of bass and treble. The pickups are shielded for less noise from lights, signs, and other electrical equipment. In addition, the 6 bridges are adjustable for string length and string height for perfect intonation and custom playing action. The Stratocaster is finished in shaded sunburst with a white pickguard, and also available in custom DuPont colors.

"Optional narrow or wide necks available at extra cost.

catalog finally arrived, the group ogled the instruments on the full-color cover, but one guitar in particular caught their eye: a red Stratocaster with gold hardware. The band were using Vox amplifiers built by Jennings Musical Industries and headed down to the Jennings' shop in central London to see if a red Stratocaster like the one they'd seen could be ordered. Luckily, the embargo was just being lifted and the custom-ordered guitar, the first Fender had shipped to the UK, arrived in early summer 1959. In the hands of Shadows guitarist Hank Marvin, the red Stratocaster caused an overnight sensation in the UK and was immediately used to stunning effect on hits like 'Apache.' Nothing like it had been seen or heard before and soon every budding rock'n'roller

in Britain and Europe was desperate to lay their hands on a real Fender guitar. Jennings were quick to see the potential. Fender guitars were a perfect match for their Vox amps and they became the first to import Fender instruments into the UK during late 1959. Before long, all The Shadows were equipped with Fender guitars and UK sales were on the rise. In a typically shrewd business move, Don Randall allowed room for a second UK distributor, Selmer, to import Fender products. Demand was huge and the Fullerton factory could hardly keep up with the orders they received for Fiesta Red Stratocasters like Hank's. It was the first time custom-color Fender guitars were ordered in bulk and gave a good indication of what was to come.

The Beach Boys play

Fender
MUSICAL INSTRUMENTS

Del Shannon plays

Fender
MUSICAL INSTRUMENTS

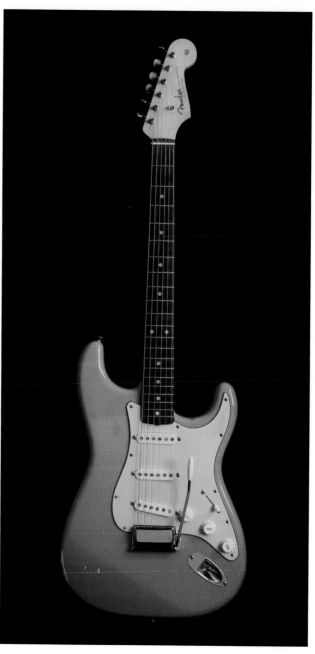

(this page, above right)
1962 – Fiesta Red

(facing page) 1962 – Candy Apple Red, factory refinish

(overleaf, left to right) 1964 – Sonic Blue, 1964 – Olympic White

The year 1958 saw the first of several cosmetic changes to the Stratocaster. Sunburst finishes switched from a two-tone black into yellow, to a three-color black, through red, into yellow. This was to bring them into line with a new six-string model, the Jazzmaster, that had just been introduced. The Jazzmaster also featured a rosewood fingerboard, which Fender Sales believed gave it a classy image, and these became standard on all Fender guitars, including the Strat, during '59. The summer months of 1959 also saw a gradual change from single-ply white pickguards to three-ply white/black/white celluloid nitrate guards. Due to the unstable nature of celluloid plastics, the center black section on three-ply guards leeches into the top and bottom layers.

These guards never look completely white, but start out with a slightly grayish tint and fade to an almost greenish hue, the shade of which is dependent on exposure to sunlight and smoky atmospheres. Collectors often refer to three-ply white nitrate pickguards as 'green guards'; these remained standard on all Strats until early 1965, when a new, completely white plastic replaced the old 'green' pickguards.

During the early '60s, Stratocaster sales soared. Fender was now an international operation, distributing instruments to all parts of the world. From Australia to Japan, Sweden, Germany and France, guitarists everywhere knew Fender was *the* name in electric solid body guitars. Rock'n'roll had exploded and splintered into various sub genres the world over and Fender instruments seemed to have found their way into all of these. Dick Dale, 'King of the Surf Guitar', developed a new, raw instrumental music on his left-handed Gold Sparkle Strat during the early '60s. Dale played through an amplifier specially developed for him by Fender, the 85-watt Showman, which he cranked to insane volume levels. He also used a Fender Reverb Unit to add a 'wet' effect and produced an unrivalled dark, menacing twang on hits like 'Let's Go Trippin'' and 'Misirlou'. In England during the late '50s, a young George Harrison drew Strats on his school books, inspired by pictures he'd seen of Buddy Holly. And although his group, The Beatles later favoured semi-acoustic guitars by Rickenbacker, Gretsch and Epiphone, "It was funny," explained George, "because all these American bands kept coming over to England and saying, 'how do you get that sound?' And the more I listened to it I decided I didn't like it. It was crap." In 1965, Harrison and John Lennon purchased a matching pair of Sonic Blue '61 Strats for the recording of the 'Help' and 'Rubber Soul' albums, putting them to excellent use on recordings like 'Nowhere Man' and 'The Word.' Folk singer Bob Dylan, who had seen Buddy Holly perform just three nights before his fatal crash, opted for a Strat when he controversially 'went electric' at Newport Folk Festival in 1965. Ike Turner, one of rock's pioneers and innovators, was seldom seen without a Stratocaster during the '60s and '70s, and another African American guitarist, born Johnny Allen Hendrix, would change the world's perception of guitar playing forever on a Stratocaster during the late '60s.

Over the last 50 years, there is hardly a guitarist who hasn't picked up a Stratocaster at some point. Such is the instrument's popularity that it sometimes alienates players who feel it too commonplace or overused. Many turn to other models in search of individuality. Most, however, return to the Strat, acknowledging that it can't be beaten as the greatest electric design of all time. It's hard to argue with an instrument that performs so well, sounds so great, looks fantastic and fits the player like a glove. Everything about the Strat is right and it has become a veritable institution among guitarists, a touchstone and an invaluable tool. It has outsold every other guitar design and its popularity remains unchallenged.

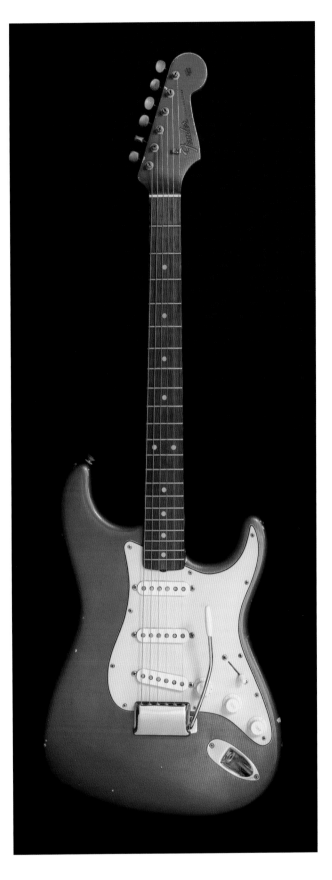

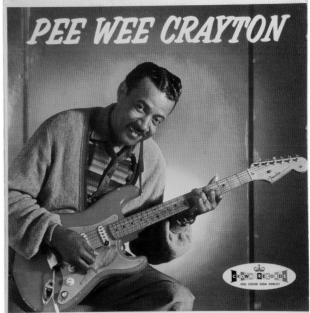

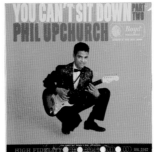

narrow panel amplifiers 1955–1964

By 1955, popular music, especially rock'n'roll, was a growth industry. The new bands liked to play loud, and as the music became more popular, live audiences grew as, in turn, did the need for louder amplification. Leo Fender was well aware of the needs of musicians and was in the process of giving them exactly what they wanted. The Narrow Panel tweed amplifiers of the mid- to late- '50s were endorsed by pretty much every rock'n'roll act across America and set standards for amplifier design that would span decades.

Stylistically similar to the Wide Panel tweed amps that had gone before, the new Narrow Panel amplifiers featured a redesigned cabinet with a thinner, narrower margin at the top and bottom of the speaker baffle. New metal nameplates that carried the Fender marque, along with the model name in a brush script, helped distinguish the new amps. The old-style, brown linen grille cloth that had been prone to tearing under touring conditions was replaced by a new, more robust woven plastic material, brown in colour with a thin, yellow stripe running horizontally. This new-style grille cloth would, in various shades, remain the standard on Fender amps for many years to come. The real difference, however, between the old and the new amps lay inside; Leo and his assistant Freddie Tavares had worked long and hard to develop the circuits. The Narrow Panels were louder than previous amps with more tonal range, and when turned up, the clean signal began to break up and distort, adding warmth and character to the sound. At full volume, the amps positively screamed, giving an overdriven effect that would be put to great use by many rock'n'roll players.

The Tremolux amplifier, introduced in mid-1955, was the first Fender to feature Tremolo – a pulsating change in volume, the speed and intensity of which can be set to produce a very pleasing effect. Tremolo had long been a feature in amplifiers made by Gibson and Danelectro, but was new to the Fender range. It would become a regular on many amps that followed.

For the bass player, Leo developed a new Bassman amp with 4 x 10" speakers and a whopping 50-watt output. Traditional double basses were being drowned out by louder guitars and drums as rock'n'roll gathered steam. Double bass and electric bass players alike were looking for more power to propel their rhythm instrument, and Leo had the answer. Guitarists also took to the Bassman and the amp quickly gained a reputation for its thick, creamy overdrive and distortion. It was loud too! A '50s Bassman amp would later form the basis for Jim Marshall's early creations in London, England. It is often said that much of the famous Marshall tone made famous by The Who, Jimi Hendrix and Eric Clapton in the late '60s was derived from the Narrow Panel Bassman.

At the top end of the Fender amp line, the Twin was radically overhauled. Raised first to 50 watts, then 85 in 1958, it became the most powerful commercially available amplifier at the time. Buddy Holly favoured these amps on his final 'Winter Dance Party' tour in 1959 and the high-powered, 85-watt Twins

remain one of the most sought-after Fender amplifiers of all time. Fender's graphic designer Bob Perine came up with a new ad during '58 which depicted himself playing a Telecaster through one of the new Twins with his five-year-old daughter Terri listening intently only inches from the speaker. Not surprisingly, this image has become known as 'The Little Deaf Girl Ad.'

The smallest amp in the Narrow Panel range – the 4-watt Champ – was to prove the real survivor. It lasted almost unchanged from 1955 until 1964 and sold in huge numbers to students and professionals alike. Its compactness, coupled with its versatile tone, has made it an all-round favourite to this day. When turned up to around halfway and above, these little amps can produce a huge overdriven sound to rival many larger models. In 1964, the Narrow Panel tweed Champ was recovered in the new-style black Tolex for just a few months until the new Blackface Champ would supersede it, finally bringing the Narrow Panel era to a close.

Champ: 4 watt; 1 x 6" speaker
Princeton: 4.5 watt; 1 x 8" speaker
Harvard: 10 watt; 1 x 8" and 1 x 10" speaker
Vibrolux: 10 watt; 1 x 10" speaker
Deluxe: 15 watt; 1 x 12" speaker
Tremolux: 15 watt; 1 x 12" speaker
Super: 20 watt; 2 x 10" speakers
Bassman: 50 watt; 4 x 10" speakers
Pro-Amp: 26 watt; 1 x 15" speaker
Bandmaster: 26 watt; 3 x 10" speakers
Twin: 50 and 85 watt; 2 x 12" speakers

THE INSIDE STORY

Why X-Ray an amplifier? True, an X-Ray doesn't show you what Fender Amps can really do, but we wanted the opportunity of showing you why Fender Amps are the best choice for musicians everywhere. First, they are constructed of only the finest components, sturdily enclosed in a rugged, heavy-duty cabinet built for hard professional use. The components of a Fender Amp, such as the heavy-duty power and output transformers and distortion-free Jensen speakers provide longer Amp life. In addition, the distinctive abrasion-resistant luggage linen covering and convenient top-mounted controls give these amps a beautifully finished appearance.

To find out how Fender Amps can really perform, visit your Fender Dealer today . . . try them . . . listen and compare. You'll prove to yourself that Fender Amps have the finest overall tone quality and will give you trouble-free top performance.

WHEN YOU BUY FENDER, YOU BUY QUALITY FROM THE INSIDE OUT!

musicmaster and duo sonic

Fender had been courting the student market since the company's humble beginnings in 1946. The appropriately named Princeton steel guitar and matching amplifier more than hinted at their inherent student status. By the mid-1950s, the line of steel guitars and amplifiers was well rounded with clearly defined upgrade paths. The Telecaster and Stratocaster guitars were aimed squarely at professional musicians, and during 1955, at Don Randall's

suggestion, Leo Fender began work on a new student model guitar.

The Fender factory was Leo Fender's domain. He was responsible for the design, research, development and manufacturing of all instruments there, but according to Randall, "Leo never made anything that wasn't requested by Fender Sales first." Don intimately understood the electrical musical instrument market. He knew what was needed, what would sell and how to

market it, and it was Randall himself who named the new instrument the Musicmaster. Don chose the name because it "sounded kind of cute." It also fitted in with the 'master' monikers, such as the Stringmaster and Bandmaster, that had gone before. Like the Champion student amplifiers and lap steels, the new name was also intended to give the young player a feeling of empowerment.

Bill Haley & The Comets' 'Rock Around The Clock' had sat at the top of the Billboard Charts for ten straight weeks during the summer of 1955, and kids everywhere wanted in on the action. The popularity of rock'n'roll and the influence it had upon aspiring musicians and their choice of instrument was not lost on Don Randall. It would prove to be a major catalyst in the future success of Fender, and the new student models would play a key role in luring budding guitarists towards the Fender brand.

The new guitar came in two configurations: the one-pickup Musicmaster and a two-pickup model named the Duo Sonic. Both featured a new, smaller-scale neck referred to as the '¾ size', designed for 'adult and young musicians with small hands.' The headstock was similar in style to that introduced on the Stratocaster a year earlier and the new guitars featured simple, single-coil pickups not unlike those found on the Strat. The body was of smaller dimensions, thinner and more compact than the Telecaster or Stratocaster, and it looked more in proportion to the younger players at which it was aimed. A simple, three-saddle bridge was designed and the guitar featured Telecaster-style tone and volume knobs with a metal pickup selector switch on the Duo Sonic only.

The first Musicmaster orders were received on 26 September 1955, but production did not commence until six months later during April 1956. Fender had been busy developing an electric mandolin and the Narrow Panel amps during 1955, and such was Leo's quest for perfection that Don would claim he was "late on nearly everything." In the first production run, Musicmasters were made in small numbers and differed slightly from subsequent models. The bodies were thicker and made from ash not alder. Pickguards were black-painted

(top) Musicmaster body being spray painted, May '57
(above) Musicmaster and Duo Sonic bodies laying out to dry in the factory, June '64
(facing page) Musicmaster with black painted pickguard from the first production run in 1956

New Fender *Musicmaster* Three-quarter Size Electric Standard

Patented adjustable bridge for each string, and string-action adjusting screws are enclosed beneath the chromed swing-type bridge cover.

Modern cutaway body design permits easy playing of all twenty-one frets.

Truss rod reinforced neck . . . easily adjustable, never warps. The new slender neck design makes possible easy fretting and faster action.

Modern head design affords straight string pull and easier tuning.

Surface plug receptacle accommodates the new Fender "Cord-Grip" plug . . . cord pivots freely for maximum playing convenience.

High fidelity pickup is fully adjustable to suit the player's tone balance requirement.

Fender
fine electric instruments

The Fender Musicmaster . . . especially designed for adult and young musicians with small fingers . . . provides all the playing qualities and design features every guitar player seeks . . . fast, comfortable neck action; excellent tone; variable string action and pickup response; plus modern cutaway design . . . See the Musicmaster three-quarter electric standard . . . play it . . . it is truly an outstanding addition to the Fender line of Fine Electric Instruments.

AVAILABLE SOON!

The DUO-SONIC ¾ Electric Guitar with two pickups and the finest Fender features.

Distributed Exclusively By **FENDER SALES, INC.** 308 E. FIFTH ST., SANTA ANA, CALIF.

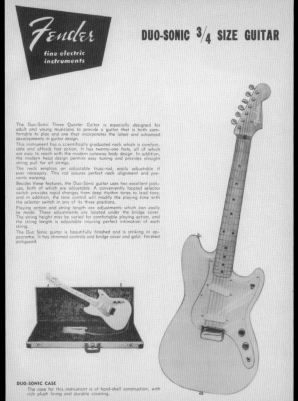

Fender
fine electric instruments

DUO-SONIC ¾ SIZE GUITAR

The Duo-Sonic Three Quarter Guitar is especially designed for adult and young musicians to provide a guitar that is both comfortable to play and one that incorporates the latest and advanced developments in guitar design.

This instrument has a scientifically graduated neck which is comfortable and affords fast action. It has twenty-one frets, all of which are easy to reach with the modern cutaway body design. In addition, the modern head design permits easy tuning and provides straight string pull for all strings.

The neck employs an adjustable truss-rod, easily adjustable if ever necessary. This rod assures perfect neck alignment and prevents warping.

Besides these features, the Duo-Sonic guitar uses two excellent pickups, both of which are adjustable. A conveniently located selector switch provides rapid changes from deep rhythm tones to lead tone; and in addition, the tone control will modify the playing tone with the selector switch in any of its three positions.

Playing action and string length are adjustments which can easily be made. These adjustments are located under the bridge cover. The string height may be varied for comfortable playing action, and the string length is adjustable insuring perfect intonation of each string.

The Duo Sonic guitar is beautifully finished and is striking in appearance. It has chromed controls and bridge cover and gold- finished pickguard.

DUO-SONIC CASE
The case for this instrument is of hard-shell construction, with rich plush lining and durable covering.

aluminium, but heavy-handed student players soon wore through the black paint, exposing the metal below.

The first advertisement for the Musicmaster ran in June 1956, but did not mention the Duo Sonic. The Duo Sonic did appear on a flyer produced at around the same time, but only as an artist's illustration. The second production run of Musicmasters included the first Duo Sonics and commenced in June 1956. Early teething problems had been ironed out and the new guitars

featured smart gold anodized pickguards, with a clear coat of lacquer for protection, and white pickup covers. Alder wood bodies were finished in a light beige colour, 'Desert Sand,' also used on contemporary steel guitars.

The $^3/_4$ guitars went through various cosmetic changes over the coming years, and although never officially offered in custom finishes, several different standard options were made available. The first major overhaul came in 1959 and coincided with the switch to slab

(facing page) 1958 Musicmaster and Duo Sonic pair – Desert Sand
(above left) 1960 pair – Tan
(above right) 1962 pair – Shaded Sunburst

(above left) 1963 pair – White with
brown pickguards

(above right) 1964 pair – White with
tortoiseshell pickguards

(facing page) 1963
pair – Red-Mahogany

rosewood fingerboards across the entire line. Desert Sand was replaced by a darker tan colour with a pinkish hue and no official Fender name. The gold anodized guards were changed to a single-ply, cream-coloured plastic and the pickup covers were now a dark brown. In July 1961, a letter sent to dealers announced that the student models would now be finished in Sunburst only. This had been requested by numerous dealers across the country who believed a Sunburst finish would have more

appeal, and would make the Musicmaster and Duo Sonic closer in appearance to the professional line of guitars. Fender Sales literature of the time suggested that the new finish would, 'contribute to the selection of these models over others.' Officially known as 'Shaded Sunburst,' it differed from the standard sunburst found on contemporary Stratocasters, Jazzmasters and Precision and Jazz Basses. It featured a deep maroon on the outer edge, fading through red into yellow, and as a cost-saving

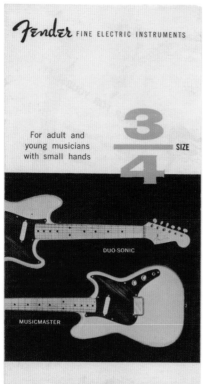

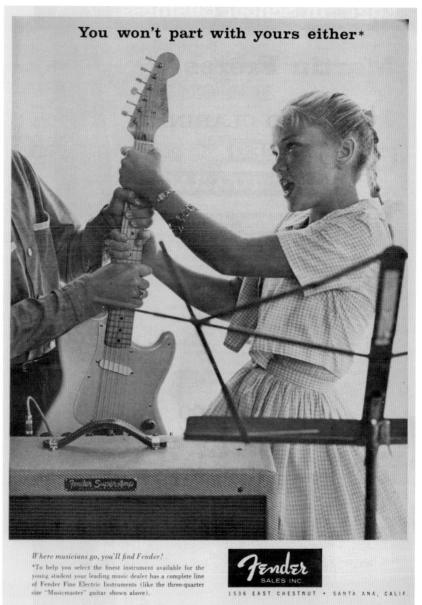

exercise, no clear coat was applied over the top as with the sunbursts on high-end models. The same maroon colour used on the Shaded Sunburst during this period also appeared on the sides of Telecaster and Esquire Customs.

During 1963, in a bid to push sales even further, Fender came up with three further stylistic variants for the ¾ scale guitars. It was the first time since the introduction of the Musicmaster and Duo Sonic that buyers were offered colour options. The Shaded Sunburst was dropped in mid-'63 and replaced by both red-mahogany and white. Red-mahogany was undoubtedly Fender's answer to Gibson's standard cherry red that was used on their popular, student-end SG Juniors and Specials. As its name suggested, the new translucent red finish was applied to mahogany bodies, but the finish used had a tendency to flake off. By 1964, mahogany was dropped in favour of poplar wood, which gave better results with the tinted red lacquer. These guitars featured white pickguards with black pickup covers. White Musicmasters and Duo Sonics usually came with three-ply, faux tortoiseshell pickguards and white pickup covers. A variant, featuring a single-ply brown pickguard, was also produced in limited numbers during fall 1963, examples of which are scarce.

In mid-1964, Fender introduced a third student model to the lineup. The Mustang was similar to the Musicmaster and Duo Sonic, but featured a reworked body with an offset waist, a new

pickguard design and, most importantly, a tremolo unit. Two plastic control knobs were mounted on a shiny, chromed control panel, which made the Mustang look positively 1960s compared to its mid-1950s older brothers. Soon the Musicmaster and Duo Sonic would receive the same facelift, and necks were offered in full-(24") or ¾-(22.5") scale lengths. All three were offered in vibrant red, white or blue by late 1964.

Although the Musicmaster and Duo Sonic were aimed at the student market

and there were some cost-saving features to enable competitive pricing, the build quality on these guitars was just as high as on the top-end models. It made shrewd business sense to offer a well-priced, quality instrument to the first-time buyer. Where other makers were quick to cut corners in production techniques and overall quality in their student guitars, Fender realized that a satisfied customer would return to the brand for their next instrument – and they usually did.

(this page, above) John Chaney and the Corral Wranglers playing at a county fair in June 1960

(overleaf) 1966 Musicmaster – Daphne Blue with 1967 Duo Sonic – Daphne Blue

(overleaf, facing page) Fender catalogs that appeared as free inserts with Downbeat magazine between 1955 and 1965, plus the 1963 new product guide at bottom left

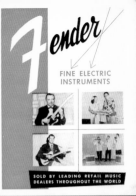

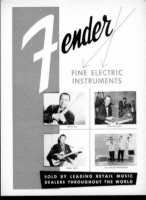

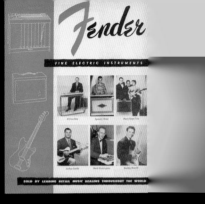

ELECTRIC MANDOLIN

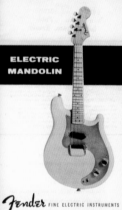

Electric Mandolin Features

The remarkable Fender Electric Mandolin is the favorite of top artists throughout the country and is now included in the instrumentation of a great many of the nation's leading musical organizations. Every mandolinist, violinist, guitarist, and other musicians will find this instrument to be an important part of their work. It is the finest instrument of its type on today's musical market.

Inset above shows Fender micro-adjustable bridges. Individual string lengths and string heights are adjustable for fast playing action and perfect string intonation.

- True Mandolin tone
- New comfort contoured body
- Accurately fretted fast-action neck
- Twenty-four frets
- Modern cutaway design
- Modern head design for straight string pull
- Beautiful natural blonde finish

DISTRIBUTED EXCLUSIVELY BY FENDER SALES, INC.
308 EAST FIFTH STREET, SANTA ANA, CALIFORNIA

Fender FINE ELECTRIC INSTRUMENTS

electric mandolin

Leo's original idea of building a family of electric stringed instruments was taking shape by the mid-'50s, and in 1956, he unveiled the latest member. No groundbreaking invention this time; the Electric Mandolin was a small, simple instrument in the now famous Fender tradition. It featured a solid body – a first for a mandolin – finished in blond or two-tone sunburst with a bolt-on maple neck, a gold anodized pickguard and a small, single-coil pickup. Unlike the conventional mandolin, Fender's offering featured only four strings and produced a thin, wiry sound when compared to fuller-sounding eight-string models. This was the instrument's real failing, as the mandolin relies on the natural chorusing effect of paired strings. The only real advantage the Fender offered over electric acoustic models by other manufacturers was an adjustable bridge, which definitely improved intonation and ease of playing.

Leo had intended his instrument for western swing bands, but these were in decline by the time the Fender Mandolin was released in early 1956. He did, however, manage to lure a few name endorsees to the new Mandolin, including Homer Burns of Homer and Jethro fame and Neil LeVang and Buddy Merrill from TV's popular Lawrence Welk Orchestra. Ultimately, the Fender was no match for Gibson-built mandolins that had dominated the market since the turn of the century and it failed to catch on.

By late 1959, the model received cosmetic upgrades including a three-tone sunburst, faux tortoiseshell pickguard and a rosewood fingerboard. A Stratocaster-style contour was also added to the front of the body at this time and it's known that a handful of custom-colour examples were produced during the '60s on a special-order basis. Serial numbers would indicate that as many as 3000 of these little instruments were produced before being discontinued in the early '70s, and although they are of limited use, they are sought-after by collectors. The build quality, like all Fenders of the time, is exceptional and a Fender Electric Mandolin, with its matching case, is a miniature collectible from the golden age of Fender.

HOMER AND JETHRO prefer Fender FINE ELECTRIC INSTRUMENTS ...choice of America's leading Artists

jazzmaster

By the mid-1950s, Fender had become a major force in the growing electrical instruments industry and Gibson, with its many professional endorsees, was the company's major competitor. During the summer of 1958, Fender unveiled a brand-new electric Spanish model to replace the Stratocaster at the top of the line; something, it was hoped, that would compete with Gibson's high-end, semi-acoustic guitars. Jazz guitarists of the day were respected, skilled musicians and nearly always touted Gibson or Epiphone instruments. Leo was well aware that guitarists looked up to these players and were influenced by their choice of instrument, and was keen to broaden Fender's horizons by breaking into this market with one of his solid-body designs. Don Randall named the new guitar the Jazzmaster in a blatant bid to target the jazz market, and although it would draw many new players to the Fender brand, precious few of these would be jazzers.

The Jazzmaster, like the Strat before, was designed from the ground up, borrowing only the basic principles of construction from its predecessor. The most radical feature was a new offset-waist body design, developed by Leo and Freddie Tavares, which was quite unlike anything previously seen on a guitar. It was a logical but daring step in an evolutionary process that had begun with the Esquire in 1950. The offset body was definitely aimed at jazz players who usually performed seated.

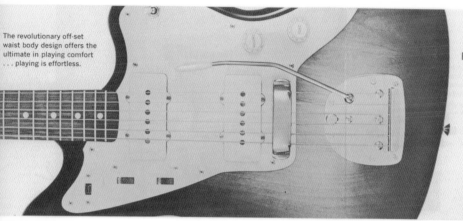

The revolutionary off-set waist body design offers the ultimate in playing comfort ... playing is effortless.

FEATURES OF THE *Jazzmaster*

- New pickups and tone circuit especially designed for modern guitar work and all other tonal requirements.
- Separate pickup tone and volume controls can be preset ... making fast pickup changes possible without need for further tone or volume adjustments.
- Enjoy the smoothest tremolo action with the new Fender "floating tremolo" ... (tremolo can be locked and arm removed or inserted again at any time).
- Adjustable floating bridge and six individual two-way bridges afford precision string intonation adjustments and custom playing action.
- PLUS these well-known Fender features ... truss-rod reinforced fast action neck with rosewood fretboard ... case-hardened, chromed parts for lasting beauty, and unequalled workmanship and finish.

THE *Fender Jazzmaster* ...

"That was another thing that just made sense," Leo told guitar historian Tom Wheeler. "Normally the player is forced to hold a guitar at an angle to play it, because it's not balanced. So it was a matter of fitting it to the rib cage... a matter of function." The design certainly gave greater comfort and balance in the seated position, but outside of recording studios, Jazzmasters were rarely played this way. The body was larger and heavier than the Telecaster or Strat and the bridge sat closer to its center, giving the instrument a longer, less compact, feel. That said, the new body design had a classy, stylish image that immediately became popular during the late '50s and would inspire many copycat designs from European and Japanese makers during the 1960s.

Another feature intended to give the Jazzmaster more of an upmarket appeal was the introduction of rosewood fingerboards. Fender's maple necks had set the brand apart from other makers during the early '50s, but by 1957, Teles, Esquires and Strats were firmly associated with country, blues, western swing and rock'n'roll players who required workmanlike guitars for hard-working environments. In a bid to change preconceptions and appeal to a more highbrow market, a 'slab' of quality rosewood was fixed to the face of a standard Fender maple neck. Truss rods ran through a channel under the rosewood cap, negating the need for walnut 'skunk stripes' and headstock plugs. Dot position markers on the neck were made from an off-white 'clay' material and a newly designed headstock, similar to the Strat but more flared at the bottom, was developed. Film footage, shot by Forrest White at the Fender Factory in '57, shows Freddie Tavares strumming

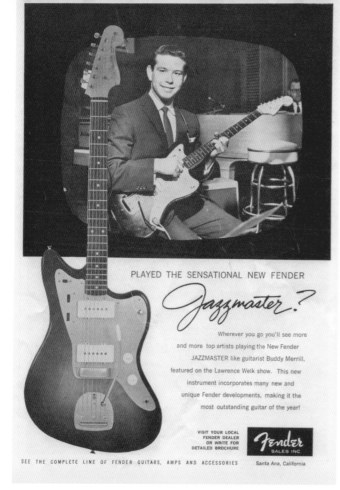

PLAYED THE SENSATIONAL NEW FENDER

Jazzmaster?

Wherever you go you'll see more and more top artists playing the New Fender JAZZMASTER like guitarist Buddy Merrill, featured on the Lawrence Welk show. This new instrument incorporates many new and unique Fender developments, making it the most outstanding guitar of the year!

VISIT YOUR LOCAL
FENDER DEALER
OR WRITE FOR
DETAILED BROCHURE

Fender
SALES INC.

Santa Ana, California

SEE THE COMPLETE LINE OF FENDER GUITARS, AMPS AND ACCESSORIES

a prototype Jazzmaster. In it, the offset body is fully developed, with controls mounted, unusually, above the strings, and the neck is made from solid maple with an early interpretation of the new headstock. The neck from this instrument has since surfaced on a late '58 production body, but it's likely that the rest of this prototype was scrapped by Fender.

The Jazzmaster featured two newly designed pickups with flat, wide coils that produced a decidedly more mellow tone than any previous Fender instrument. "Leo was trying to get more of a jazz sound than the high, piercing Telecaster sound," claimed production manager Forrest White, while Leo Fender commented: "The pickup wasn't so deep, and it was wider, thinner, more spaced out. See, the more spaced out the coil is – the wider the spectrum under the string – the warmer the tone." The Jazzmaster certainly had a warm, sweet tone, but with less bite than the Telecaster or Strat, and it found favour with many musicians during the late '50s and early '60s looking for an alternative sound, look and feel from a Fender guitar. To aid the Jazzmaster's tonal range, Leo developed a circuit that he borrowed from the lap steel guitar that Forrest White had brought to the factory during 1951. It enabled the player to switch between pre-set lead and rhythm tones. In the lead setting, both pickups were enabled – either individually or together – with volume and tone controls positioned close to the bridge. The rhythm circuit, which employed the neck pickup only, was activated by flicking a switch on the upper bout and adjusted via two roller pots positioned, like those on the prototype, above the strings.

(preceding page) 1958 – Sunburst
(below) the factory at 500 South Raymond Avenue in 1959

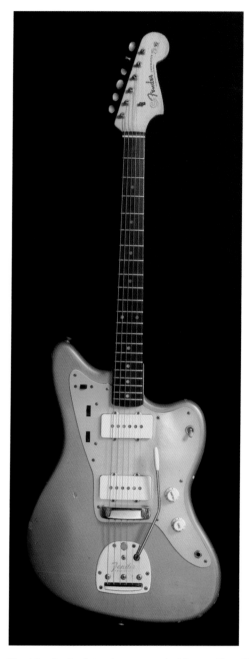
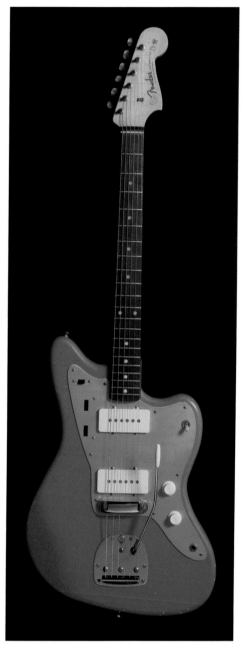

The idea looked good on paper, but in practice, the extra electronics had a tendency to dull both output and tone.

Leo also developed a new Tremolo that worked on a completely different principle to his Strat design. Instead of a combined bridge and Tremolo unit, Leo opted for a system that employed a single spring housed under a large, flat, chromed tailpiece. The strings passed over a separate floating bridge that rocked in its mounts as the Tremolo arm moved up and down. The new system had a gentler, more subtle action than the Strat which suited certain styles of playing better, but it had a major failing that would become apparent with the passing years. Fender had designed his new Tremolo and bridge for string gauges of .12 and above.

(above, left to right) 1958 – Gold, 1958 – Red, 1958 – Sunburst with prototype maple neck

(facing page, main picture) 1958 – Blond

(facing page, inset center) Buddy Emmons – on pedal steel – leads an improvised jam session at the factory circa 1959 – standing behind from left to right are Forrest White, George Fullerton and Leo Fender

(facing page, bottom) dot inlay position markers being inserted into Jazzmaster necks in 1959

Heavy by today's standards, these strings were standard fare on guitars during the '50s. By the early to mid- '60s, many players had begun using lighter-gauge strings, as they enabled string bends not possible with heavier gauges. When lighter-gauge strings were fitted to Jazzmasters, the bridge became problematic and strings often popped out of their saddles with heavy-handed playing. This problem largely resulted from the shallow break angle that Jazzmaster strings have as they pass from the tailpiece over the bridge. Although devices have been developed to alleviate the problem, it is a flaw that has given the guitar a bad reputation among guitarists since the mid-'60s, when sales started to dwindle. Telecasters and Stratocasters – with strings that passed through the body, giving an acute break angle and improved sustain – never suffered the inherent problems of the Jazzmaster, proving that even a genius of Leo's stature was capable of mistakes.

Despite this, the Jazzmaster found favour with many name players and enjoyed its heyday as the company's flagship guitar during the late '50s and early '60s. Luther Perkins, from Johnny Cash's band, was an early endorsee and used a Jazzmaster on many Cash recordings and live dates, including the live 'At Folsom Prison' album. A young Buddy Merrill appeared regularly on the Lawrence Welk TV show during the

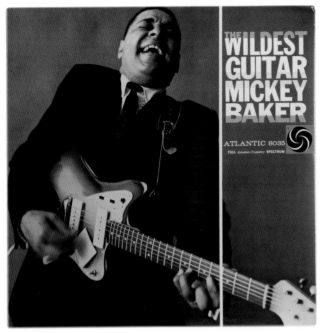

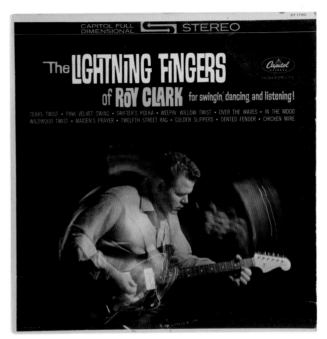

late '50s playing a Jazzmaster and his endorsement may well have inspired a new instrumental group who formed in Tacoma, Washington during 1958. The Ventures were Fender endorsees who set a trend for many instrumentalists that would follow. They employed a Precision bass, Stratocaster and Jazzmaster on all their early hits and lead guitarist Bob Bogle, used a Jazzmaster to great effect as the lead instrument on the band's 1960 smash 'Walk, Don't Run'. Wayne Moss twanged a Jazzmaster on the signature riff to Roy Orbison's 1964 chart-topping 'Oh Pretty Woman' and soul singer Clarence Carter was seldom seen without a Jazzmaster in the '60s. Gospel-soul band leader Pop Staples used a Jazzmaster throughout the '60's and early '70s on all his recordings with the Staple Singers, and countless surf groups found the sound and image they were after with a Jazzmaster.

The first ads to depict the Jazzmaster appeared during the summer of 1958. They featured a prototype instrument with an early rosewood board, which, as a hangover from maple board production, still retained the walnut plug feature at the headstock. It also had black pickup covers and chromed barrel knobs like those used on Telecasters. The first mention of the guitar on a Fender price list appeared in July 1958, just in time for summer trade shows where prototypes were displayed. It

included the Jazzmaster guitar with Tremolo and dual wide-range pickups at $329.50, as well as a non-Tremolo version for $299.50. It's unlikely that the non-Tremolo Jazzmaster was even prototyped and its presence on the mid-'58 price list remains something of a mystery. Production instruments began to leave the factory during the fall of 1958. These sported gold aluminium pickguards – like those seen on contemporary Precision basses, Duo Sonics and Musicmasters – and a new three-tone sunburst with black edges fading through red into yellow. The earliest production runs used a red paint that was susceptible to fading with exposure to UV rays, and with aging, these often appear as an almost two-color sunburst. A long, plastic-tipped Tremolo arm, Stratocaster-style control knobs and the obligatory chrome bridge cover completed the Jazzmaster. Blond examples, and custom-finished guitars with gold guards, were made available via special order, but these were few and far between. In early 1959, Fender switched to a celluloid nitrate plastic for Jazzmaster pickguards. These were four-layer, with an imitation tortoiseshell effect on the top and a sandwich of white/black/white below. Custom-finished Jazzmasters usually employed three-ply white/black/white nitrate guards from this point until 1965. To improve much-needed shielding for the wide, flat pickups and electronics, a

thin sheet of aluminium and brass trays, shaped to fit interior cavities, were installed under the pickguard. By the end of 1959, all Fender guitars and basses had adopted the rosewood fingerboards first introduced on the Jazzmaster. Three-tone sunburst, with tortoiseshell guard and rosewood fingerboard, remained the standard finish on Jazzmasters until the mid-1970s, but by the early '60s, custom-finished Jazzmasters had become increasingly popular.

Generally speaking, the standard finish for Fender's professional six-string guitars during the 1950s was see-through blond for Telecasters and Esquires, and sunburst for Stratocasters and Jazzmasters. The Precision Bass was finished in blond between 1951 and 1954, followed by a switch to sunburst from late 1954 onwards. Student range Musicmaster and Duo Sonic guitars were finished in Desert Sand from 1956 – 1959, changing to a light tan from 1959 – 1961. As with any rule, there are always exceptions and rare instruments produced during the 1950s, sporting non-standard finishes, would pave the way for a regimented custom-color scheme introduced by Don Randall at Fender Sales during 1961. By the mid-1960s, custom-color Fenders were not uncommon, especially on offset-body instruments

from the Jazzmaster, Jaguar, Jazz Bass, Bass VI and Electric XII family. As pop music became more colorful, so too did the instruments and Fender custom-color guitars offered musicians the chance to stand out from the crowd.

The earliest example of a Fender electric Spanish guitar produced in a solid color dates back to the very first production run of Esquires in early 1950. These were finished in black with white pickguards, most likely to disguise the cheap, lightweight pine bodies that invariably featured knot-holes. Very few pine Esquires were built, as bodies were soon made from quality ash. Leo settled on a see-through blond finish for these, which highlighted the natural grain. He claimed: "There was a big trend towards instruments with blond finishes on the body. Epiphone was very popular, and some of them were just about as blond as you could make an instrument. People seemed to like that look." There are one or two known instances of early '50s Telecasters produced in metallic colors, but those were almost certainly one-off special-order instruments. Fender used DuPont nitrocellulose car paints, widely available across America, to finish their instruments, and from September 1956 onwards, price lists announced that any Stratocaster, Telecaster, Esquire or

Shot on location in London, England

GUITARS, BANJOS, AMPLIFIERS, KEYBOARD INSTRUMENTS AND ACCESSORIES

SANTA ANA, CALIF. 92701

FOR A **FREE** CATALOG WRITE TO: FENDER MUSICAL INSTRUMENTS, DEPT. DB-5, 1402 EAST CHESTNUT, SANTA ANA, CALIFORNIA 92701

(facing page) 1964 – Sunburst

*(overleaf, left) 1959 – Sunburst,
1962 – Black, 1963 – Lake Placid
Blue*

(overleaf, facing) 1963 – Shell Pink

Precision Bass could be ordered 'in custom DuPont Ducco finishes at five per cent additional cost.' But what had led to this change in policy?

With the arrival of the Stratocaster in 1954, Fender introduced its now famous two-color sunburst, and by way of promoting the new guitar, several early Strats were gifted to name players. These often featured custom finishes such as Bill Carson and Pee Wee Crayton's red guitars with gold anodized guards or Eldon Shamblin's gold Strat that featured a standard single-ply white guard. Gretsch had also begun to offer colored finishes in 1954 as standard options on several of their guitars and these perfectly suited the more flamboyant musical era that was just beginning. By the mid-1950s, performers often sported brightly-colored suits, so why not have the matching guitar? In 1955, Fender displayed custom-finished Precision Basses at trade shows in colors including blue and a peachy shade of pink. Color footage of the 1957 NAMM show features a gold Strat with a white pickguard and a one-off Stratocaster built entirely from clear Lucite plastic with gold hardware, dubbed the '$1,000 guitar.' Red, gold and black are perhaps the most common custom colors on late '50s

Fenders, but rare original examples in pale blue, metallic green, off-white and beige have surfaced. The red seen on '50s instruments differs from those offered during the '60s and Bill Carson often described the color as 'Cimarron Red' as it matched the interior of the famed Cimarron Ballroom in Tulsa, that belonged to Fender endorsee Leon McAuliffe.

In July 1961, Fender Sales finally issued their first official custom-color chart. It featured 14 color chips and also gave mention to blond – a non-standard finish on everything but the Telecaster. All 15 tasteful shades could be ordered on any guitar in the professional range at an additional five per cent of the standard-finish price. The first chart included Black and Olympic White, a metallic gold called Shoreline and metallic silver called Inca. There were two pastel greens: the pale Surf Green and the darker Foam Green. There were also two pastel blues: Sonic and the slightly darker Daphne. Sherwood was a dark metallic green and Lake Placid was a deep metallic blue. The shades of red were Fiesta, which was a mid-color with an almost pinkish hue, and Dakota, which was darker, plus a deep pink metallic called Burgundy Mist. One final color intended for female players – or brave men – was a subtle

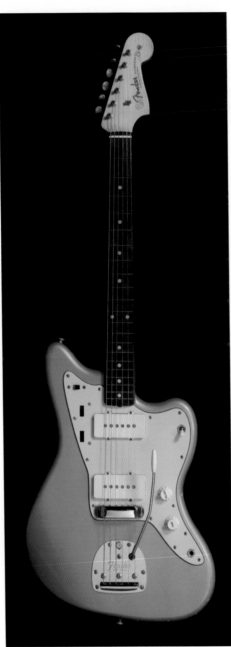
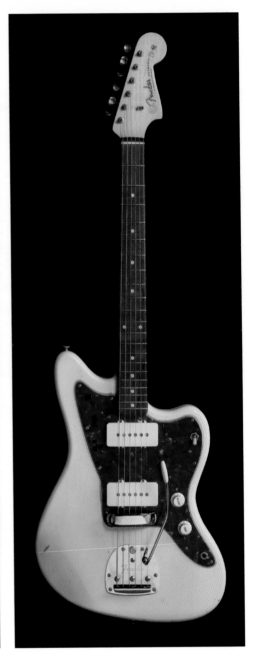

pastel, Shell Pink, and it remains the rarest of all the official Fender custom colors. Original examples are incredibly scarce as Shell Pink was rarely ordered. It was replaced on color charts in November 1963 by a new metallic shade, Candy Apple Red, which would prove to be one of Fender's most enduring custom-color options.

In England during the early 1960s, there was unprecedented demand for custom-color Fenders, especially Fiesta Red guitars, as every young rock'n'roller did their best to emulate Hank Marvin from the Shadows. Fender could hardly keep up with orders for Fiesta Strats from the UK and many sunburst guitars arriving on British shores were dispatched by their importers – Jennings or Selmer – for unofficial refinishes prior to being sold to unsuspecting youths. These so-called 'Selmer' refinishes can command higher values than standard factory-finished instruments, despite the fact that they are refinished and non-original. However, Fender did offer a refinishing service where instruments could be returned to the factory for a new coat of paint and upgraded parts, such as new pickguards or control knobs. These instruments often feature decals from a later era than the component parts. Matching numbers were often stamped into the body (under pickguards) and necks to ensure that correct components were remarried after the refinishing process.

During 1965, Fender Sales reorganized their color chart, replacing some of the unpopular choices with new options.

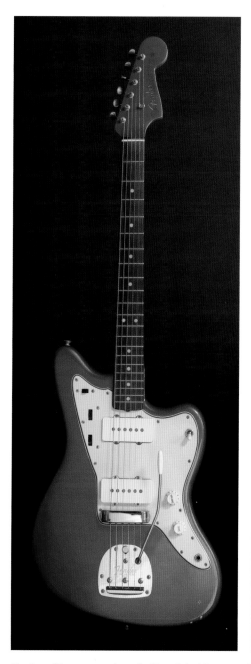

Daphne Blue was replaced with a light blue metallic called Blue Ice, Shoreline Gold became Firemist Gold Metallic (a darker, less subtle shade), while Burgundy Mist was replaced with a dark, almost black, metallic called Charcoal Frost. Sherwood Green was switched with Ocean Turquoise Metallic, the seldom-ordered Surf Green was replaced with subtle Teal Green Metallic and Inca Silver was replaced by a darker Firemist Silver Metallic.

Custom-color Fender guitars from the early and mid-'50s are incredibly rare and even those from the late '50s are seldom seen. They are highly prized by collectors and command values far in excess of standard-finished instruments from the same era. It takes a trained eye that

has studied hundreds of original guitars to accurately spot the genuine article from the fakes that abound. Even original undercoats and primers have become an exacting science, known only by a few. Early '60s custom-color Fenders are rare too, but largely down to the introduction of color charts in '61, dealers began to order custom-color instruments as stock items for music shops. By late 1964, Fender's Mustang, Duo Sonic and Musicmaster guitars appeared in Olympic White, Dakota Red and Daphne Blue as standard finishes, which shows how popular solid colors had become on Fender Instruments. That said, any custom-color Fender guitar or bass from the golden age is a rarity today and coveted by players and collectors alike. Certain colors are less common than

 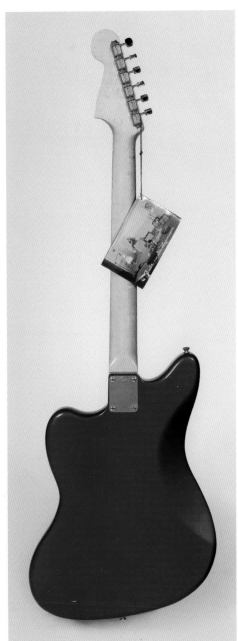 

others and some are more sought after by collectors. Custom-colored Telecasters and Esquires are far rarer than Jaguars, Jazzmasters or Strats and custom-order Precisions turn up less frequently than Jazz Basses. Headstocks, featuring a matching color applied to the face, were seen on a handful of instruments produced during the late '50s, 1960 and 1961, but became standard on all custom-finished Jazzmasters, Jaguars, Jazz Basses and Bass VIs from mid-1962 onwards. Custom-colored Electric XIIs, Bass Vs and Coronados always featured matching headstocks, while Stratocasters, Telecasters and Precision Basses bearing these are impossibly rare. Shades of the same color can vary wildly as cellulose paints are prone to fading and discoloring with age.

It's common for a Lake Placid Blue to fade to a color resembling Ocean Turquoise, or an Olympic White to turn a creamy yellow. Clear top coats that were applied to give custom finishes depth and lustre have a habit of turning a golden yellow, which can dramatically affect the original color underneath, and unfaded examples of Fender custom finishes are today the most highly prized.

The topic of Fender finishes is worthy of a book of its own and there are a disproportionate number of custom examples shown within these pages, compared to standard guitars. These are presented in order to display the breadth, and artistry, of the products produced by Fender during the company's creative heyday.

Prior to the incorporation of Fender Sales in 1953, advertising for Leo's company was limited to say the least. F.C. Hall had been reluctant to spend money on trade ads and, much to Leo's annoyance, less than a dozen small advertisements ran between 1946 and 1953. The creation of these was overseen by Don Randall, and with the advent of Fender Sales in which he held a large stake, Don began to take out full-page ads in *Downbeat*, *Music Trades*, *International Musician* and *Country & Western Jamboree*. Don continued to develop most of the ideas himself, aided by various out-of-house design companies, but by 1955, he brought in Stan Compton to assist him with the job. Don and Stan soon decided it was time that Fender engaged the services of a

professional outfit to handle the company's ads and catalogs. They struck gold in 1957 when they chanced upon the Perine/Jacoby agency.

Bob Perine was a fantastic art director and a talented photographer. His ideas and designs for Fender between 1957 and 1969 did a lot to change the public perception of the company and electric guitars in general. In Perine, Randall and Compton, Fender now had a formidable marketing team that was the envy of all other guitar manufacturers. "I worked closely with Bob and supervised him, but only up to a point. He worked well on his own," claimed Randall in later years. Bob brought a sophisticated, artistic vision to the company's literature, evidenced in his earliest ads from late '57 and his first catalog design, the 1958 – 1959 full-line. Bob persuaded Compton to spend extra money producing a brochure with a full-color cover and the results were worth every penny. Crew-cut models posed among an array of Narrow Panel amps, table and pedal steels and electric guitars artistically hung from strings. Compared to the staid, stodgy image makers like Gibson and Epiphone portrayed through their sales literature, Perine's work was stylish, colorful and modern, and it set Fender apart from its rivals. Perine designed a new Fender logo for the 1958 – 1959 catalog, as he'd noticed the company had been using no less than 13 different types of trademark. He felt it was time to integrate into one uniformed design. Upon seeing the new catalog, Leo was unhappy with the 'F' in the new logo and summoned Bob to the factory. In Perine's own words: " 'You see Bob,' said Leo 'It should be like the curve of a woman's back: it has to be just right. Higher here, a little lower there. I don't think you've got it yet.' Having no answer for such subjectivity, I laughed, which I don't think Leo appreciated. After all, hadn't he been dictating the subtle curves of guitar bodies for nearly a decade? 'So you get the curve right and you're okay,' he said. When I told Randall about the meeting he simply replied, 'That's Leo.' " Spurred on by Leo's advice, Perine perfected a new company logo that was trademarked in 1960. The new bolder, thicker logo met with Leo's approval and was soon incorporated as the standard on all Fender literature. The launch of the Jazz Bass in 1960 saw its first use on a headstock decal, and by 1965, all Fender guitars and amplifiers carried the new logo, which has prevailed to this day.

One of Perine's enduring ad campaigns was simplicity itself. It depicted Fender owners from all walks of life in bizarre settings with their beloved instruments, accompanied by the strapline: 'You Won't Part With Yours Either.' This popular series ran for many years and included skydivers, surfers, skiers, jet pilots, football players, skateboarders, tank drivers and deep-sea divers all posing with Fender instruments. Perine often starred in his own ads playing Strats, Teles or Jazzmasters. He had learned to play guitar while in the navy during World War Two, so the Fender job was a dream ticket. When targeting the youth market, Bob often included his three daughters, Jorli, Lisa and Terri (and their high school friends) in photo shoots for ads and catalogs, creating a Californian vision of Utopia in which everyone played a Fender guitar. His 1957 Ford Thunderbird was a regular fixture too. Bob Perine's esthetic, attention to detail and genuine passion for the brand played a big part in shaping the Fender image during the late '50s and '60s, and he undoubtedly played a huge role in the company's success during its golden age.

The year 1962 saw changes to the rosewood fingerboards on Jazzmasters and all other guitars in the Fender range. The thick 'slab' rosewood boards that were flat on the bottom surface, where they were fixed to maple necks, were replaced with a thinner curved board during the summer of '62. This saved money by using less rosewood, but Leo also believed this construction method would counteract differences in expansion and contraction that occurred between the two woods on slab-board necks. By mid-'63, he opted for an even thinner piece of rosewood and this style of construction lasted well into the 1970s. The Jazzmaster went on to sell well, but not to the jazz guitarists Fender had envisaged. It became a firm favourite with garage and surf bands during the early '60s, its cresting body shape suiting them well. It has since been adopted by countless alternative rock bands in search of something different from the Fender look and sound. Leo had tried, and failed, to better his previous creations, but succeeded in producing a beautiful, well-loved, if somewhat quirky, instrument that has endured the test of time.

(facing page) Bob Perine with some of his work at the 1967 NAAM show

(this page) 1962 – Shoreline Gold

brown / brown grille amplifiers 1959–1961

The next phase in Fender amplification was an important step forward. It was ushered in during 1959 with the development of the new Vibrasonic amp. Leo had something different in mind: a new patented amplifier and cabinet design that would soon replace the Narrow Panel amps.

Most guitarists were now performing standing up in front of their amplifiers near the front of the stage, and were free to move around and perform for the crowd. Changing amp settings during performances proved difficult with the older Narrow and Wide Panel Fender amps, with guitarists having to lean over to adjust controls. Always keen to accommodate the needs of the musician, Fender developed a new amplifier chassis that displayed the control knobs across the front of the amplifier 'for convenience of operation.' This simple switch made a big difference for the player and, by 1961, all Fender amplifiers – save one – would change to this new arrangement.

With the new cabinet design came a new covering material. Players had been complaining that their tweed amps began to look tatty after a few months on the road. Lacquered tweed was replaced on the new-style amps with a tough, heavily textured vinyl fabric called Tolex, made by the General Tire And Rubber Company in Ohio. Tolex could cope better with the ever-changing conditions equipment was being subjected to. The earliest Tolex used by Fender between 1959 – 1961 was pinkish-brown in color and complemented by the same dark brown grille cloth that had been employed on the Narrow Panel tweed amps since 1955. The front-mounted controls sat on a newly designed faceplate, brown with white script, and a new, larger Fender nameplate made from flat steel sat proudly in the top left-hand corner of the speaker baffles. The earliest examples of the new-style amps used small, round metal control knobs, but these were soon replaced by brown plastic knobs. Five more amplifiers had joined the Vibrasonic in the new 'Professional' series by 1960 and these ran concurrently with several tweed amps still in production. The brown Tolex, brown grille styling was the first in a gradual changeover of the Fender line, and by 1961, all but the Champ had been replaced by the new front-facing control panel amplifiers.

Rarest of the brown Tolex/brown grille cloth amps was the Twin. It was the last to join the newly styled combos in June 1960 and was produced in limited numbers. The cabinet was smaller than later Twin amps, which necessitated the speakers being placed at opposite corners instead of side by side. The old-style leather handles looked out of place on the new amplifiers, so a modern, moulded plastic handle was developed to complete the new look. 'Dog bone' handles were mid-brown and featured a raised Fender logo and ridges for extra grip. They were soon added to the larger tweed amps, whose leather handles were prone to breaking under touring conditions. Early-style brown Tolex/brown grille combos are easily recognizable by the sharp, non-radiused edge that runs across the top edge of the cabinets; all Fender amps that followed would feature a rounded-off top edge.

By 1959, it seemed Leo Fender had the 1960s all mapped out.

Announcing the New
FENDER VIBRASONIC AMP

- DUAL CHANNEL CIRCUIT
- NEW FUNCTIONAL STYLING *
- LANSING 15" SIGNATURE SPEAKER
- RUGGED VINYL COVERING
- NATURAL "VOICE-LIKE" VIBRATO CHANNEL *

* Patent Pending

The Fender Vibrasonic Amplifier is one of the finest musical instrument amplifiers ever offered to the buying public. It offers the musician tremendous distortion-free power, plus one of the most advanced circuits in the amplifier field. In addition, the Vibrasonic Amp employs the famous 15" Lansing D-130 Signature Speaker which is recognized throughout the country as one of the finest obtainable for amplification purposes.

This circuit is dual-channel design—normal and vibrato—with separate volume and tone controls for each. An outstanding feature of the vibrato channel is the pleasing effects that can be achieved. The Vibrasonic vibrato circuit duplicates with fidelity the vibrato of the human voice inasmuch as the pitch is raised and lowered at varying speeds that may be selected, and to a smaller degree the volume is intermittently increased and decreased. Every musician will readily appreciate the amplification qualities made possible with this feature.

The Fender Vibrasonic Amp introduces a new concept in amplifier design. The inputs and channel controls are neatly mounted across the front of the amp providing easier access and conforming to the desire of many musicians to have the amplifier placed in back of them while playing. With the control panel mounted on the front, necessary control changes are convenient to make and the control position marks easier to read.

The over-all appearance of the Fender Vibrasonic Amp is sleek and modern in every respect and is enhanced by the rich textured vinyl fabric covering. This material is extremely tough and is abrasion and scuff resistant and is washable. The amplifier cabinet is made of ¾ inch woodstock and lock-jointed corners to assure more than adequate strength to take hard professional use. The grill cloth is the latest style plastic material, and is of such porosity as to allow considerably more sound to pass without muffling and without loss of high frequencies as is ofttimes found with ordinary grill cloth.

Another outstanding feature of the Vibrasonic is the single units parts panel on which are mounted practically all of the small parts including the condensers and resistors. These small parts are securely attached to this panel through brass eyelets into which they are soldered. Each is held securely in place and not allowed to vibrate or rattle. This eliminates a great source of amplifier failure and guarantees that your Fender Vibrasonic Amp will give long faithful service.

All the features mentioned above combine to provide the musician with the finest portable musical instrument amplifier ever developed and will set the standard others will seek to achieve in the future. Safety codes for all states are equaled or exceeded, and each amplifier is guaranteed to give complete customer satisfaction. This guarantee is backed by our many years of successful business relationships with music dealers and their customers throughout the world.

Pro: 25 watt; 1 x 15" speakers
Vibrasonic: 25 watt; 1 x 15" speaker
Super: 30 watt; 2 x 10" speaker
Bandmaster: 30 watt; 3 x 10" speakers
Concert: 40 watt; 4 x 10" speakers
Twin: 85 watt; 2 x 12" speakers

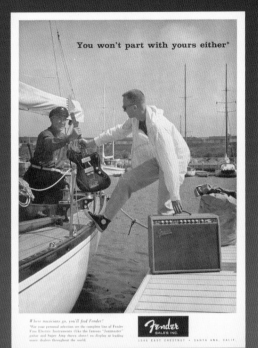

jazz bass

By January 1960, the Fender family of electric instruments included 13 amplifier models, 11 steel guitars and six different six-string guitars, but only one electric bass. The Precision Bass was considered to be the industry standard and Fender seemed to have the market cornered.

The electric bass had already had a huge impact on the music scene and Fender Sales were doing excellent business with the Precision. So in 1959, it was logical that Don Randall requested a new bass design from Leo: "We wanted an upscale model to put on the market. The Jazz bass wasn't Leo's idea, particularly, it was more of a marketing idea, something we wanted to expand the line." Leo Fender told guitar historian Tom Wheeler: "Well, it's like a car, you know. You come out with the standard model, then you have the deluxe model, a Cadillac version."

The earliest examples of the Fender Jazz appeared in March 1960, but the new bass didn't appear on a price list until July of that year. At $279.50 for the standard sunburst finish, it was $50 more than the standard Precision. The name and offset body styling, were a follow-through from the Jazzmaster guitar, and it's likely that the name was chosen to appeal to jazz musicians in a move to draw more players away from acoustic double basses into the electric bass field. Leo's new design certainly had a stylish and sophisticated look, with its chromed control

FULL RANGE BASS RESPONSE • RAPID TECHNIQUE • NEW "OFF-SET" WAIST BODY DESIGN

NEW! The Jazz Bass not only incorporates individual two-way micro-adjustable bridges for perfect string intonation and heights but also employs adjustable damping arms for any degree of sustained tone.

NEW! Dual pickups have two pole pieces for each string. These provide instant string response and full tone during string vibration. Tandem tone and volume control for each pickup permit mixing of the pickups plus further bass and treble boost whenever desired by the player.

NEW! 1-7/16", that's the actual size of the Jazz Bass neck at the nut . . . more slender than most any guitar. This revolutionary neck design facilitates rapid playing technique of the most difficult musical passages. In addition, it is truss-rod reinforced to assure perfect neck alignment at all times.

FENDER JAZZ BASS

Another Fender First!

The Jazz Bass is Fender's newest addition to the field of electric basses and represents the standards by which others will be compared. It offers the musician greater playing comfort, faster playing action, and the finest bass tone reproduction. The "off-set"* waist design contributes greatly to the playing ease and comfort of the musician. In addition, the portability and light weight of the Jazz Bass will be readily appreciated by every bassist. Be sure to try this outstanding new instrument at your Fender dealer.

*Patent Pending

Fender
SALES, INC.

SANTA ANA, CALIFORNIA

Sold by leading music dealers throughout the world

A WINNING COMBINATION

The all-new Bassman Amp and the already popular Fender Jazz Bass or Precision Bass, go together in perfect combination. The new Bassman Amp was designed especially to accommodate these two fine electric basses and gives the finest performance available to bassists.

The Bassman Amp incorporates an enclosed speaker with a separate amplifier chassis unit. The use of the enclosed 12" Heavy-Duty Custom Design speaker with its special baffle*, makes the Bassman distortion-free, allowing the player to use his full bass notes and ample volume. Another new Bassman feature is the incorporation of dual channels; one bass, and the other normal for use with guitar or other instrument. The chassis, or amplifier portion, may be top-mounted as shown or may be used separately.

The Jazz Bass is Fender's newest addition to the field of electric basses and represents the standards by which others will be compared. It offers the musician greater playing comfort, faster playing action, and the finest bass tone reproduction. The "off-set"* waist design contributes greatly to the playing ease and comfort of the musician. In addition, the portability and light weight of the Jazz Bass will be readily appreciated by every bassist.

Try the Fender electric basses and the Bassman Amp at your Fender Dealer.

*Patents Pending

Fender's new Speaker Enclosure offers the finest amplified sound reproduction. Comparison proves its smoother response in all frequency ranges . . . distortion-free even at higher volume levels. The speaker Projector Ring* eliminates cancellation of front and rear radiation, permits greater speaker efficiency and optimum enclosure performance.

The Bassman is equipped with special Tilt-Back Legs* which enables the sound to reach the farthest point in any room or hall. The tilt-back feature prevents sound absorption where played in a carpeted room or a place where sound absorption is a problem.

Dual pickups have two pole pieces for each string . . . provides instant string response, full tone during string vibration. Tandem tone and volume control for each pickup permit mixing of the pickups plus further bass and treble boost whenever desired.

1⁷⁄₁₆", that's the actual size of the Jazz Bass neck at the nut . . . more slender than most guitars. This revolutionary design facilitates rapid playing technique on the most difficult musical passages. And it's truss-rod reinforced to assure perfect neck alignment.

SOLD BY LEADING MUSIC DEALERS THROUGHOUT THE WORLD

Fender
SALES, INC.

1546 EAST CHESTNUT • SANTA ANA, CALIFORNIA

plate, pickup covers and faux tortoiseshell pickguard.

A new neck, narrower at the nut than the Precision, offered players a very different feel, and the closer string spacing allowed for faster bass runs and greater ease of playing. The neck tapered out towards the body, to give regular spacing at the bridge, and has become a favourite with many bass players since its introduction. The Jazz bass featured a brand-new headstock logo created by Bob Perine, bolder and more visible than previous designs, featuring gold lettering within a thin black outline. Every new Fender model launched after this point would carry the updated decal, which has become known as the 'transition' logo. Its use spanned the period between the old-style 'spaghetti' logos of the '50's and later-style logos used by Fender in the late '60s and '70s.

The Jazz featured two single-coil pickups, wired in sequence to give a noise-cancelling humbucking effect like the single split pickup on the Precision. Each had eight individual pole pieces – two for each string – that gave a clear, punchy tone, strong in the mid-range, which offered a good alternative to the Precision. Pickups were initially controlled by a pair of dual concentric 'stack' knobs that allowed for adjustment of volume and tone on each control, one for each pickup. This feature was dropped by early 1962 in favour of a simpler system with three plastic knobs – a volume for each pickup and a smaller knob that controlled tone for both. The Jazz bass bridge was similar to the Precision, but early examples featured a new system for dampening individual strings. Felt pads could be raised or lowered to mute the sustain of the strings, and to conceal the unsightly device, a large chromed bridge cover bearing an embossed Fender 'F' was designed. The mutes proved unpopular with players, who preferred to dampen strings instinctively with their hands, and were dropped from the bass in early 1963, but the bridge cover that hid them survived into the '70s and beyond.

(preceding pages, left to right) 1960 – Blond, 1960 – Sunburst, 1964 – Sunburst

(this page, above and right) George Fullerton supervises boxed guitars and amps being loaded onto a truck at the factory in 1960

(facing page, left to right) 1962 – Fiesta Red, 1965 – Firemist Gold, 1965 – Candy Apple Red

(overleaf facing pages, left to right) 1965 – Foam Green, 1960 – Blond left-hand model, 1962 – with original brown Tolex case

As the Jazz Bass was launched during 1960, Don Randall was on the offensive to take the Fender brand to a global audience. In postwar Europe, American GIs had been spreading the news about what was going on back home. Rock'n'roll took an early foothold in Germany as 45s, often shipped over by loved ones and friends, kept soldiers up to date with the latest sounds. In Britain, Bill Haley's 'Rock Around The Clock' had hit the number one spot in 1955, and as Elvis Presley burst into the charts during early 1956, teenagers simply couldn't get enough of American rock'n'roll. Emulating the sounds they heard, however, was virtually impossible, as electric guitars and amplifiers were unavailable in the UK. Buddy Holly toured

Britain in 1958, playing his space-age Stratocaster. The tour served to fan the flames of the new youth movement and gave many teenagers their first glimpse of a Fender.

Trade sanctions that had prohibited the import of US-made electrical and musical goods into Britain were being lifted during 1959 and Don, eager to strike while the iron was hot, attended his first international music fair in Frankfurt, Germany, that year. It was a big step for Fender Sales and was key to opening doors across Europe. Fender's first export market had been Canada, where the full Fender line was being distributed as early as 1957, but by 1960 distribution arrangements were in place in the UK and Germany. Don

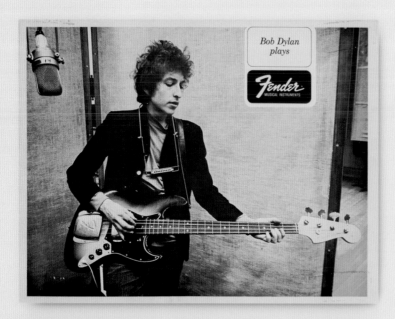

quickly began to build up a global network of distributors and dealers eager to sell Fender product. Before long, Fender Sales were distributing to all corners of the globe from their Santa Ana facility. By opening up markets in Europe, Australia, South Africa and Japan, Fender would become America's largest musical instrument exporter by the early '60s.

The Jazz Bass certainly benefited from Fender's new global distribution. John Entwistle of The Who was an early British endorser, as was Noel Redding of The Jimi Hendrix Experience, who was rarely seen without his sunburst Jazz during the band's heyday in '66 and '67. In America, Bob Dylan was famously pictured with a Jazz Bass shortly after

'going electric' in 1965, a pose that would have been intended to provoke folk purists, angry at his change in direction and instrument choice. Rick Danko, from Dylan's backing group The Band, favoured a Jazz and even The Beatles used one during the recording of 'Abbey Road' in 1969. Bassist Larry Graham pioneered a new technique of slapping the strings of his Jazz Bass on late '60s hits with Sly And The Family Stone, and by the end of the decade, the instrument was established as a classic Fender design. Leo had done it once again. He had created another instrument that would sit at the top of its field, side by side with the Precision. Fender's domination of the bass market was set to continue for quite some time.

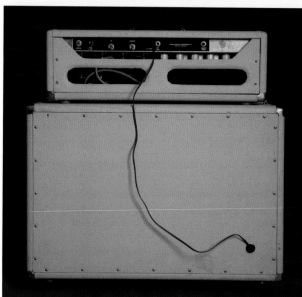

blond / oxblood grille amplifiers 1960 – 1962

Soon after the introduction of the brown Tolex amplifiers, with their forward-facing controls, Fender introduced yet another new amp design where the amplifier section and the speakers would be housed in two separate cabinets. The amplifier sat 'piggyback' on top of the speaker cabinet, held firmly in place by chromed anchor plates and mounting knobs. Breaking the larger combo amps into two sections supposedly made for easier portability. Fender also claimed in early literature: 'The amplifier sections may be used remotely, allowing the speaker portion to be placed at any point away from the player while having the control section nearby or completely offstage.'

The new Piggyback amps were intended to sit at the top of the line and a new, textured blond Tolex, with a striking, deep maroon 'oxblood' grille cloth, was selected to set them apart from the brown combos. Dark brown control panels with white script, white plastic knobs and darker brown 'dog bone' handles finished off the new look. As the 2 x 12", 85-watt Twin combo also resided near the top of the line, it became the only combo to receive the blond/oxblood treatment.

It was a new model, the Showman amp, that prompted breaking the amplifier and speaker cabinet into two separate units. The Showman was essentially an 85-watt Twin amp, minus it's vibrato channel, paired with a single 12" or 15" JBL speaker, but problems had arisen when the amp was mated with anything other than 2 x 12" speakers. The enormously powerful amplifier head had a tendency to blow speakers, so Fender developed a complex baffle system for the new speaker cabinets today known as 'bass reflex'. The new closed-back speaker cabinet, allowed better flow of sound and improved low frequency response. While it prevented speakers from blowing, it added extra weight, hence the separate amp and speaker cabinet design. Upon its release in September 1960, there wasn't a guitar amp to rival the Showman. At $600 for the 1 x 15" version, it was a serious investment for any musician, costing more than twice the price of a new Fender Stratocaster.

The Piggyback amps featured another Fender first: tilt-back legs. These were chromed metal struts that could be angled backwards and allowed the amplifier to be tipped back onto the rear edge of the speaker cabinet. This projected the sound forwards and upwards 'to reach the farthest point in the room or hall in which it is being played.' The new amps also featured nickel-plated corner protectors which were soon applied to the larger combos in the Fender range. Guitar amplification was becoming larger, heavier and louder.

Tremolux: 30 watt amplifier; 1 x 10" or 2 x 10" speaker
Bandmaster: 40 watt amplifier; 1 x12" or 2 x 12" speaker
Bassman: 50 watt amplifier; 1 x12" or 2 x 12" speaker
Showman: 85 watt amplifier; 1 x12" or 1 x 15" speaker
Twin: 85 watt; 2 x 12" speakers

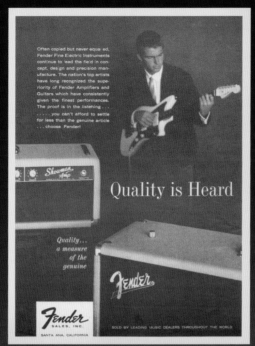

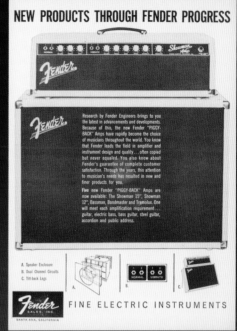

FENDER VI BASS GUITAR

The new Fender Six-String Bass Guitar is the finest available on today's market. The Bass Guitar offers an entirely "new-sound" to every playing group as it is tuned one octave below the standard guitar. Numerous new tone combinations are made possible by three full range pickups, each controlled by a two-position switch enabling the player to select the pickups individually or in any combination. This remarkable new guitar incorporates all the Fender developments including the comfort-contoured "off-set" body design, smooth tremolo action, floating bridge, and extra-slim faster neck. The Bass Guitar is a fine addition to the Fender line of Fine Electric Instruments and answers the demand for a high-quality Six String Bass Guitar. In addition to all its outstanding features, it is beautifully finished in shaded sunburst, and is also available in custom DuPont colors.

THESE OUTSTANDING FEATURES . . .

. . . make the new Bass Guitar an attractive and fine quality instrument. The Bass Guitar has been designed to create new sound combinations for the soloist and playing group. The Fender Bass Guitar employs the standard six-string guitar tuning; chord structures and fingering are identical to the guitar. Thus, both guitarists and bassists will find the instrument easy to play and adapt to their present orchestrations and instrumentations.

Fender SALES, INC.

FINE ELECTRIC INSTRUMENTS

SANTA ANA, CALIF.

bass vi

Following hot on the heels of the Jazz Bass, Leo Fender launched a brand-new addition to his family of stringed instruments during 1961. The new guitar was somewhere between a Jazzmaster-style six-string with Tremolo and a Fender Jazz Bass. Although officially named the Fender VI, it is more commonly referred to as the 'Bass Six.' The concept behind the new instrument was not completely original and it's more than likely that it was intended to plug a hole in the market. The New Jersey Danelectro company had pioneered a six-string bass – Model 1376 – during 1956. The instrument had become popular with session guitarists and several Nashville producers, who used the 'Dano' to great effect to double up acoustic bass parts, often muting the strings. This technique was called 'tic-tac' bass and it gave records more punch. By the '60s, it was frequently used to double up electric bass, as evidenced on many Beach Boys recordings and surf instrumentals. Six-string basses, sometimes referred to as 'baritone guitars', are usually tuned to E-A-D-G-B-E, an octave lower than a standard guitar. Many players, however, prefer tuning to B-E-A-D-G-C, which offers lower notes on the bottom strings.

The Fender VI featured a 30"-scale length, halfway between a guitar and a full-scale electric bass. Its long 21-fret neck was narrow at the nut, like the Jazz Bass, which meant that the strings were grouped closely together. The body was offset, like a Jazzmaster, and it shared the same combined tailpiece/Tremolo unit with a redesigned, deeper bridge that allowed for extra string

(above) 1963 – Fiesta Red against Blond Tolex case

(facing page, left to right) 1962 – Sunburst, 1962 – Lake Placid Blue

(overleaf, left to right) 1966 – Foam Green, 1962 – Shoreline Gold, 1961 – Sherwood Green

(overleaf facing pages, left to right) 1963 – 'Champagne' Sparkle, Jack Bruce of Cream with his early Sunburst model in 1966, 1963 – Olympic White, 1963 – Fiesta Red

adjustment. Like the Jazz Bass, volume and tone controls were mounted to a chrome control panel and pickup switching was possible via a new hexagonal plate with three sliding switches. The Bass VI featured three specially designed pickups with chrome mounting rings. The standard finish was sunburst with a faux tortoiseshell guard, but a high proportion of custom-color examples exist, perhaps produced in an effort to promote sales. After the release of the Fender Jaguar during 1962,

changes were made to the Fender VI to bring it in line with the new six-string: an extra 'tone modification,' or 'strangle' switch, was added to the pickup selector plate, which offered a deep tone; pickups were redesigned, like the Jaguar, with notched metal sides; and Leo's fascination with muted strings was indulged with the addition of a bridge mute akin to the type also introduced on the Jag.

The Fender VI found favour with many British musicians during the '60s. Former Shadows bassist Jet Harris,

featured one as the lead instrument on his chart-topping 1963 hit 'Diamonds'. Eric Haydock of the Hollies, and John Entwistle of The Who regularly used Fender VIs, and Jack Bruce played a sunburst Fender VI in Manfred Mann before forming Cream with Eric Clapton and Ginger Baker in 1966. During his stint in Cream, his bass received its now-famous psychedelic paint scheme courtesy of Dutch art collective The Fool. Peter Green used a Bass VI during his time with Fleetwood Mac and Beatles guitarists George Harrison and John Lennon favoured the Bass VI when accompanying Paul McCartney as he switched to piano for songs like 'Hey Jude', 'Let It Be' and 'The Long And Winding Road'. In America, the Fender VI was a popular studio instrument and appeared on countless recordings during the '60s. It was endorsed by Buddy Merrill, Neil LeVang and Billy Strange, and was used to produce the famous deep twang heard on Glen Campbell's 'Wichita Lineman'.

Although the Fender VI proved to be a great studio tool, it never caught on as a live guitar, due in some part, to its split personality. Its narrow neck meant that the strings were too closely spaced for most bass players, while its heavy-gauge strings ruled out most styles of conventional guitar playing. While plucked chords are possible, strumming the Fender VI is not advisable. It is fantastic for producing deep lead guitar parts and makes a versatile bass for players with smaller hands but, ultimately, it fell between two stools for most musicians and subsequently sold in small numbers.

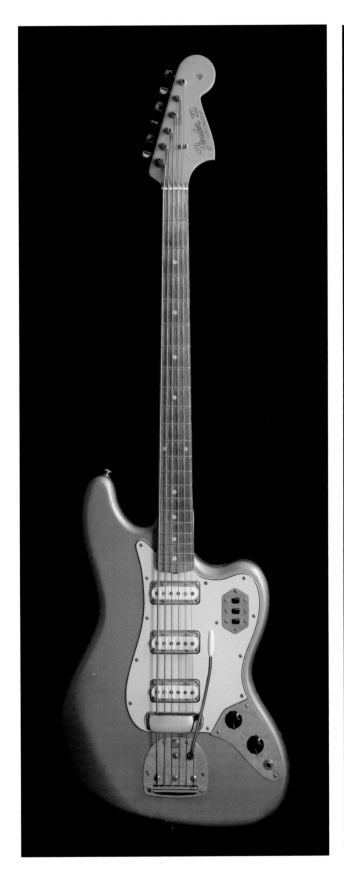

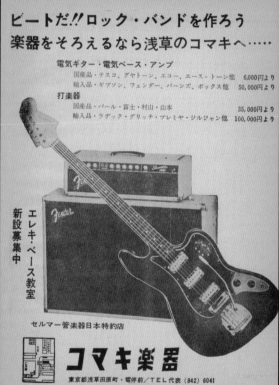

brown / oxblood grille amplifiers 1961-1962

During 1961, the brown Tolex Fender amps in the 'Professional' series started to appear with maroon 'oxblood' grilles instead of the earlier brown style. Reasons for the switch are unclear, but this short-lived variation lasted only a few months. Just five models are known to have been produced in this format, which is often confused with the earlier brown Tolex with brown grille cloth era. Glimpses of these rare combos appeared in the 1961

full-line catalog, which showed the Vibrasonic and Concert, but only the '61 mini fold-out catalog displayed the full range. Essentially unchanged from the earlier brown Tolex/brown grille 'Professional' series, the only amp from that era not present in the new configuration was the Twin, which switched to blond Tolex with oxblood grille at around the same time.

'Dog bone' handles were still present but it was becoming apparent that these were not up to Fender's usual standards. The plastic used became brittle and prone to cracking under the weight of heavy amplifiers. British amp manufacturer Jennings Musical Industries (JMI) would borrow the 'dog bone' design for their own range of VOX amplifiers but employed a more pliable plastic that gave better, but still less than perfect, results. Unbroken examples of the brown Fender 'dog bone' handles are rare today. This short-lived range saw the last appearance of the Bandmaster as a combo; it was redesigned as a Piggyback during 1961 when it too received the blond/oxblood treatment.

Pro: 25 watt; 1 x 15" speaker
Vibrasonic: 25 watt; 1 x 15" speaker
Super: 30 watt; 2 x 10" speakers
Bandmaster: 30 watt; 3 x 10" speakers
Concert: 40 watt; 4 x 10" speakers

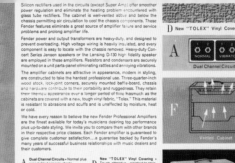

jaguar

Launched in spring 1962, the Fender Jaguar could hardly be described as a new design. It was essentially a revamped Jazzmaster with a shorter-scale neck, newly designed pickups and an adapted tone circuit. It did offer one 'Fender first,' in the shape of a new string mute that sat under the standard Jazzmaster-style bridge. The mute – a small piece of foam mounted on a chrome plate that could be flipped up under the strings – was gimmicky and deemed surplus to requirements by musicians used to dampening strings with the palm of their hand. Consequently, it is usually seen in the off position or completely removed from the guitar. These minimal changes to the Jazzmaster design placed the Jaguar at the top of the Fender range. It was priced at $379.50, compared to the Jazzmaster at $349.50, the Stratocaster at $259.50 and the bargain-priced Telecaster at only $209.50.

But why make the changes to the Jazzmaster? Some guitarists complained that Jazzmasters felt long and unwieldy compared to Strats and Teles. This was due to the bridge being placed nearer to the center of its offset body, which pushed the neck away from the player. A shorter 24"-scale length certainly combated the problem and Leo also felt that the new neck would find favour with fans of Gibson instruments which usually employed the 24-inch scale. Other guitarists claimed that the mellow Jazzmaster pickups lacked

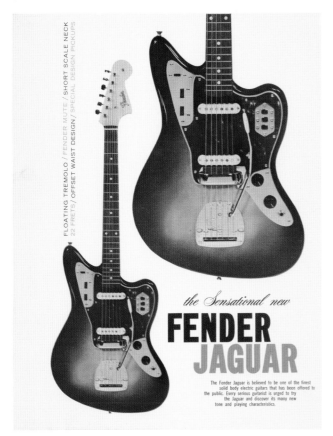

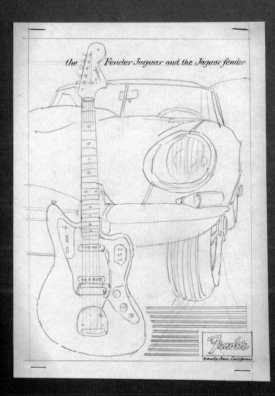

the Fender Jaguar and the Jaguar fender

Fender
Santa Ana, California

the bite they were used to from a Fender guitar, so rather than update the design, a new model in the same styling was created. To set it apart from the Jazzmaster, the Jaguar's control knobs and switches were mounted on three separate chrome plates and a new larger, flared-out headstock was designed. The headstock carried Bob Perine's redesigned Fender logo that first appeared on the Jazz Bass – seen here for the first time on a six-string.

The new patented, 'wide range' pickups looked similar to those featured on Stratocasters, but Leo designed a chrome metal cradle, with notched sides, in which the pickup sat. This new design was intended to reduce hum and interference, while concentrating the magnetic field under

(facing page, top to bottom)
Bob Perine's mock-up for an early Jaguar ad, Fender stand at a 1963 teen fair

(above, left to right) 1962 – Sunburst, 1965 – Black

(overleaf, left) 1965 – Sherwood Green

(overleaf, right) Carl Wilson of The Beach Boys with his Olympic White Jaguar

the strings. It resulted in bright, trebly sounding pickups with more output, but a thinner overall sound than previous Fender guitars. The electrics were as per the Jazzmaster, with dual lead and rhythm circuits, both with designated tone and volume controls switchable via the upper bout control panel. The Jazzmaster pickup selector was replaced by three slider switches, mounted on a hexagonal plate, similar to the one employed on the Bass VI. Two switches turned the pickups on and off, while a third, often referred to as the 'strangle' switch, allowed for a simple tone modification that cut treble frequencies via a tone capacitor.

Like the Jazzmaster, the standard finish on the new, high-end six-string was a three-color sunburst with a faux tortoiseshell pickguard. Necks were maple with slab rosewood fingerboards and clay dot markers. However, only the very earliest Jaguars feature slab board necks, as the new curved rosewood boards were introduced only a few months after the model's introduction, during the summer months of 1962. From commencement of production, Fender made small batches of Jaguars in custom color finishes. Prior to '62, custom-color guitars were specifically ordered and seldom seen as stock items hanging on the walls of music shops. The Jaguar would be one of the first Fender instruments to change that perception.

The new guitar quickly found favour with instrumental surf groups. Not only did it have the sound they were after but its shape and style suited the genre perfectly. With its cresting-wave body shape and flashy, automobile-style chrome parts, a custom color Jaguar in Foam Green, Sonic Blue or Candy Apple Red would become *the* Surf guitar – a genuine 'babe magnet' for young guitarists. Carl Wilson from the Beach Boys was one of the most famous exponents of the Jaguar and was seldom seen without his Olympic White Jag with matching headstock, during the band's early years. It soon became commonplace for bands like the Beach Boys, to order matched sets of custom-color Fender guitars. This would usually comprise of a Fender bass – Precision or Jazz – a Stratocaster and a Jaguar or Jazzmaster with a full backline of Fender amps to complete the look. During the early '60s, Fender equipment was unrivalled in terms of quality, reliability and image. The new decade had arrived in full color and Fender had the matching tools to create the musical backdrop.

Left-handed Jaguars and Jazzmasters were made available during late 1963, and in the same year, a new moulded case was introduced by Fender for its professional six-string models. Made by Bulwin, the new case, often referred to as the 'sunglasses case', was reddish-brown molded plastic, with plush orange interiors and twin storage pockets. A gold Fender logo embossed onto the outside of the case proudly boasted the quality of the contents, but injection molding for this sort of usage was in its infancy and the new cases were a heavy, and expensive, option. They retailed at $80 for the Jaguar, 50 per cent more than the standard Tolex-covered case.

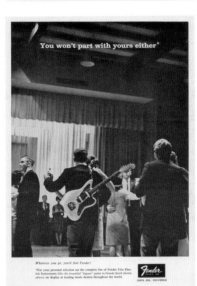

February 1964 saw the introduction of custom neck sizes on the Jaguar, Jazzmaster and Stratocaster. The standard 1⁵⁄₈" width B neck was now joined by a narrow 1¹⁄₂" A neck, a 1³⁄₄" C neck and a 1⁷⁄₈" D neck. All non-standard neck widths could be specially ordered for an extra five per cent on retail price. A and C widths are rare, while D necks were almost never ordered.

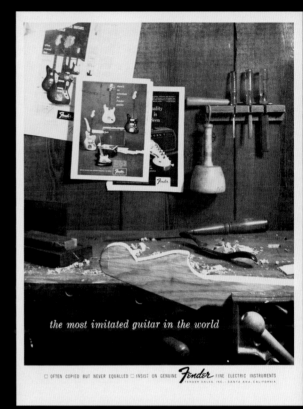

the most imitated guitar in the world

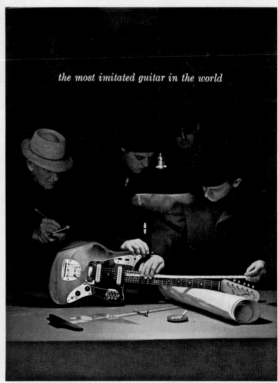

the most imitated guitar in the world

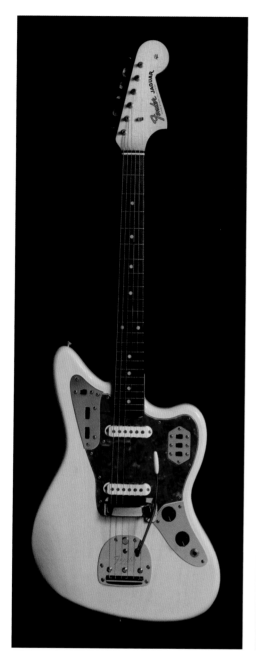

Surf music and the Fender Jaguar enjoyed their heyday between 1962 and 1965. For that brief period, the pair seemed inseparable, so much so that it would lead to the Jaguar becoming an unpopular choice by the late '60s as surfing sounds faded away to be replaced by heavier rock. With its abundance of chrome and impractical string mute, the guitar began to look dated and it has never been afforded the timeless status given to the Telecaster or Stratocaster designs. Nonetheless, like the Jazzmaster, the Jaguar has since found favour with alternative bands looking for a Fender guitar with a different sound and image. Very much a product of the 1960s, the Fender Jag has its own unique appeal among players and collectors.

(facing page) 1965 – Inca Silver
(this page, left to right)
1963 – Blond, 1965 – Fiesta Red,
1964 – Olympic White

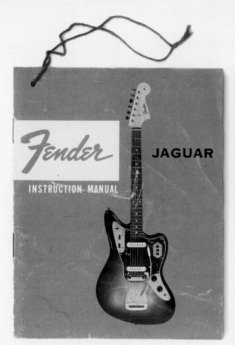

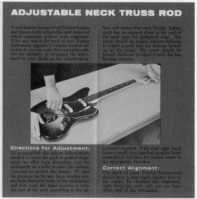

*(top left) early '60s Jaguar
instruction manual*

(above) 1964 – Lake Placid Blue

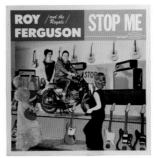

fender facts

Fender Facts was a four-page periodical newsletter launched by Fender Sales during 1962. It was similar in style to Gibson's *Gibson Gazette* and was mailed out to Fender dealers and customers who had subscribed via warranty registration cards. Running for a total of 17 issues until 1969, it informed readers of new models, accessories and changes to the Fender line. Issue 5 from November 1963 (shown above) introduces the new Candy Apple Red custom color as well as the availability of Jaguars, Jazzmasters and the Bass VI in left-handed versions. Also on offer was the new Fender Clock for $11.99 and the 'Handy Stand,' a device for holding a guitar or bass in the playing position while leaving the musician free to move about the bandstand. Today, these newsletters are very scarce and provide a valuable insight into the company's history.

brown/wheat grille amplifiers 1961–1963

HOW TO ENJOY YOUR NEW FENDER CUSTOM-ENGINEERED AMPLIFIER

Between 1959 and 1963, Fender experimented with various color combinations across the amplifier line. Tolex was available in different shades, as was the grille cloth material that Fender had been using since the Narrow Panel tweeds were introduced in 1955. In 1961, Fender discontinued all but one of the tweed Narrow Panel amps by redesigning the Princeton, Deluxe and Vibrolux for the updated cabinet. The 1961 full-line catalog displayed Fender amplifiers in five different color combinations. At the top of the line, the Piggyback amps and the Twin featured blond with oxblood grilles. The larger combo amps appeared in both brown with oxblood and brown with brown grilles, while the smaller combos carried a new brown with wheat grille combination. This left the little 4-watt Champ as the only survivor of the Narrow Panel tweed era.

Textured brown Tolex, now a darker tone than that seen on earlier amps, was matched with a new, wheat-colored grille cloth, brown faceplates and brown plastic control knobs. This made for a combination that was both tasteful and attractive. Brown with wheat grille amplifiers used the old-style leather handles from the tweed era and lacked any sort of Fender badge on the speaker baffle. The only subtle nod to the amplifier's origin was a small script under the model name that read 'FENDER ELECT. INST. CO.'

By 1962, the Pro, Vibrasonic, Super and Concert amps switched from their brown/oxblood grille image to the new brown/wheat style. These larger combos all featured a flat metal Fender logo on the baffle board and dark brown molded plastic 'dog bone' handles. By mid-1963, the unreliable 'dog bones' were finally replaced by a new, more efficient strap handle in dark brown plastic with nickel-plated ends. This enduring design would soon feature on all Fender amplifiers.

The February 1963 issue of *Fender Facts* heralded the launch of a brand-

new Fender combo, the last to receive the brown/wheat grille treatment. The Vibroverb was a compact, 35-watt unit that utilized 2 x 10" speakers. It was similar in specification to the Super, but the real breakthrough lay in the onboard reverb, an important first on any Fender amplifier. 'The new Vibroverb enables the player to obtain the 'expanded-sound' effect without having to use a separate reverb unit.' A newly designed foot switch was provided to enable on-off switching of both reverb and vibrato effects, something that would

become a common feature on Fender amplifiers over the coming years. It was also the first Fender combo to utilize the tilt-back legs previously reserved for the Piggyback amps.

Princeton: 12 watt; 1 x 10" speaker
Deluxe: 15 watt; 1 x 12" speaker
Pro: 25 watt; 1 x 15" speaker
Vibrasonic: 25 watt; 1 x 15" speaker
Super: 30watt; 2 x 10" speakers
Vibrolux: 30 watt; 1 x 12" speaker
Vibroverb: 35 watt; 2 x 10" speakers
Concert: 40 watt; 4 x 10" speakers

fender acoustics

Roger Rossmeisl was an extremely gifted guitar designer and builder. Born in northern Germany in 1927, he was the son of a skilled musician and luthier named Wenzel Rossmeisl, who branded his instruments 'Roger' in honour of his son. The young Rossmeisl spent the war years studying the art of guitar making at Mittenwald School near the Austrian border and, in 1945, he graduated as a Master Guitar Maker, aged just 18.

After some years working alongside his father in Berlin, Rossmeisl wrote a letter to Ted McCarty, president of Gibson guitars in America, and was offered a position with the firm in 1952. His short stint at Gibson was unsuccessful and he produced only one arch-top jazz instrument. Rossmeisl emigrated again, this time to the West Coast of America, where he landed a job at Rickenbacker in early 1954. Rickenbacker had been producing lap steels and amplifiers since the early 1930s, but had recently been sold to the ambitious Francis Hall during 1953. Hall had watched the growth of Fender – both as boss of Radio-Tel and via his partnership in Fender Sales – and was eager to have his

own company in the growing electric guitar business. Rossmeisl's arrival at Rickenbacker was perfectly timed and he was responsible for most of the designs that the company produced over the following eight years. These would form the cornerstone of Rickenbacker's output for the next half a century. Beginning, in 1954, with the Combo series of solid-body guitars, Rossmeisl went on to design and develop the Capri range of semi-acoustics in the late '50s and early '60s. These would become famous in the hands of The Beatles, ensuring Rickenbacker's future as a guitar maker for decades to come.

Fender had toyed with idea of producing acoustic guitars since the early '50s and the 1952 fold-out catalog featured

STANDARD GUITAR

Beautiful mahogany finish, rich full tone, fast action adjustable neck, unique neck and head design for modern appearance and ease of playing.

Available in three sizes:

17R—Standard size, birch body, large frets, good tone. Available in light or dark finish.

300R—Mahogany body, special neck with tension rod, exclusive head design, professional frets, rosewood fretboard, wonderful tone.

• 400R—Same as 300R but larger cases available.

an intriguing picture showing four acoustic models. Two of these looked like outsourced instruments built by another manufacturer, while the other two – almost certainly prototypes – featured Fender-style necks, with rosewood fingerboards, and Telecaster-style headstocks. These instruments – the 300R and 400R – remain a mystery and never appeared on price sheets or any other sales literature. During the late '50s, Fender Sales, under the guidance of Don Randall, purchased the Regal brand name. They ordered acoustic guitars to be produced under that banner, by the giant Harmony company in Chicago, for distribution alongside the Fender

line of electrics. At the time, Harmony was the largest supplier of stringed instruments in the world and built guitars for several distributors under brand names such as Silvertone, Stella and Vogue. Though the Regal brand gave Fender a financial interest in the acoustic guitar market, Leo still considered the possibilities of producing his own range of acoustics. Many of his favourite western swing and country artists used acoustic guitars and a revival in folk music was driving increased sales for rival makers like Martin and Gibson.

By the early '60s, Leo was giving the matter serious thought. He wanted an instrument good enough to carry the

Fender name and, by coincidence, Roger Rossmeisl paid a visit to the Fender plant in 1962. Dissatisfied with his position at Rickenbacker, he offered his services to Leo and was hired on the spot. Plans were immediately put in place for a new line of Fender acoustic guitars and Leo and Roger worked closely on the design of these new instruments. The principal difference that would set the new guitars apart from other manufacturers offerings was the employment of bolt-on necks with Fender-style headstocks and fully adjustable bridges. No acoustics had been built like this before and the new instruments would certainly cause a stir upon release.

Fender ACOUSTIC INSTRUMENT CO., INC.
1560-1580 Missile Way, Anaheim, California / 871-9680

Roger R. Rossmeisl

Leo Fender

Fender ACOUSTIC INSTRUMENT CO., INC.
1560-1580 Missile Way, Anaheim, California / 871-9680

*(preceding page) 1964 concert with
(inset) Roger Rossmeisl*

*(facing page, top to bottom) acoustic
guitar production in 1966, Ray
Davies of The Kinks with his Malibu*

The new design featured a large, internal wooden
block that sat under the neck, through which four
long, neck-fastening screws passed. A metal tube,
usually camouflaged with brown paint, ran inside the body
in line with the neck, acting as a backbone for the
instrument. This design, although filed for patent by
Leo in 1963, had been used during the early part of
the 20th century by the Larson Brothers on several of
their highly revered acoustic instruments and it's thought
that Leo may have borrowed the idea from those. It gave the
body rigidity and prevented necks pulling forward with
age, a common problem on acoustics. Unfortunately,
the wooden block and metal tubes made guitars heavy
and had a detrimental effect on their sound. These were
issues Leo was not used to facing with his solid-body
instruments and consequently, the acoustic field was one
he would never master.

The new designs were first unveiled at the National
Association of Music Merchants show in Chicago during July
1963. They also appeared in that month's price list,
although instruments weren't officially available until later
in the year. The first two models to enter production were
the King (later Kingman) at $350 and the slightly wider-
bodied Concert at $325. Both were stylish Rossmeisl
designs and early examples featured solid spruce tops, with
rosewood back and sides, rosewood fingerboards with clay

Tex Ritter
plays

Fender
MUSICAL INSTRUMENTS

dot markers and tortoiseshell pickguards. Rossmeisl
would later incorporate several features he'd used on
Rickenbacker guitars, including gold pickguards and
chequered bindings, onto the new acoustics.

Initially built at the overcrowded Fender factory at
500 South Raymond Avenue, plans were soon underway
for a dedicated acoustic manufacturing facility nearby on
Missile Way in Anaheim. The new plant was up and
running by January '64, and by December of that year,
the smaller-bodied Palomino was introduced at $199.
April 1965 saw the addition of two budget-priced
instruments: the $159 Malibu and the all-mahogany
Newporter at only $129. The acoustic lineup was
completed in July 1965 with the introduction of two
12-string models that featured Fender's new 'hockey stick'
headstock: the Shenandoah at $290 and its smaller-
bodied, cheaper cousin the Villager at $185.

Fender's artist liaison department did a fantastic job
pushing the acoustic range on name players during the
'60s, and for a while, it seemed as if almost every country
artist favoured the new bolt-on neck design. Johnny Cash,
Tex Ritter, Faron Young, The Carter Family, Wanda Jackson
and Charley Pride all posed with Fender acoustics, and it
was hard to watch a country music TV programme during the
mid to late '60s without spotting one. Canadian folk
singer Ian Tyson, of Ian & Sylvia fame, regularly played
a Fender Kingman,and Ray Davies of The Kinks used his
Fender Malibu throughout the mid-1960s. Bob Dylan and

(preceding pages, left to right) 1965 Shenandoah, 1968 Villager, 1967 Palomino

(overleaf) Wildwood promtional shot featuring Bob Perine's daughter Jorli

(overleaf facing page) 1970 Songwriter flyer plus extracts from the 1970 acoustic guitar catalog

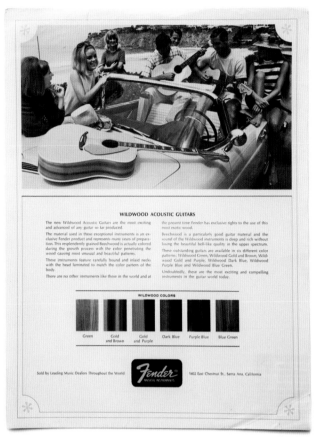

Robbie Robertson were captured jamming on Fender acoustics in a London hotel room in the legendary *Eat The Document* film, and for a while, it seemed as if the Fender range of acoustics might take off.

During mid-1966, the Fender King was renamed the Kingman and a new model, named the Wildwood, appeared. The Wildwood was essentially a Kingman that sported a brave new finish for a Fender instrument. To achieve this unique finish, beech trees were injected with colored dyes during growth, and once harvested, the wood was sliced into thin veneers and carefully applied to backs, sides and headstocks of standard Kingman acoustics. The results were both dramatic and colorful and Fender literature claimed that 'no two Wildwood guitars are exactly alike.' Wildwood acoustics were initially offered in six brightly colored shades, but by 1967, as the process was introduced to the Coronado range of semi-acoustic electric guitars, the range was pared down to just three shades: Wildwood I – Rainbow Greens; Wildwood II – Rainbow Blues; and Wildwood III – Rainbow Golds. "They were beautiful guitars," Don Randall told guitar historian Tony Bacon, "but they never went any place, never caught on." March 1968 saw the introduction of an optional gray sunburst, named Antigua, on the 12-string Shenandoah model, and in July of the same year, one final new model – the Redondo – was introduced. It was essentially a Newporter with a spruce top instead of mahogany.

Optional sunburst tops were offered across the line in 1969, and by 1970, black too became an option.

One little-known variant of the Fender acoustic range is the Songwriter, a small, parlour-sized guitar that never went into production. Designed by Roger Rossmeisl, only two prototypes were built, by Phil Kubicki in 1969, who states that "one was given to Bobbie Gentry and the other to Carl Perkins". Aimed at female players, the Songwriter was planned to be available in seven 'colors of the '70s' and, although a promotional flyer promised 'the famous Fender sound from a new guitar about as portable as a tennis racquet', the instrument never saw the light of day. Another Fender rarity.

By 1971, Fender had abandoned production of their own acoustic guitars and, once again, switched to outsourcing instruments that would carry the Fender name. The acoustic designs of Roger Rossmeisl and Leo Fender remain one of the company's less successful but nonetheless interesting diversions. Over the passing years, they have gained an unfair reputation as inferior instruments, largely due to the added weight of wooden neck blocks and metal body braces. While it's true that they never rivalled Gibson, Martin or Guild acoustics produced during the '60s, these Californian-built guitars from the golden age are great-sounding, highly playable guitars with a decidedly Fender look and feel.

Fender Songwriter

The lightweight heavyweight in 7 fashion colors. The famous Fender sound from a new guitar about as portable as a tennis racquet.

Fender ACOUSTIC GUITARS

fender reverb units

this is **ECCO-FONIC . . .**

Echo had become an important effect for both vocalists and guitarists during the 1950s. Guitar players including Les Paul, Chet Atkins and Scotty Moore from Elvis Presley's band had all used echo to great effect on recordings during the early to mid-'50s. In 1959, Fender bought in pre-made tape echo units from the Ecco-Fonic company, housing them in tweed cases for sale under the Fender brand name.

Reverb was a similar effect that gave an excellent approximation of sound reverberating around a large room or hall. Hammond had developed an effective system that employed long springs to give the desired sound for their range of organs and it was this design that Leo Fender licensed for his reverb unit. In typical fashion, Leo adapted and improved on the original Hammond design, adding dwell, mixer and tone controls that gave an impressive array of 'expanded' sounds. He housed his new design in what looked like a small Fender amplifier that could be matched with any type of amp, PA system or studio setup to add the best portable reverb available during the early '60s. Launched in July 1961, the Fender Reverb unit became an instant hit with surf bands and instrumental groups, adding its characteristic wet, splashy sound to many recordings of the day. The opening crescendo of The Chantays 'Pipeline' and The Surfaris 'Wipeout' are prime examples of a Fender Reverb unit in action.

The earliest reverb units came in brown Tolex with wheat grilles, but Fender soon offered these in blond with oxblood grilles to match the Piggyback amps and 85-watt Twin from the Professional series. By 1963, Fender began adding onboard reverb to several of their combo amps including the Twin, which now became the Twin Reverb. Further variants of the reverb unit in blond with wheat grille and black with silver grille cloths ensured that any Fender amp could be partnered with a matching reverb unit during the 1960s.

(facing page) 1959 Ecco-Fonic introduction flyer

(facing page bottom, left to right)
1962 – brown / wheat grille,
1962 – blond / oxblood grille

(this page bottom, left to right)
1963 – blond / wheat grille,
1966 – blackface / siver grille

fender sparkle finishes

Sparkle finishes are something of an enigma among Fender collectors. While it is known that these were offered by Fender on a strictly custom-order basis during the 1960s, there is no supporting literature and very few facts to go on. What is known is that sparkle finishes were not applied at the Fender factory, but outsourced to auto spray shops close by. This in itself adds more confusion, as although Fullerton was a center for hot-rodding and customizing automobiles in Southern California, little information is available on exactly how, where or by whom these guitars were painted.

Sparkle finishes became popular on hot rods and custom cars during the mid- to late '50s and it was logical that customers would request these on guitars. Gretsch had offered sparkle finishes on their Silver Jet and custom Duo Jet guitars between 1955 and 1966, but these were applied with the celluloid plastic that the company used to cover drum sets. Fender sparkle finishes featured heavy metal flakes of varying sizes, much larger than those seen in standard Fender metallic colours. These required special spraying equipment that Fender did not carry. Sparkle finishes were usually, but not always, shot over an existing paint scheme, more than likely a second or rejected finish that acted as a primer for the sparkle coats. It is also possible that customers returned their pre-owned guitars to Fender to receive sparkle finishes after purchase. One known example of this was when Dick Dale's band The Del-Tones, returned a Jazzmaster, Strat and Precision Bass for matching green 'Surfburst' finishes. Perhaps the most famous examples of Fender sparkle finishes were a pair of Silver Sparkle Telecaster Customs that featured matching headstocks and black checkerboard binding. These were built by Fender in 1964 for Buck Owens and his guitarist Don Rich; a third matching instrument was also built for George Fullerton. As automobile refinishers had little or no knowledge of the standard procedures used by Fender, sparkle finishes vary wildly. They are undoubtedly the work of different spray artists or spray shops and counterfeits are hard to detect. Each instrument must be judged on its own merits and history to determine originality.

Buck Owens and his band play

*(facing page) 1964 Musicmaster –
'Tangerine' Sparkle*

*(this page above, left to right) 1958
Jazzmaster – 'Surfburst', 1965
Jazzmaster – Blue Sparkle, 1965
Jaguar – Green Sparkle*

*(this page, left) Dick Dale & His
Del-Tones with matching 'Surfburst'
guitars*

blond / wheat grille amplifiers 1962 – 1964

Surf music sprang up on Fender's doorstep in Southern California and swept across America and the rest of the world during the early 1960s. Influential rock'n'roll artists like The Ventures, Duane Eddy & Santo and Johnny proved a vocalist wasn't necessarily a key ingredient for a rock band and many youngsters followed suit, forming their own instrumental groups during the early part of the '60s. Fender guitars and amplifiers were the weapon of choice and surf music became a perfect advertisement for the Fender sound. A typical early surf band would usually consist of drums, a Fender bass, a Stratocaster and possibly a Jazzmaster. Fender Piggyback amps were de rigueur and considered a must by any surf groups who could afford them. Essential to the surf sound was a Fender Reverb unit, which gave the music atmosphere and edge; built-in reverb was not yet standard on Fender amps.

Bands such as Dick Dale & His Del-Tones, The Surfaris, The Bel Airs, Eddie & The Showmen and The Beach Boys, all hailing from Southern California, were the big exponents of the new surf sound and all relied heavily on Fender equipment. The new Fender Jaguar guitar, launched in 1962, quickly became a favourite with surf groups and a new series of Fender amplifiers released in 1962 would prove popular too.

For the second and final phase of blond Tolex-covered amps, Fender replaced the oxblood grille with wheat-colored grille from late 1962. The wheat grille complemented the blond Tolex perfectly and made for striking, classy-looking amplifiers very much in keeping with the image and style of the times. Like the blond/oxblood combination before, the blond/wheat styling was reserved for the Piggyback amps and the Twin. The blond/wheat amps initially featured a rough Tolex, with brown faceplates and white plastic knobs. However, with the arrival of smooth black Tolex and black faceplates on Fender combos during late 1963, the blond/wheat range adopted a smooth blond Tolex, a black faceplate and black, numbered control knobs for its final incarnation.

Ever keen to push their products, Fender Sales regularly set up stands at popular teen fairs during the early to mid '60s. Kids would visit the Fender display to pick up a free catalog, price list or custom color chart. They could even try out a real Fender guitar through a Fender amp, often showing off a lick they'd learned from one of the instrumental hits of the day. Californian surf, sea and sun, set to the twang of a Fender guitar, was a match made in heaven.

Tremolux: 30 watt amplifier with 2 x 10" speaker cabinet
Bandmaster: 40 watt amplifier with 2 x 12" speaker cabinet
Bassman: 50 watt amplifier with 2 x 12" speaker cabinet
Showman: 85 watt amplifier with 1 x 12" or 1 x 15" speaker cabinet
Dual Showman: 85 watt amplifier with 2 x 15" speaker cabinet
Twin: 85 watt; 2 x 12" speakers

mustang and mustang bass

The Mustang was an important, and long overdue, addition to the Fender range when it first appeared in July 1964. It bridged the gap between the entry-level student models and the Professional range of guitars. Priced at just $189.50, it sat neatly between the $159.50 Duo Sonic and $209.50 Telecaster. It was, however, $20 more expensive than the one-pickup Esquire from the Professional range and found favour with many semi-pro musicians on a budget.

Don Randall had long been requesting a student model guitar with a Tremolo and Leo finally relented with the Mustang. Essentially a Duo Sonic with a vibrato unit, Fender spent some time working on the new design. He wanted a simple, affordable Tremolo that functioned properly, but one that could be mounted to the top of the guitar with minimal routing to the body. As usual, Leo succeeded and the Mustrang Trem fulfilled all the requirements. The unit featured a Jazzmaster-style bridge, with simplified bridge saddles, designed to cope with heavy-handed playing.

The standard student body shape was adjusted slightly to give it an offset waist, in keeping with recent Fender models. A new pickguard was designed to complement the new body shape, which featured a Telecaster-style sweeping curve across the top bout of the guitar. It was made from either faux tortoiseshell or a new style of three-ply plastic with a white pearloid top, black center and plain white underside.

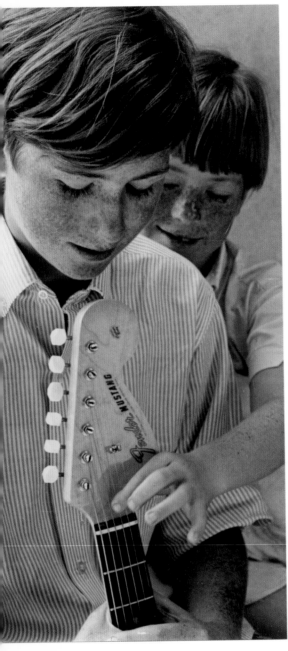

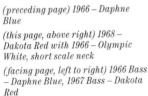

(preceding page) 1966 – Daphne
Blue

(this page, above right) 1968 –
Dakota Red with 1966 – Olympic
White, short scale neck

(facing page, left to right) 1966 Bass
– Daphne Blue, 1967 Bass – Dakota
Red

Volume and tone controls were mounted to a chrome control
plate that negated the need for shielding under the pickguard.
The Mustang featured two pickups identical to those
employed on the Duo Sonic, but instead of a single pickup
selector, it featured two sliding switches that offered tone
settings for lead and rhythm playing as well as an 'off' option
in the center position.

The Mustang was offered in a choice of three colorful
standard finishes: Dakota Red, Olympic White and Daphne
Blue, the full names being dropped in favour of Red, White and
Blue for simplicity and ease of ordering. The Mustang was
also available in two scale lengths: a short 22.5" scale like
the Musicmaster and Duo Sonics, or a slightly longer 24"

scale like the Jaguar. The longer-scale length won the day and orders for short-scale Mustangs were virtually non-existent. Both new necks featured the now-popular larger headstock design with a transitional Fender logo in gold with black edging. By the end of 1964, the cosmetic changes introduced to the student range via the Mustang were carried over to both the Musicmaster and Duo Sonic, bringing all three guitars into line.

Don Randall was proved right when the Mustang became an overnight success. Its arrival was well timed and it fought off many cheap, imported instruments competing for similar space in the now-congested student guitar market. As the British invasion of the Amercan music scene gathered pace through 1964, guitar sales were at an all-time high and Fender struggled to keep up with demand. By late 1964, the Fullerton factory was playing catch-up as it raced to fulfil orders for the Mustang.

By the end of 1964, Leo had begun work on a bass model that would complete the range of Fender student guitars. The Mustang bass, with its short 30" scale length, was the perfect companion to the successful Mustang guitar and it filled yet another gap in the market for a professionally made, solid-body student bass. Many other makers were now offering budget-price bass guitars, but Fender had been slow to enter the field, seemingly happy to remain dominant at the top end of the market.

*(this page, below) 1968 –
Competition Burgundy*

*(facing page, left to right)
1968 – Olympic White, 1968 –
Competition Orange, 1968 –
Competition Burgundy*

*(overleaf) 1969 Bass – Competition
Burgundy, 1968 Bass – Competition
Orange, 1969 Bass – Competition
Red*

*(overleaf, inset) Rolling Stone
Bill Wyman with his Competition
Orange Mustang Bass*

Leo developed a new split pickup for the Mustang Bass, much smaller than that used on the Precision, but still capable of producing a good, solid bass tone. The bridge was a new design, too. Four fully adjustable bridge saddles sat on a large chrome plate that allowed for four individually adjustable string mutes. Body styling was very similar to the Mustang guitar, with controls mounted on a chrome plate. Finally launched in July 1966, early examples came in Red or Blue with a white pearloid pickguard, or White with a faux tortoiseshell pickguard.

In May 1969, the Mustang guitar and bass lines received new 'Competition' paint schemes that replaced the Red, White and Blue options. These came in three striking combinations with 'racing stripes' that ran diagonally across the contour on the front of the body and matching headstocks. The options were Competition Red (metallic red with white stripes), Competition Orange (light orange with dark orange stripes) and Competition Burgundy (a shaded metallic blue with pale blue stripes).

The Mustang Bass found favour not only with students but also experienced players with smaller hands. Bill Wyman of The Rolling Stones used both Competition Burgundy and Competion Orange basses during '69 and '70, and by the late '70s, many punk and new wave bands had adopted the small, affordable bass.

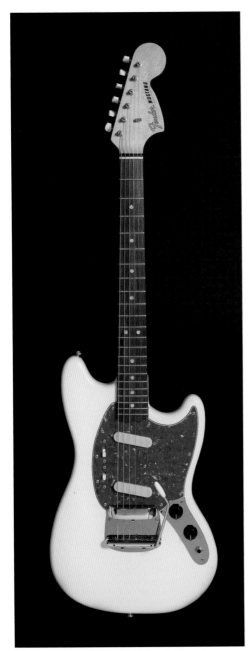

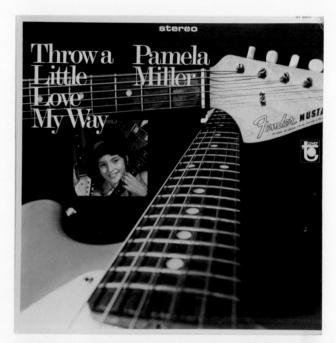

The choice of professionals and students

Fender Fine Electric Instruments

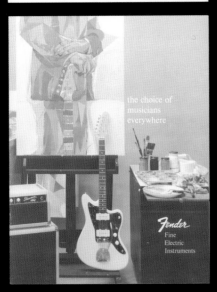

the choice of musicians everywhere

Fender
Fine
Electric
Instruments

Fender FINE ELECTRIC INSTRUMENTS / 1965-66 CATALOG

Fender FINE ELECTRIC INSTRUMENTS CATALOGS 58-65

blackface amplifiers
1963 –1968

If you look at a live photograph of any blues, rock or country band playing during the mid- to late '60s, the chances are they will be playing through a backline of Fender Blackface amps. Only Vox and, later, Marshall would pose a serious threat to Fender's stronghold as market leaders during this most important era in rock music's history. From The Rolling Stones to The Byrds, Muddy Waters to Moby Grape, Jefferson Airplane to The Lovin' Spoonful and Buck Owens to The Band, everybody, it seemed, was playing through a Blackface Fender amp during the 1963 – 1968 era . Even The Beatles used Blackface Fender Showman amplifiers during the 1966 recording sessions for 'Revolver.'

Fender's Blackface amplifiers are regarded by many as the most versatile and useable the company ever made. The switch to black Tolex covering, black faceplates with white script and black numbered knobs came in mid- to late 1963. Dick Dale later claimed it was he who first persuaded Fender to make black amplifiers, but its more than likely other musicians were also complaining about how dirty their old tweed, blond and brown amps looked after regular touring. JMI (one of Fender's UK distributors in 1963) had begun using black covering on their Vox amps as early as 1961, but as rock music grew and its environment changed, a move towards a more durable, scuff-resistant covering was inevitable and long overdue.

The first black Tolex amps appeared in mid-1963 and ran alongside the blond/wheat styling of the Piggyback amps and 2 x 12" Twin combo. The earliest examples, like most of the brown/wheat combos before, lacked any sort of Fender logo on the grille cloth. Soon, however, a new raised chrome metal logo was worked up which incorporated Bob Perine's redesigned Fender script with a tail that ran under the word Fender. The black amps featured a new silver grille cloth and black plastic strap handles with nickel-plated ends. These were the most rugged Fender amps to date and were capable of withstanding pretty much anything that could be thrown at them. By late '64, the whole Fender range had been brought into line with all amps covered in the same style. Only the Princeton and Bassman amplifiers stood out with their short-lived white plastic knobs. It was the first time since the Narrow Panel tweeds that the Fender amp line received a uniform look.

Several new models were introduced during the Blackface era, but none more important than the Twin Reverb launched in late 1963. Essentially the old, 85-watt Twin amp with onboard reverb, the Twin Reverb would go on to become one of the all-time classic amplifiers; an industry standard and workhorse that would grace stages all over the world for decades to come.

Elsewhere in the Blackface range, other models were offered in standard and revamped versions. The Champ was offered with vibrato as the Vibro Champ, whilst the Princeton, Deluxe, Pro and Vibrolux were all offered in standard or reverb-equipped versions. Fender had all bases covered. Every style of musician was catered for with the new Blackface range, and all were great-sounding amplifiers. Groove Tube

Your new *Fender* custom-engineered Amplifier

founder and amp expert, Aspen Pittman, described the Deluxe Reverb as "the amp I would choose if I were stranded on a desert island and could only have one. Small, simple to operate, sounds terrific for any kind of music and gets great overdrive distortion when turned up." High praise indeed, which could be applied to any amplifier from the Blackface era.

Champ: 5 watt; 1 x 8" speaker
Vibro Champ: 5 watt; 1 x 8" speaker
Princeton: 12 watt; 1 x 10" speaker
Princeton Reverb: 12 watt; 1 x 10" speaker
Deluxe: 20 watt; 1 x 12 speaker
Deluxe Reverb: 20 watt; 1 x 12" speaker
Pro: 25 watt; 1 x 15" speaker
Vibrolux: 30 watt; 1 x 12" speaker
Vibrolux Reverb: 35 watt; 2 x 10" speakers
Vibroverb: 40 watt; 1 x 15" speaker
Pro Reverb: 40 watt; 2 x 12" speakers
Super Reverb: 40 watt; 4 x 10" speakers
Twin Reverb: 85 watt; 2 x 12" speakers
Tremolux: 30 watt amplifier with 2 x 10" speaker cabinet
Bandmaster: 40 watt amplifier with 2 x 12" speaker cabinet
Bassman: 50 watt amplifier with 2 x 12" speaker cabinet
Showman: 85 watt amplifier with 1 x 12" or 1 x 15" speaker cabinet
Dual Showman: 85 watt amplifier with 2 x 15" speaker cabinet

THE NAME
THAT MAKES
THE DIFFERENCE

Often copied but
never equalled,
Fender Fine Electric
Instruments are in
constant demand by
the world's top
musicians. Look to
the Fender signature
for quality.

Fender
SALES, INC.

Santa Ana, California

Feel the difference...

Hear the difference

Enjoy comfortable
fingering...smooth
playing...fast action
...on the world's
finest guitars.
Plug into the greatest
musical instrument
sound system in the
world. Now you have
the perfect combi-
nation. That's what
makes the difference.
*At your nearest leading
Music Dealer.*

Fender
MUSICAL INSTRUMENTS
SANTA ANA, CALIFORNIA

FREE CATALOG / Write Fender Musical Instruments, Dept. F-5, 1402 East Chestnut, Santa Ana, California

PREFERRED BY LEADING ARTISTS ... EVERYWHERE

Comparison proves their Superiority

Jazzmaster

Fender 12-String

Duo-sonic

Mustang

Musicmaster

Bass VI

Jaguar

Stratocaster

Telecaster

Esquire

Jazz Bass

Precision Bass

Mandolin

Fender SALES, INC.

cbs takeover

On Tuesday, 5 January 1965, Fender Musical Instruments and Fender Sales Inc were sold lock, stock and barrel for $13,200,000 to CBS – the mighty Columbia Broadcasting Systems conglomerate. Talks between the two companies had begun during the summer of 1964, but were kept under wraps by Leo and Don until close to the final sale.

The Fender operation had grown out of all recognition during the early '60s and the pressures of running a large factory, with hundreds of staff, were beginning to weigh heavily on Leo's shoulders. In 1963, he made a serious proposition to sell his share in the business to Randall for $1.5 million and Don began to draw up a prospective agreement. With time to reflect upon the possible risks, Don convinced Leo that the pair would be better off selling the company to a third-party cash buyer. They had taken Fender as far as they felt they could, without ploughing huge sums back into the business, and an enduring streptococcal infection meant Leo's health was not at its best. The timing of their decision could not have been better; the guitar business was about to explode and it's unlikely that Leo and Don could have coped with further expansion without third-party funding.

Ironically, it was a CBS television appearance that set the ball rolling. When The Beatles made their first US appearance on the Ed Sullivan show on 9 February 1964, it became the most widely watched television programme of all time, with over 73 million viewers. The group looked and sounded like nothing that had gone before and suddenly every kid across America wanted a guitar. This had a colossal impact on not only the music industry but popular culture as a whole. Orders flooded into Fender from all corners of the world and the demand for electric guitars and amplifiers was overwhelming. "We were the largest dollar-volume producer in the world at the time we sold to CBS," claimed Leo. "We were also selling something like 80 per cent of all the basses of professional quality in the world. On one of our guitars, the Mustang, we were 15 million dollars back-ordered. That's a successful little guitar." As Fender and other established guitar manufacturers struggled to keep up

with increased demand, a host of new makers, mainly from the Far East, stepped forward vying for a piece of the action. The Beatles and the British invasion had triggered the biggest boom the electric guitar market would ever see, but what seemed like good business for music companies during the mid-'60s would have its downsides. Leo was happy with the steady growth he'd achieved with Fender, but the new challenge was daunting and prompted preliminary talks with potential buyers during early 1964.

The first to express an interest were The Baldwin Piano Company based in Cincinnati – keen to break into the burgeoning electric guitar market, they began discussions with Fender during April 1964. Don handled negotiations while Leo remained in his lab at the factory, but talks began to break down when it became clear that Baldwin had no interest in buying either Leo's acoustic guitar business or the Fender Rhodes keyboard concern. Baldwin, obviously looking for a bargain-basement deal, would later buy into the more modest Burns guitar company based in London, England. As the Baldwin deal started to fizzle out, a period of discussion began between Leo and Don about Fender becoming a public corporation offering shares for sale. But soon the pair were introduced to executives from CBS, keen on the idea of acquiring Fender. CBS was an enormous corporation in control of over 40 different companies, most of which were in the entertainment field. They had recently purchased the New York Yankees baseball team for $11 million and controlled the giant CBS television and radio stations and Columbia records, who, through CBS laboratories, had introduced the 33 $^1/_3$ long-playing album during 1948.

Don's negotiations were conducted through the Columbia Records Division of CBS, via an acquisitions team headed up by Jon Lorenz and legendary music industry executive Clive Davis. Several meetings took place in New York through September '64 as terms for a deal were hammered out. Columbia initially came at Don with low offers for the Fender operation, but after a thorough audit of the company's accounts and business practices by CBS, a glowing report was submitted to executives, which led to greatly improved terms. An agreement was reached during October. CBS eventually offered a staggering $13.2 million in return for the acquisition of the Fender guitar and amplifier factory, Fender Sales, the Fender acoustic plant, the Fender Rhodes keyboard division and the VC Squire Company that Don and Leo had purchased a few years earlier for the production of Fender Strings. Don had pulled off an unprecedented deal, the like of which had not been seen in music instrument history. In the space of 18 short years, the Fender business partners had built something quite incredible and they were about to be rewarded handsomely for their efforts. There was, however, an atmosphere of anticlimax surrounding the sale. There was no way up from this point, only down. "Leo wouldn't even go back to New York and pick up his check, wouldn't go back for the closing," explained Don. "I picked up his share of the booty and deposited it in his bank for him. He was busy working at Fender." When asked by Tom Wheeler many years later if he regretted the sale of Fender, Leo replied in typically nonchalant fashion: "No, I don't think so. A company like we had was sure a job, I'll tell you – it was so big. And then we had so many doors to lock up each night; George (Fullerton) had a career just to lock up at night."

The pair had made over five million dollars each from the sale, and it was agreed during negotiations that both Leo and Don's services were to be retained by CBS for five years after the buyout. Don's skills in sales and distribution were the ones CBS were interested in, and while he set up offices in both New York and Fullerton, Leo quietly moved to a new workshop a few blocks away from the South Raymond factory on Elm Street; a place where he could work alone at his own pace, uninterrupted by the goings-on at the CBS-owned factory. As soon as the sale was completed, plans were underway for the construction of a huge new manufacturing plant that would sit adjacent to – and dwarfing – the old factory buildings. All manufacturing of electric guitars and amplifiers was moved into the new factory building while the old units would be turned into a repair center, research and development departments and general storage for the main plant. CBS executives in suits and ties wasted no time examining the product range of their new acquisition, suggesting changes and new product lines.

Headstock decals on Fender guitars had seen a gradual changeover to Bob Perine's bolder 'transition' design (first used on the Jazz Bass in 1960), but by early '66 the old-style 'spaghetti' logos associated with pre-CBS production had been completely phased out . Old-style 'green' nitrate pickguards used on Stratocasters, Telecaster Customs and custom-finished Fenders were also discontinued soon after the takeover. Celluloid nitrate was flammable and Fender began replacing it with a stark white plastic, more durable and less prone to fading. Stratocasters were the first to feature white guards soon after the CBS takeover, with other models making the switch during the course of 1965 as stocks of the old green guards depleted.

Another CBS-instigated change, more obvious to potential customers, was a redesigned headstock seen on Stratocaster and Jazzmaster models produced from December 1965 onwards. These were enlarged to bring them in line with the Jaguar and Mustang, and incorporated the transition Fender logo in an early move by CBS to push Fender's branding. The new

headstocks, with larger logos, would be more visible on TV screens and stages. Necks on high-end models – Jaguars, Jazzmasters and Jazz Basses – were given white binding that ran down the edges of the fingerboard from mid-'65 onwards. The range of custom-color finishes available for Fender guitars was also revised during early 1965. 'Pre-CBS' has become a term used by dealers and collectors of Fender instruments to give a natural demarkation point after which quality begins to drop. Instruments made before the takeover will generally command higher prices than those produced during the CBS era. Strictly speaking, the only pre-CBS guitars and amplifiers made in 1965 were those built on Monday, 4 January. It's certainly true that, by the early '70s, a Fender guitar was not built to the same

standards demanded by Leo Fender, Forrest White or George Fullerton. But the drop-off in quality did not happen overnight. Fender, under CBS, continued to strive to produce instruments of quality throughout the 1960s and into the '70s. However, Fender's new owners were new to guitar making and quickly started making crucial mistakes. Wood was no longer carefully selected and seasoned, and there was a noticeable drop in the quality of paint finishes, especially on sunburst guitars. Pickups were now made to a cheaper specification and didn't sound as good as earlier units, and corners were being cut elsewhere in production techniques. As demand for Fender instruments grew, and production increased, it became harder and harder for CBS staff to monitor quality properly.

(page 209) 1966 Jaguar – Sunburst
with bound neck

(preceding pages, left to right)
1966 Stratocaster – Sunburst, 1966
Stratocaster – Candy Apple Red,
1966 Telecaster – Candy Apple Red

(this page, above and right) the vast
new CBS plant stands alongside the
original nine factory units at 500
South Raymond Avenue, Fullerton

marauder

'An electric guitar without pickups?' announced Fender in an opening salvo from their first full-line catalog since the CBS takeover. The instrument in question was the Marauder and it remains something of a mystery, as it never made it past the prototype stage, despite being featured in company literature and offered to dealers as a stock item. The guitar's premature appearance, before adequate field-testing, was indicative of the new regime now in place at Fender. CBS executives tripped over themselves rushing to get the new instrument to market in a bid to cash in on potential sales, and the move proved disastrous for the ill-fated Marauder.

Intended to sit at the top of the line, the new six-string featured a radical concept where four specially designed pickups were concealed beneath the pickguard. The only drawback was that the idea didn't work. Though the instrument was a product of Fender's research and development department, the pickups were the invention of one Quilla 'Porky' Freeman, a western swing musician who hailed from Missouri. Steve Soest, of Soest Guitar in Orange County, inspected a Marauder prototype during the early '70s and claimed: "The pickups were over-wound to compensate for the distance from the strings. And you know how unshielded, high-impedance, single-coil pickups sound when they're turned up around any electrical interference source? They hummed rather loudly!"

It's believed only five of the concealed-pickup Marauders were built before the idea was scrapped. Two of these – a sunburst Tremolo model and a Blue Ice Metallic non-Tremolo guitar – were pictured in the 1965 – 1966 Fender full-line catalog and featured white pearloid pickguards, Stratocaster bridge/Tremolo units and Jaguar-style pickup selection and control knobs. The body shape was similar to the Jazzmaster and Jaguar, with stretched, more pronounced cutaway horns. Necks too were Jazzmaster in style, with 21 frets, but fingerboards were bound and featured large Gibson-esque, block position markers, the first sighted on a Fender instrument. The Marauder appeared on the July 1965 price list and a custom-finished Tremolo model was priced at $502, twice the price of a non-Tremolo sunburst Strat. The high price didn't deter orders being placed, but all of these were returned, marked 'cancelled', once the decision was made to drop the Marauder before a single production instrument had been built.

In an attempt to revive the failed model, Gene Fields from Fender's R&D department worked on a second round of prototypes during 1966. These featured three exposed pickups and various switches to turn them on or off and activate tone circuits, like those found in a Jaguar. The first instrument from this run was finished in Lake Placid Blue and included a new, single-sided headstock designed by Fields. It employed a German carve running along the bottom edge and would be revived in the 1970s for his Fender Starcaster design. Of the eight prototype instruments made in the revised Marauder series, four featured regular fretted fingerboards while four more were produced with angled

'slant' frets. This gimmick, intended to enhance playability, did little to help the Marauder make it into production. The slant-fret idea was later adopted by Rickenbacker, and the Marauder was once again consigned to the reject pile.

(facing page) first of the second-series prototype Marauders from 1966 – Lake Placid Blue, (facing page, inset top) order cancellation from 1968 after the model had been abandoned, (facing page, inset bottom) 1965 catalog featuring two series-one Marauder prototypes

(this page, above) 1966 – Sunburst second-series prototype with slanted frets

electric xii

Prior to 1964, electric 12-string guitars were virtually unheard of. Acoustic 12s had been popular with folk and blues players since the 1930s and by the early '60s, were enjoying a surge in popularity due to the folk music boom. But it was a single instrument presented to one of The Beatles that would start a huge trend for electric 12-strings during the mid 1960s.

Although Gibson and Danelectro had developed 12-string electrics during the early '60s, it was the California-based Rickenbacker company that would launch the first commercially successful model. Soon after their first prototype was built in 1963, a second was presented to George Harrison during The Beatles first US tour in February 1964. George was thrilled with the new instrument and immediately started using it in the studio and on stage. Beatle recordings, such as 'A Hard Day's Night' and 'You Can't Do That,' instantly brought the chiming electric 12-string sound to a mass audience. Guitarist Jim McGuinn rushed out to buy a Rickenbacker 12-string after seeing George with his in the *A Hard Day's Night* movie and the guitar soon became an integral part of the sound of his new band The Byrds.

Fender were quick to start work on their offering in this rapidly growing market. The new guitar was launched in June 1965, just as The Byrds hit number one in the US singles charts with 'Mr Tambourine Man', an electrified cover of Bob Dylan's song that relied heavily on the 'jingle-jangle' 12-string sound. The Byrds would spearhead a folk rock movement during the mid '60s and electric 12s proved to be a key ingredient. The band's record label, and new Fender owners CBS even managed to place a Firemist Gold prototype 12-string with Byrds vocalist Gene Clark in time for The Byrds' second-ever TV performance. Fender's timing seemed perfect.

The new model was a follow-through in the Jazzmaster–Jaguar tradition, with a similar offset body design. It featured two split pickups, a four-way rotary tone selector

FENDER and ASTRONAUTS IN SESSION—This candid photo was taken during a recent recording session at RCA-Victor studios . . . The Astronauts, recording for a new album and a single, are using, in addition to their regular Fender Showman amps, the Bassman amp, Super/Reverb amp, Jazz Bass and Jaguars; also the new Fender-Rhodes electric piano and the Matador 12-string guitar.

(preceding page) 1965 –
Firemist Gold pre production model
as featured in the 1965 catalog

(this page, top) Buddy Merrill with
prototype (right) 1965 – Sunburst

(facing page, left to right) 1966 –
Olympic White, 1965 – Sonic Blue,
1966 – Fiesta Red

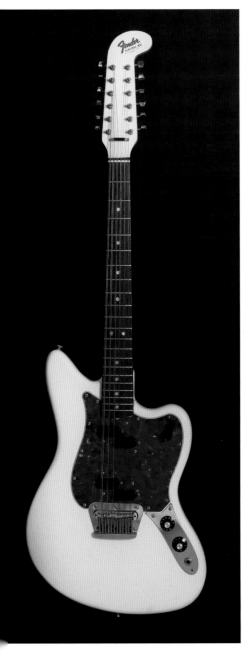
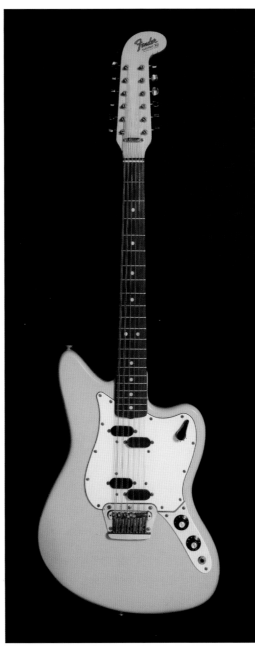
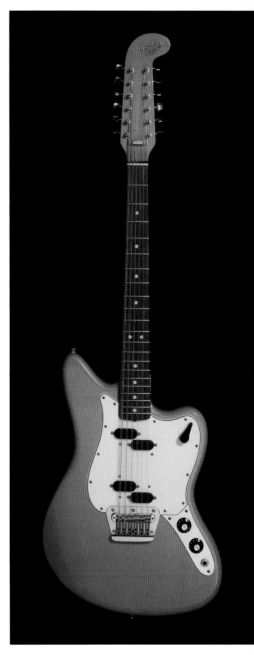

(that offered both pickups individually, together or together in out-of-phase mode) along with volume and tone controls mounted on a chrome plate. The real plus that the Fender 12 offered over its rivals was a fully adjustable 12-saddle bridge which meant the guitar could be set up for perfect intonation and ease of playing. Leo Fender was behind the superb design work that went into the new bridge and it was to be one of his last designs for the company as it was sold to CBS. The instrument, like the Fender VI before it, received an uninspired name choice, 'Electric XII,' although an article from the time describing a factory visit by surf band The Astronauts suggested that the new guitar was originally

due to be named the 'Matador.' Over time, the Electric XII would become affectionately known as the 'hockey stick', due to its unusual and ungainly headstock design.

An early prototype XII, given to long-term Fender endorsee and 'test-driver' Buddy Merrill, sported a Mustang-style pickguard and pickup selectors, while others featured white control knobs and string guides placed higher up the headstock than on production models. The standard finish on production Electric XIIs was sunburst and the first production run featured white pearloid guards with black volume and tone knobs similar to those found on Blackface Fender amps, although

(this page, left to right) Fender publicity shot featuring another pre production Electric XII, Bob Dylan with his Sunburst Electric XII

(facing page, left to right) 1966 – Candy Apple Red, 1965 – Sunburst, 1965 – Lake Placid Blue

pickguards were soon changed to faux tortoiseshell on sunburst instruments. Many custom-color examples were produced during the first couple of years' production, in a tactic employed by CBS to drive sales of their newer, or harder to sell, guitars. The 1965 and early '66 models featured pearl dot inlays on rosewood fingerboards, but this had changed to block inlays with binding by mid-'66. Block-inlayed Electric XIIs are rare and catalogs and serial numbers would suggest that Fender reverted back to using earlier-made dot-inlaid necks during the late '60s. The guitar became a firm studio favourite, but never really caught on as a live instrument. Although Beach Boy Carl Wilson and John Pisano from Herb Alpert's Tijuana Brass

performed with pre-production Electric XIIs during the mid-'60s, the guitar seemed destined to remain behind closed studio doors. Bob Dylan was pictured during 1965 playing the same sunburst XII that appeared in the '65 catalog and folk singer/songwriter Tim Buckley regularly endorsed the guitar. Pete Townsend of The Who often used a Fender Electric XII for recording and Jimmy Page played the Led Zeppelin classic 'Stairway To Heaven' on one, though neither guitarist appeared in public with the guitar. Velvet Underground guitarists Lou Reed and Sterling Morrison bought a pair of Electric XIIs, employing them to great effect on songs like 'What Goes On' and 'Beginning To See The Light' from the band's eponymous third album.

Electric XIIs are clearly evident on later Velvet Underground recordings, like 'Rock And Roll' and 'Who Loves The Sun,' proving that the guitar was an important instrument during the band's later years.

By 1967, the 12-string fad was fading fast. Many other manufacturers had jumped on the bandwagon, but Rickenbacker remained market leaders by gaining early, high-profile endorsements from The Beatles and The Byrds, the foremost exponents of the 12-string sound. By 1969, the model had been dropped from the Fender line, although it's unlikely that any new parts were built after 1967 and overstocks of unused bodies and necks would be sawn up to create a strange new instrument, the

(overleaf, left to right) 1966 – Blue Ice, Pete Townsend of The Who with his Sunburst Electric XII

(overleaf, facing pages left to right) 1966 – Candy Apple Red with block and bound neck, 1966 – Blue Ice with block and bound neck

'Custom,' during 1969. The Fender Electric XII remains one of Fender's unsung classics. It's possibly the most playable and versatile electric 12-string ever made, and while it lacked some of the characteristic chime made famous by Rickenbacker 12s, it has proved to be an enduring, underrated gem from Fender's golden age.

You
won't
part
with
yours
either

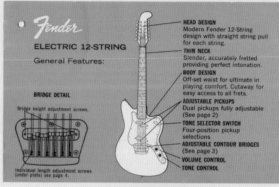

Fender

ELECTRIC 12-STRING

General Features:

BRIDGE DETAIL

Bridge height adjustment screws.

Individual length adjustment screws (under plate) see page 4.

HEAD DESIGN
Modern Fender 12-String design with straight string pull for each string.

THIN NECK
Slender, accurately fretted providing perfect intonation.

BODY DESIGN
Off-set waist for ultimate in playing comfort. Cutaway for easy access to all frets.

ADJUSTABLE PICKUPS
Dual pickups fully adjustable (See page 2)

TONE SELECTOR SWITCH
Four-position pickup selections

ADJUSTABLE CONTOUR BRIDGES
(See page 3)

VOLUME CONTROL

TONE CONTROL

'66 slab-body precision bass

During 1966, an interesting Fender instrument appeared that would forge a path many would later follow. Fender's UK distributor Arbiter placed a special order for a new style of Precision Bass. In many ways, this order and the guitars that arrived in the UK during the summer months of '66 could be seen as the first Fender reissue.

The basses featured slab bodies finished in blond, similar to those used on Precisions up to 1954. They also sported maple fingerboards – another throwback to '50s production – and a three-ply black/white/black pickguard, the first black guard employed on a Fender guitar since 1954. With a split-coil pickup, the instrument mixed early and late '50s P-Bass ingredients to produce something previously unseen, but with more than a nod to the past. It's believed that two batches of 25 instruments were produced. The first, during spring of '66, featured black pickguards and a second batch, made in the fall, employed faux tortoiseshell guards. Exactly who ordered these, or why, remains a mystery to this day, but the basses proved popular with British bands of the day, including The Who, The Move, Amen Corner and The Tremeloes.

(left) 1966 slab body Precision Bass – Blond

(above) John Entwistle of The Who with a slab-body Precision in London on 12 November 1966

coronado

The Coronado marked a huge turning point for Fender. Not only was it the first non-solid-body electric guitar produced by the company but it was also the first time Fender appeared to be chasing after their main rival Gibson.

The instrument was designed by Roger Rossmeisl at the request of CBS shortly after their takeover. The new owners of Fender were keen to broaden the company's product range and thought nothing of going after the semi-acoustic market that was dominated by other makers such as Gibson, Gretsch, Rickenbacker and Guild. If they could make them, why couldn't Fender? The move would prove to be a mistake and it did

nothing for Fender's image in the music marketplace. For the first time since 1950, Fender looked like market followers, not market leaders. There was much discussion, and a lot of indifference, among dealers and music store owners upon the instrument's launch in early 1966.

The first mention of the new thin-line acoustic-electric guitars appeared as the cover story to the November 1965 issue of *Fender Facts*. The instrument was still un-named at that stage, and although rumours of it becoming either the Fender 'Fantasy' or 'Aztec' circulated, it finally arrived in January '66 as the Coronado. It was more than likely named after a small city that lies just outside San Diego, not far from Fullerton, which translated from its native Spanish means 'the crowned one.'

INTRODUCING...

...THE SENSATIONAL NEW FENDER CORONADO GUITARS AND BASS

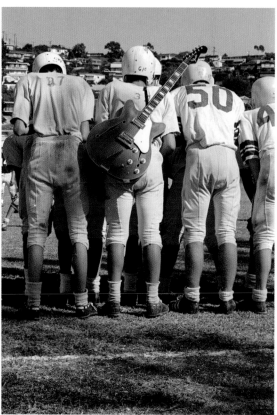

(above, left to right) Fender Fantasy prototype, 'You won't part with yours either' ad out-take featuring a pre-production Coronado, Roger Rossmeisl and Monk Montgomary discuss the Coronado Bass, December 1966

Sticking to the principles that Rossmeisl had employed with his acoustic guitar range, the new line of semi-acoustic guitars also featured bolt-on necks – something previously not seen on semis. Like all of Rossmeisl's work, the guitar's styling was classy and elegant, although somewhat reminiscent of Gibson's ES 300-series guitars. It was a striking design featuring the now iconic Fender headstock and large stylised f-holes. A new Tremolo unit was developed as well as new, 'full-range,' single-coil pickups that were outsourced from Rowe Industries (famous for producing pickups under the DeArmond brand name). Keen to push the new model, CBS offered the guitar in several configurations: one- and two-pickup models – with or without Tremolo – a 12-string and a single-pickup bass. Standard finishes were Sunburst or Cherry Red and custom colors became an option from October 1966. All two-pickup models featured block-inlaid bound necks, while the one-pickup six-string and bass received

only pearloid dot inlays. By June '67, a two-pickup bass, along with Wildwood versions of the 12, six-string and dual-pickup bass, were offered.

Retailing at $319.50 ($25 more than a custom-color Stratocaster), the two-pickup Coronado was priced to take on its rivals, specifically the two-pickup Gibson ES 330 at $325 and the two-pickup Rickenbacker 330 at $339.50. Like the acoustic line before it, the Coronado failed to gain acceptance with musicians who were set in their ways, expecting hollow-body instruments to feature set (glued-in) necks. Although the standard of workmanship was high, the instruments felt cheap and somewhat flimsy by Fender standards. They were more akin to the Asian copies that were starting to flood the market than the home-grown, workmanlike Fender instruments players were used to. Fender's artist relations department did a good job pushing the Coronado onto musicians, who often posed with the guitars for publicity shots, but the model failed to catch on.

(above, left to right) 1966 XII – Blue Ice, 1966 XII – Cherry, 1967 XII – Firemist Gold

(below) 1967 XII – Sunburst

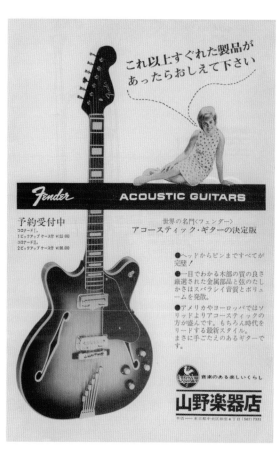

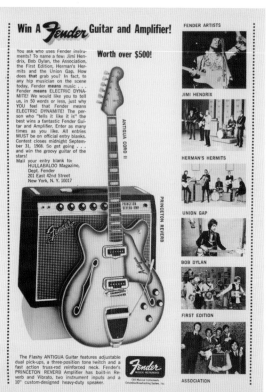

When a young man's fancy turns to music...

he has Fender in mind.

There's a complete selection of Fender Guitars and Amps at your nearest leading music dealer.

The new line of Fender Solid-State Amps.   *Fender* MUSICAL INSTRUMENTS   SANTA ANA, CALIFORNIA

FREE CATALOG / Write Fender Musical Instruments, Dept FT-11-1402 East Chestnut, Santa Ana, California 92701

(preceding pages, left to right) 1968 – Antigua, 1968 – Wildwood II

(this page, left to right) 1967 Bass I – Sonic Blue, 1968 Bass II – Cherry

(facing page) Coronado production at the CBS plant, 1966

October 1967 saw the introduction of the Coronado's final variant: the Antigua. This was Fender's last-ditch attempt to push the model and, like the Wildwood guitars, was simply a different color scheme. These instruments featured a new style of sunburst – pale gray fading through to a darker gray at the edges – that is sometimes referred to as 'Grayburst.' The new color was born out of necessity, rather than a creative decision. It had been devised to cover up burn marks and scorches

that were caused during the binding process. Fender finally gave up on the Coronado in 1971 when the last of the Antigua-finished guitars were dropped from price lists. Though it is said that Roger Rossmeisl oversaw some of the highest standards of quality control during the CBS era with his Coronado range, the instrument remains an unpopular choice among guitarists. It fell between two schools of thought – Fullerton and Kalamazoo – but held little appeal for the devotees of either.

bass v

Five-string electric basses are commonplace today, but Fender's Bass V was the first ever made and remains something of a curio from the early CBS era.

It was the first Fender stringed instrument produced with little or no design input from Leo himself and was launched alongside the Electric XII and ill-fated Marauder during the summer months of 1965. The idea behind the new instrument was a simple one, but unlike Leo's designs, the concept was ill-thought out and failed to catch on. The Bass V added an extra string, a top C, to the conventional four-string bass so that musicians could reach higher notes without having to move up and down the fretboard. The extra string gave players a greater range, within easy reach, making complex bass patterns more easily achievable.

The Fender VI had offered similar opportunities to players since its launch in 1961, but most bassists found the neck too thin and the strings too close together. The Bass V offered decent string spacing, a full 34"-scale length and the opportunity for fatter tone via heavy-gauge strings. What Fender's R&D department failed to get right were the proportions of the new instrument. Five strings meant that fewer frets were required, but not thinking the new idea through properly, designers stretched and elongated the body design to meet a short, 15-fret neck. To accommodate the extra machine key, the Bass V also featured a longer headstock and the end result was ungainly and ugly. At almost three inches longer than a Precision Bass, the new instrument looked deformed and stretched compared to other Fender basses. A 20-fret neck, with a more proportioned body, may have fared better and has since become a conventional layout for five-string basses.

The standard finish for Bass Vs was sunburst with a faux tortoiseshell pickguard, but like most of the new CBS designs, Fender manufactured an array of custom-color examples – with matching headstocks and white pickguards – in a bid to push sales. The bass featured an unusual split-pickup design with a two-pole section for the bottom strings and three-pole pickup for the top three. Dot-inlaid fingerboards were standard during '65 and early '66, but later examples received the block-and-bound neck treatment popular on other late-'60s Fenders. The shorter neck design necessitated the need for a specially commissioned neckplate, longer than those used on regular solid-body Fenders. Study of Jim Werner's list of Fender serial numbers and date stamps indicates that Bass Vs commenced with neck plate number 600000, and it would appear that around 1000 of these rare basses were produced between mid-1965 and 1970, when it was finally dropped from Fender price lists.

Legendary Motown bassist James Jamerson, who usually used a Precision Bass, and Led Zeppelin's Jean Paul Jones, most associated with a Fender Jazz, are perhaps the only two musicians of note spotted with Bass Vs during its short life span. According to Fender historian Richard Smith, Leo Fender had no knowledge of the instrument's existence when asked about it during the mid-1980s. This was hardly surprising, as the Bass V wasn't much more than a failed CBS experiment.

(facing page) 1965 – Candy
Apple Red

(this page, left to right) 1966 – Ocean
Turquoise, 1967 – Sunburst

(this page, bottom left) John Paul
Jones of Led Zeppelin with a late
'60s Bass V

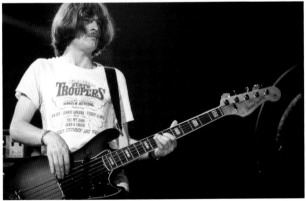

cbs changes

By mid-1966, Fender had become a gigantic operation, virtually unrecognizable from the one Leo and Don had sold to CBS just months before. Guitar making was now big business and output had increased dramatically. Don Randall wrote to Forrest White in December 1965 congratulating him on an unprecedented 80 per cent increase in production on the previous year. Fender had bolstered their line of stringed instruments with several new guitar and bass models since the takeover and even began manufacturing a range of banjos during early 1966. April of that year also saw CBS purchase the Ohio-based Roger drum-manufacturing operation to ensure that the company had all bases covered. Production of all Fender electric guitars and amplifiers now took place in the enormous $2.7-million CBS factory which, George Fullerton claimed, "...seemed too small, even at the time of completion. Several areas of the operation still had to be housed in other locations. There was a constant change of operational proceedings, as well as personnel positions and responsibilities." Fender was not the only company experiencing such an upheaval; Gibson, Rickenbacker, Gretsch and many other makers were all struggling to

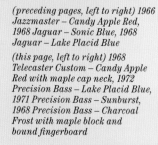

(preceding pages, left to right) 1966
Jazzmaster – Candy Apple Red,
1968 Jaguar – Sonic Blue, 1968
Jaguar – Lake Placid Blue

(this page, left to right) 1968
Telecaster Custom – Candy Apple
Red with maple cap neck, 1972
Precision Bass – Lake Placid Blue,
1971 Precision Bass – Sunburst,
1968 Precision Bass – Charcoal
Frost with maple block and
bound fingerboard

keep apace with increased demand and it was beginning to show in the quality of instruments produced from 1966 onwards.

Immediately after the takeover, CBS began actively pushing Fender products via their myriad of media channels. Columbia recording artists regularly posed with Fender equipment in photo shoots or on TV shows. Ads ran on CBS radio stations with catchy jingles that proclaimed: "A picky guitar picker picks a Fender." Columbia Records Division even released a compilation album of CBS artists, entitled 'It's Happenin' Here At Fender!,' with a cover that was a blatant ad for Fender products. Print ads for Fender guitars now ran in a wide range of publications, including titles such as *Boys' Life Scout Magazine*, as CBS targeted new audiences. Fender was now a powerful global brand, the biggest in the music equipment field and next

to Gibson *the* name in electric guitars. Pop music had become the largest growth market in the entertainment industry during the mid- to late '60s and even kids' TV programmes, such as The Monkees, The Banana Splits and The Archie Show, promoted guitar playing to the youth market. The flipside to this candy-coated coin was the emergence of heavy rock, pioneered by groups like Cream, The Who, The Stooges and Led Zeppelin. These groups promoted a new style of guitar playing to a new style of guitarist and a brand-new audience. Volume was the essential ingredient and CBS staff made sure Fender catered for heavy rock musicians with amplifiers now advertised as 'Ear Splitter!' or 'The Heavies from Fender,' alongside Fuzz-Wah pedals and the Fender Blender overdrive unit.

Further cosmetic changes began to appear on Fender guitars, with

increased branding high on the CBS agenda. By fall 1965, a large Fender 'F' was now stamped into all guitar and bass neckplates and newly designed machine keys also carried a Fender stamp. Necks on the Jaguar, Jazzmaster and Jazz Bass, which had been bound with dot inlays during late 1965, began to feature large perloid block inlays from the spring of 1966. While the Electric XII, Bass VI and Bass V had bypassed the dot and bound phase during '65, these all featured block and bound necks by mid-'66. From January 1967, maple fingerboards, with black blocks and binding, were offered as an unpopular option on the Jaguar, Jazzmaster, Jazz Bass, Bass VI and Bass V, and examples of these are, not surprisingly, rare. Although maple fingerboards had been a custom option on Telecasters, Stratocasters and the Precision Bass since the early to mid-'60s, January '67 saw these

(above) 1967 custom-built Jaguar featuring contoured back with flat edge bound top, angled bridge pickup and pearloid pickguard

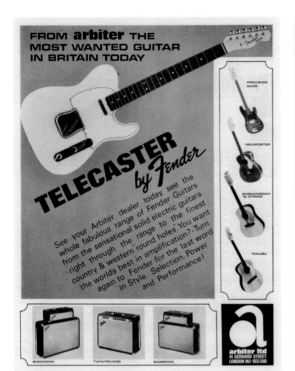

reintroduced as an official option and one that became instantly popular. Headstock decals gradually changed from the transition-style logo to a new CBS design during 1967. The CBS Fender logo – black with gold edging – was designed to stand out, and by late '67, almost all model names appeared in bold capital letters on headstocks, ensuring no one would mistake a Fender for a Gibson or vice versa.

Fender paint finishes also went through changes during the late '60s. Nitrocellulose paints, which had been used since the late '40s, were now deemed unstable, weak and prone to fading. Fender finishes had employed thin coats of cellulose paint, prone to scratches and wear with heavy use, and it was not uncommon for the clear lacquer on Fender necks to completely wear through after months and years of constant playing. That said, players liked the feel of cellulose; it had a natural quality that bonded well with maple necks and gave a smooth playing action. Body finishes often faded with exposure to direct sunlight and wore through to the primer coats and wood beneath with heavy use. Fender looked for a harder-wearing

finish that would maintain the instrument's appearance while being easier to apply and so switched to polyester during the course of 1968. Heavy coats of the new paint were applied to give instruments a 'thick-skin' finish, and although it certainly proved more durable than cellulose, the new instruments felt plastic and cheap compared to older ones. Bodies sounded less resonant and somehow suffocated by the finish, while maple fingerboard guitars offered the player a completely different feel to the cellulose-finished guitars. Many musicians felt that Fender instruments lost much of their character in this simple but important change. As polyester finishes became standard on Fender instruments, many of the company's custom-color options were dropped during 1969, leaving only Black, Olympic White, Blond, Sonic Blue, Candy Apple Red, Lake Placid Blue, Ocean Turquoise, Firemist Gold, Firemist Silver and Sunburst in the existing range.

In 1968, Fender introduced an optional Tremolo unit for the Telecaster guitar that could be either factory fitted or retro fitted by existing owners. If Leo had ever envisaged the

Telecaster with a Tremolo, he would certainly have designed one for it. Despite this, CBS staff settled on a Bigsby-made unit – once again stamped with a Fender 'F' – in a move that would surely have upset Leo, if indeed he still cared. As if to symbolize the end of Fender's golden age, CBS dropped the company's pioneering electric guitar, the Esquire, from the line during 1970, deeming it surplus to requirements. Times had changed, but not necessarily for the better.

(this page, left) necks and bodies await assembly at the CBS factory in 1966, the Fender warehouse in 1968

(this page, above) 1969 Jazzmaster – Sunburst

(facing page, left to right) 1972 Jaguar – Blond, 1969 Stratocaster – Olympic White with rare matching headstock, 1972 – Telecaster Custom – Candy Apple Red with tremolo unit

(facing page bottom, left to right) Forrest White, Freddy Tavares, George Fullerton, Leo Fender and Don Randall in 1966

(overleaf, left to right) 1968 Jazz Bass – Lake Placid Blue, 1972 – Bass VI – Blond

(overleaf, facing page) mini catalogs 1952 – 1968

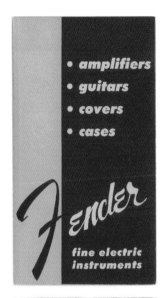

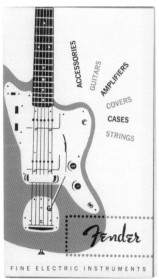

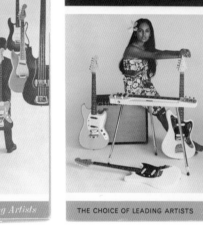

jimi hendrix

On 24 September 1966, an unknown guitarist landed at London Airport armed with one change of clothing and a Fender Stratocaster. Within nine months, he had turned the whole music scene on its head and guitar playing would never be the same again. Born Johnny Allen Hendrix on 27 November 1942 in Seattle, Washington, he acquired his first guitar at age 15, a cheap $5 acoustic, and by 1959 he had his first electric, a Supro Ozark. Hendrix was obsessed with rock'n'roll and blues and idolized Elvis Presley, who he'd seen perform in Seattle during '57. After a brief stint in the army in 1961–1962, Hendrix turned semi-pro, then professional, learning the ropes backing artists including Sam Cooke, Chuck Jackson, Jackie Wilson, The Isley Brothers and Little Richard. It was during this time that he became attached to the Fender brand, playing first a Duo Sonic, then Jazzmasters, and eventually settling on a Stratocaster. Jimi played left-handed, usually playing right-handed instruments flipped upside down in a move that became his trademark throughout the '60s. During mid-'66, Jimi formed his own band Jimmy James And The Blue Flames. He was almost immediately spotted at the Cafe Wha in New York by ex-Animals bassist Chas Chandler, who wasted no time in bringing Hendrix to the UK where he believed he could make him a star.

Bassist Noel Redding and drummer Mitch Mitchell completed the lineup for The Jimi Hendrix Experience and the trio caused an overnight sensation in the UK and Europe. Mid-'60s London

proved to be the perfect place for Hendrix to hone his style and sound, and early recordings such as 'Hey Joe' and 'Purple Haze' showed exactly what he was capable of. Jimi could make a guitar sing and talk to the listener like no guitarist before him or since. Such was his command of fuzz and feedback that he made it a part of the language of the music. His flamboyant stage antics often involved playing the guitar with his teeth or behind his head, and not wishing to be upstaged by The Who, Jimi set fire to his Stratocaster at The Experience's first major US show – Monterey International Pop Festival – in June 1967. From this point onwards, Hendrix became an international star whose light shone brightly for just a few short years before his final concert in September 1970.

Long-term Fender Sales rep Dale Hyatt told guitar historian Tony Bacon: "When guys like that come along, we couldn't build enough guitars. As a matter of fact, I think Jimi Hendrix caused more Stratocasters to be sold than all the Fender salesmen put together." Hendrix was undoubtedly the greatest electric guitar player of all time and his endorsement of the Stratocaster speaks volumes. Though there were occasional sightings of Hendrix with a Gibson Flying V, SGs and even a Les Paul, the Stratocaster was always his favorite, the guitar on which he could express himself best. Only the Strat was capable of keeping up with his seemingly boundless capability, and since his death in 1970, no player has truly rivalled him.

(facing page, left to right) 1969 Stratocaster – Sunburst, Jimi Hendrix with his white '66 Strat in 1967

(this page, below left) playing a white 1965 Jazzmaster alongside Cornell Dupree while backing Wilson Pickett at an Atlantic Records launch party, New York, 5 May 1966

rosewood stratocaster and telecaster

Fender had built special, one-off instruments for name endorsees since the company's humble beginnings in the 1940s. Leo knew that looking after musicians who promoted his products was vital to the company's success. As the late '60s rolled in, rock music had grown into a gigantic business and CBS were acutely aware of the importance of product placement as they chased after several name acts. In 1968, Don Randall met with The Beatles at their Apple headquarters in Saville Row, London, and an arrangement was made to supply the group with a full complement of Fender equipment including guitars, keyboards and amplifiers for the recording of their new album 'Let It Be'. Back in Fullerton, at Fender's research and development department, the idea was hatched to build special, one-off versions of the company's best-loved six-strings, made entirely from expensive, heavy rosewood. These instruments were some of the most lavish solid-body designs Fender would ever produce and it was decided that a prototype Telecaster would be presented to George Harrison and a matching Stratocaster to Jimi Hendrix.

Roger Rossmeisl came up with the concept and developed the construction method, while his assistant, Phil Kubicki, hand-built the bodies and necks. "We built two bodies and necks for each instrument and finished

one of each. We selected the best parts to make each guitar," explains Kubicki. Bodies were made by sandwiching two slabs of thick rosewood together, with a thin layer of maple running through the center. To alleviate weight, Kubicki hollowed out chambers in the rosewood slabs. Black three-ply guards complemented the dark rosewood bodies, and as a finishing touch, old-style 'spaghetti' logos were applied to the headstocks of both prototypes. George's guitar was finished first and dispatched to London in time for the recording of the new Beatles record in early '69. The accompanying *Let It Be* film shows George using the guitar almost exclusively and, upon seeing the movie, Kubicki recalls: "I nearly jumped out of my seat!"

Largely down to the exposure that the Telecaster received via George Harrison's patronage, Fender launched a short-lived production model in May 1969. It retailed at $375.00, $105 more than the standard Tele. Sadly, Jimi would never receive his guitar. As Kubicki explains: "The Strat for Jimi was kept by us in the R&D department. They were trying to deliver it and then he died. We held onto it for two or three months after his death and then Roger told me that it got requisitioned and that I was to take it to the front office at Fender. I left it with a secretary there and never saw it again."

(facing page, left to right) 1969 Rosewood Stratocaster specially built for Jimi Hendrix, George Harrison with his Rosewood Telecaster at the 'Let It Be' recording sessions in January 1969

(this page) 1969 production Rosewood Telecaster

silverface/aluminium trim amplifiers 1968 – 1969

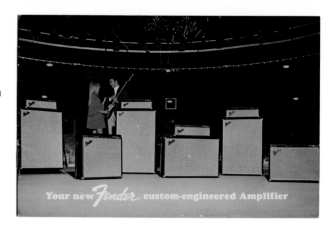

Your new *Fender* custom-engineered Amplifier

After the CBS buyout in early 1965, Fender began to develop a new line of solid-state, transistorized amplifiers loosely based on some of its best-selling and most-loved tube models. Transistors were used to replace 'old-fashioned' tubes. They were small, cheap to produce and were being heralded as the future for amplification. Their inherent light weight meant that amplifiers could be built to more portable specifications. Fender were testing the water, the technology was new and many amplifier manufacturers were quick to jump on the solid-state bandwagon. Problems, however, lay ahead. Early manufacturing difficulties led to many of the new solid-state amps being returned to the factory for repair work. Even when working properly, the sound that the new amplifiers produced was harsh and tinny compared to the warm, lush overtones produced by Fender's vacuum tube designs. The Fender name was still synonymous with reliable, quality tube amps and the new line did not catch on. Dealers and players alike were in agreement that Fender tube amps were what they wanted and the new solid-state amplifiers would prove to be poor sellers. The move towards solid-state technology had caused friction between CBS executives and factory staff. Don Randall claimed that CBS "didn't know an amplifier from a full moon" and long-standing factory foreman Forrest White eventually resigned over quality-control issues in December 1966. Available between mid-1966 and 1971 only, the transistorized solid-state amps are not considered part of Fender's golden age.

By the late '60s, ambitious rock bands were playing large auditoriums and stadiums with huge PA rigs and complex lighting setups. A single guitarist would often be seen playing through more than one Fender amp or a stack of Dual Showman cabs to get the desired volume needed to fill the theatre. Marshall amps, with their multiple 4 x 12" speaker stacks, were giving Fender a run for their money and a new breed of amplifier builders, often from the UK, were appearing with names like HiWatt, Sound City, Kustom and Orange. Amplification was getting bigger and louder as rock music continued to grow.

By 1968, the Blackface Fender amp lineup looked positively pre-CBS and the not-so-new owners at Fender were looking to spruce up the range. Having tried and failed with something completely different in the solid-state amps, CBS staff were keen to update the look of the tube amp line without causing too much disruption to production techniques or public perception. The changes were simple, intended not to mess with a tried-and-tested formula. The black control plates were replaced by new, brushed aluminium panels, with pale blue block capital fonts. The new control panels captured the bright lights at concerts and, like the chromed Fender logos, shone out from the back of stages everywhere. Black Tolex/silver grille cloths, strap handles and black numbered knobs remained, but there was one other addition, a small legacy from the solid-state range. The new Silverface amps

featured the same aluminium trim that ran around the edge of the speaker baffle on the solid-state amps. Wedged between the grille cloth and cabinet lip, the aluminium trim gave a smart touch to this early version of the Silverface models. Fender were probably using up leftover stocks from the failed solid-state range, but those didn't last long, as the aluminium trim was dropped from the amp line during 1969. This short-lived incarnation of Fender amplifiers would be the last to appear while Leo Fender and Don Randall still had connections with the company. During a visit to London in 1968, Don had supplied The Beatles with a complete backline of the new Silverface amps with aluminium trim. It was these amplifiers that powered the band's final public appearance on the roof of their Apple offices in London on 30 January 1969.

Leo's amps had come a long, long way from the honky-tonk bars and clubs of Orange County in the late 1940s. In 20 short years, his amplifier designs had shaped the sound of popular music and played a big part in dictating the path it would take. His willingness to listen to musicians who told him what they needed from a guitar amplifier had paid off. It's doubtful he could have ever imagined how much influence his designs would have upon popular music and, in turn, popular culture. But as the years pass, and we look back on his early designs, we can only marvel at the genius of Leo Fender.

Champ: 5 watt; 1 x 8" speaker
Bronco: 5 watt; 1 x 8" speaker
Vibro Champ: 5 watt; 1 x 8" speaker
Princeton: 12 watt; 1 x 10" speaker
Princeton Reverb: 12 watt; 1 x 10" speaker
Deluxe Reverb: 20 watt; 1 x 12" speaker
Vibrolux Reverb: 35 watt; 2 x 10" speakers
Pro Reverb: 40 watt; 2 x 12" speakers
Super Reverb: 40 watt; 4 x 10" speakers
Twin Reverb: 85 watt; 2 x 12" speakers
Bandmaster: 40-watt amplifier with 2 x 12" speaker cabinet
Bandmaster Reverb: 45-watt amplifier with 2 x 12" speaker cabinet
Bassman: 50-watt amplifier with 2 x 12" speaker cabinet
Showman: 85-watt amplifier with 1 x 15" speaker cabinet
Dual Showman: 85-watt amplifier with 2 x 15" speaker cabinet
Dual Showman Reverb: 85-watt amplifier with 2 x 15" speaker cabinet

telecaster thinline

Prior to the CBS takeover, a hollow-bodied Fender electric guitar was unthinkable. Leo had reinvented the wheel, as far as electric stringed instruments were concerned, and remained steadfast in his approach towards manufacturing techniques. With the new regime came a new approach to Fender's research and development process, and following the launch of the Coronado in early 1966, Fender executives turned to the existing range of guitars to see if there were suitable candidates for the semi-acoustic treatment. Contoured body designs with rounded-off edges ruled out all but one model: the Telecaster. During '59, the Telecaster Custom had been given edge-binding to give it the appearance of a high-end semi-acoustic, so producing a hollow-bodied version seemed logical. A prototype instrument, built in early '67, featured a fully hollow body. It was constructed in a similar manner to Fender acoustics of the day with a solid spruce top and zebra-wood back. The instrument was incredibly lightweight, although the absence of any f-hole gave it a deceptively solid appearance. It's unclear why this design was not pursued. Perhaps designers felt that heavy necks might unbalance the guitar.

During early 1968, Roger Rossmeisl developed a new design for a semi-acoustic Tele. It would be launched over the summer months as the Telecaster Thinline. Assisted by Virgilio 'Babe' Simoni in Fender's wood shop and body department, Rossmeisl used an ingenious technique he had developed at Rickenbacker where a solid slab of mahogany or ash was cut to the shape of the body, then flipped onto its front. Acoustic chambers were then hollowed out from the back with routing equipment that also left a stylized f-hole in the front of the guitar's body. A flat piece of matched timber was then glued to the back of the hollowed body, giving it the appearance and strength of a solid-body instrument but with improved weight and semi-acoustic sounds. Phil Kubicki built prototypes in Fender's R&D department while Roger Rossmeisl designed an elegant new pickguard that allowed for the Thinline's single sound-hole. Electrics were as per the standard Telecaster, with two single coil pickups and simple tone and volume control. Necks were of all-maple construction, but unlike the maple necks of the '50s, these featured a maple cap fingerboard applied to the face of the maple neck, doing away with the need for mahogany skunk stripes and headstock plugs. As demand for maple boards on Fender instruments grew during the late '60s, a return to '50s-style production techniques occurred in late 1968. A late-'60s Fender decal (with only the Telecaster name) was applied under a clear coat of polyester lacquer. Available in natural mahogany or ash finishes from July '68, sunburst became a standard option from October of the same year. Custom DuPont finishes were also offered at five per cent additional cost.

The Telecaster Thinline was a welcome addition to the Fender range. It offered players everything they wanted

from a Tele in a lightweight package with a light, springy tone. It is one of the few post-CBS creations worthy of golden age status and found favour with several musicians upon release. Curtis Mayfield, usually associated with Stratocasters, adopted the Thinline as his main guitar during the late '60s and early '70s, and Sly Stone was a regular endorsee during the same era. In 1971, Fender redesigned the Thinline to incorporate Gibson-style humbucking pickups and it lost much of its early appeal. The guitar remains a fine example of Roger Rossmeisl's legacy.

(preceding pages) 1967 hollow body Telecaster prototype

(facing page) 1968 – Sunburst

(this page, left to right) 1969 – Ash, 1970 – Yellow, 1968 – Candy Apple Red

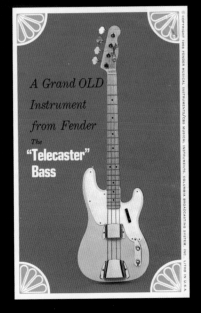

telecaster bass

Perhaps inspired by the slab-bodied Precision Basses produced for Arbiter during 1966, Fender launched the Telecaster Bass in 1968. It was a straight reissue of the early-'50s Precision and would mark the first, but not the last, time Fender would revisit one of their earlier designs. Musicians were already starting to look back with nostalgia at the pioneering days of rock'n'roll. Many newer groups, such as Creedence Clearwater Revival and The Band, were returning to traditional values in music and the Telecaster Bass seemed like a well-timed and welcome reintroduction to an old friend. A flyer announcing the new model proclaimed: 'Recently, pros and veterans in the music field have rediscovered the revolutionary features, the playing advantages, the great *sound* of the Telecaster Bass. In response to this activity, Fender has recreated this fine bass instrument – building it as it was built a generation ago.'

Barring a few minor differences and, of course, the name change, the Telecaster Bass was a fairly accurate reproduction of an early '50s Precision. It included the primitive two-saddle bridge, single-coil pickup, the unique pickup and bridge covers and a blond slab body. The pickguard, however, was made from single-ply white plastic, not black, which gave the appearance of a 1954 – 1957 P-Bass. To give the instrument more of a retro feel, Fender used a transition-style logo on the headstock with 'TELECASTER BASS' in small capital letters underneath, like the decals of the '50s.

Keen to keep up with the trends of the day, the late '60s saw Fender experiment with many new color schemes for their instruments. The Telecaster Bass would not escape this treatment, and during 1968, it was offered – along with the Telecaster six-string – in Paisley Red and Blue Flower options. Inspired by the previous 'summer of love' in 1967, and the hippy movement of the time, these schemes offered a fun diversion from the traditional finishes available on Telecaster guitars and the new bass. The finish was achieved by gluing heavily textured pieces of wallpaper to the front and back of the guitar's body. As there were no body contours to contend with, this was a fairly straightforward process on Telecaster models. The body edges were then sprayed pink for the Paisley instruments and blue for the Flower option. A thick polyester clear coat was used to seal the bodies, which were then given transparent plastic pickguards so as not to detract from the finish underneath. The new finish was striking, but had a major flaw. The textured nature of the wallpaper meant that it was unstable and cracks soon began to appear in the clear top coat. Often huge pieces would fall off, exposing the wallpaper or wood underneath. Today, pristine examples are hard to find and the short-lived Paisley and Blue Flower guitars were dropped from the line during 1969. Custom-color Telecaster Basses were also made available, but are rare finds today. In early 1972, CBS replaced the single-coil pickup with a large, ugly humbucking type in a move to revive sales for the Telecaster Bass, but production had ceased by the end of the decade.

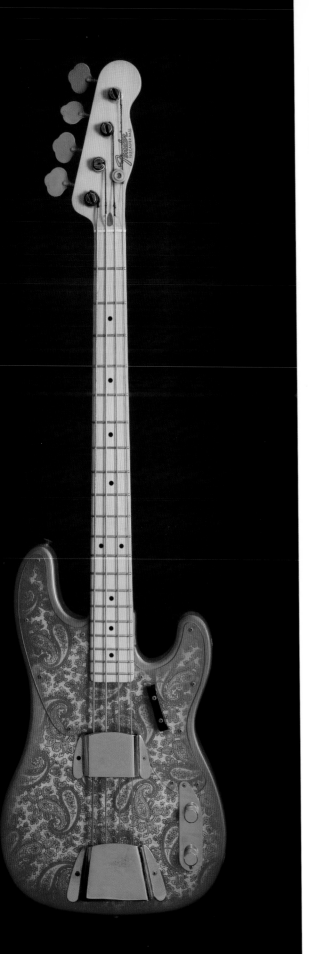

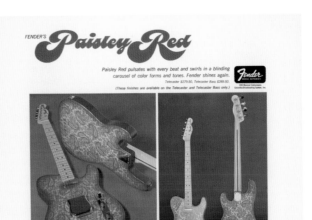

(preceding pages, left to right) 1969 Telecaster Bass – Blond, Fender guitar stand fronts from top – 1956, 1957, 1961, 1962, 1963, 1964 – 1967

(this page, left) 1968 Telecaster Bass – Paisley Red

(facing page, left to right) 1968 Telecaster – Paisley Red, 1968 Telecaster – Blue Flower

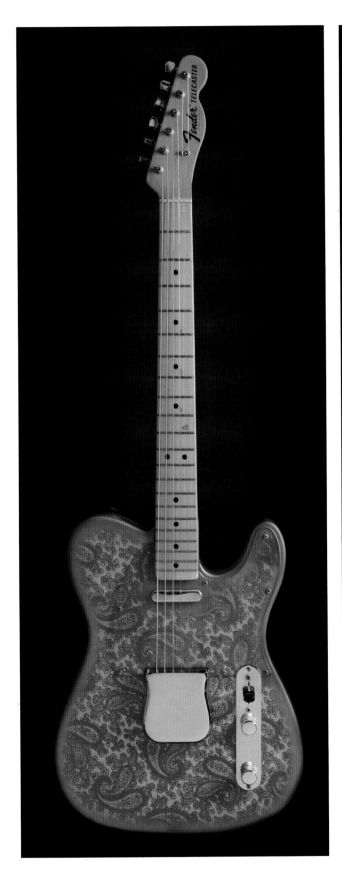

ltd and montego

The LTD and Montego models were the brainchild of Roger Rossmeisl. They were high-end, hand-crafted jazz guitars that would sit at the top of the Fender price range during their short production run between 1968 and 1972. Rossmeisl had done good work for Fender, designing both their acoustic range and the Coronado semi-acoustics. Neither of these projects fulfilled his real passion for handmade jazz guitars, and in 1968, CBS let him loose on two new designs, both of which carried the hallmarks of his formal training in Germany.

Intended to rival the likes of Gibson's Super 400 and guitars by high-end makers such as D'Angelico, the LTD would fail to catch on with jazz players. This was largely due to the ever-present bolt-on neck that Rossmeisl had employed on his previous creations for Fender. That said, the new guitar boasted outstanding build quality and lavish design which retailed for $1200 in July 1968 – the price of five Telecasters.

All LTD and Montego instruments were hand-built by Rossmeisl and his assistant, Phil Kubicki, at Fender's research and development department in one of the original pre-CBS buildings at South Raymond Avenue. Even the pickups and electrics were designed and handmade by Freddie Tavares in the adjoining building, and in many ways, the LTD and Montego could be described as the first Fender Custom Shop instruments. "The LTD guitars were made as prestige items, they weren't intended as a profit source, more 'look what we can do,' a marketing tool if you like," says Phil Kubicki.

The LTD was offered in either a sunburst or a natural finish and featured gold-plated hardware, pearl inlays (featuring reversed Fender 'f's to form heart shapes), ebony fingerboards, Grover Rotomatic machine heads and pickguards made from specially imported Italian Mazzucchelli celluloid. The hand-carved spruce top and maple back of the body featured one of Rossmeisl's specialities – the 'German carve' – a technique often employed by his father when building acoustic instruments. Rossmeisl had used the German carve on several of his Rickenbacker designs, passing it on to one of his apprentices there, Semie Moseley, who went on to set up Mosrite guitars. Semie later claimed that Rossmeisl taught him everything he knew about guitars and the German carve featured on several Mosrite guitars, including the famous Ventures model.

As its name suggests, the LTD was produced in very limited numbers and Phil Kubicki estimates that he and Rossmeisl completed less than 40 instruments. Most of these feature labels inside, hand-signed by Rossmeisl, but later examples are signed by Kubicki on the underside of the solid top.

The Montego utilized the same body shape and general outline as the LTD, but was built to slightly lower specifications. Montego bodies were outsourced and assembled in Germany with pressed spruce tops and maple back and sides. Construction of necks and final assembly took place at Fender's R&D department. Available with one or two pickups, simpler inlays and chrome hardware, these elegant guitars retailed at $700 for the single-pickup version

and $800 for the twin pickup. Kubicki estimates that less than 100 Montegos were built.

Sadly, CBS let go of Roger Rossmeisl in 1972. Phil Kubicki resigned from his position shortly after and the productive R&D team of the late '60s had been dismantled. Kubicki went on to develop the successful and highly regarded Factor Bass and Roger died in his homeland of Germany in 1979, aged just 52.

(facing page) 1972 LTD – Sunburst
(this page, above) 1969 Montego II – Sunburst

bronco

Launched in November 1967, the Fender Bronco seemed more the brainchild of overzealous CBS executives seeking to maximize profits than the company's research and development department. Fender had offered lap-steel guitars with Champ amps as matched 'student sets' since the late 1940s, so it seemed logical, and long overdue, that they do the same with a guitar and amp set.

Designed for 'the beginning student to enter the rich world of music,' the Bronco set comprised of a one-pickup Fender electric guitar with Tremolo and a hard case, plus a 5-watt tube amplifier with an 8" speaker and built-in vibrato. At just $265.50, it was a salesman's dream and if any potential buyer was still unsure, it's likely that a free can of Fender guitar polish and a Fender chord book were thrown in to seal the deal.

The Bronco guitar used a regular body from the Mustang, Duo Sonic and Musicmaster range finished in bold Dakota Red with a single pickup positioned close to the bridge. The neck too was from the same family line, but to cut down on costs, a newly-designed pickguard was made from a single piece of three-ply white/black/white plastic, which dispensed with the need for a chromed control panel. A cheap, and suspiciously non-Fender, combination Tremolo and bridge unit was also employed. The amplifier was a Silverface Vibro Champ in disguise, with only its bright red 'BRONCO AMP' moniker to hide its true identity.

Little thought had gone into the new guitar and its oddly shaped pickguard rendered it the ugly ducking of the Fender student range.

swinger

Virgilio 'Babe' Simoni began working for Fender in 1953, aged just 16. By the mid-1960s, he had risen to the position of Product Manager for stringed instruments. He was a skilled worker and well respected within the company, but in 1969, he was presented with a problem. Fender had large stocks of unwanted parts from some of their less successful models and Babe was given the task of using these up in a creative way. Two new models, the Swinger and the Custom, were developed and produced on the factory floor under Babe's supervision, without involvement from Fender's R&D department.

Born out of the need to save costs and recycle unwanted parts, the first of two 'bits-er' instruments was the Swinger, sometimes referred to as the Arrow or Musiclander. The Swinger was basically a vehicle to use up piles of short-scale (22.5") necks intended for the student range of guitars. Since late '64, Fender had offered Musicmasters, Duo Sonics and Mustangs in either short-scale or longer 24"-scale length options. The shorter-scale necks had proven unpopular, and by 1969, CBS found themselves with hundreds of over-stocks from '66 and '67 production runs. "Instead of using the (usual) headstock design, I made it more rounded, like an acoustic, then somebody came along and cut the end off – made it look like a spear," claimed Simoni.

The new headstock design was certainly striking and, to match it, an equally unconventional body shape was conceived. A regular Musicmaster body was run through a band saw, which sliced a graceful curve into the bottom end near the strap button, and another small slice was cut from the left horn. Leftover Bass V bodies were also used as blanks for the Swingers, but required more woodworking to achieve the new body shape. These have telltale routes for the Bass V pickup concealed under their pickguards. Regular Musicmaster parts were used to complete the guitars and the end results were surprisingly attractive. The Swinger was a small, basic student model, but it was

well-suited to female guitarists and younger players.

It's estimated that Simoni produced between 300 and 600 Swinger guitars in six shades: Daphne Blue, Dakota Red, Black, Lake Placid Blue and Candy Apple Red with white pearloid guards, or Olympic White with a faux tortoiseshell guard.

A late '60s, CBS-style Fender decal is all that usually appears on Swinger headstocks. Those that do carry the model name do so by virtue of a clear plastic sticker with black lettering – an indication of the guitar's transient nature.

The Swinger never appeared in any Fender literature and it's likely that they were handed direct to Fender sales reps to sell off on the road. In response to a letter sent to Fender in 1978 enquiring about a Swinger, Freddie Tavares wrote: "I finally solved the mystery, and can tell you that Fender did build a guitar like the one shown... the guitar, named Musiclander, came into being without the usual development process which is conducted by the R&D Department... this incident makes me feel like an orphan in a company I have been with for more than a quarter century, because I never heard of this guitar until your enquiry."

(facing page, left to right) 1969 – Daphne Blue, 1969 – Black

(this page, left to right) 1969 – Dakota Red, 1969 – Olympic White, 1969 – Lake Placid Blue, 1969 – Candy Apple Red

Fender Musical Instruments

1966-67 CATALOG

Fender

ELECTRIC GUITARS / STEEL GUITARS / AMPLIFIERS / BANJOS / ACCESSORIES

Fender Musical Instruments...ON THE GO!

1968 CATALOG

Fender Custom

...new in shape and sound

Fender lovin' care

1969 Catalog

custom

For Fender's second 'bits-er' guitar, Simoni was presented with a different challenge. It came at around the same time that both Leo Fender and Don Randall were terminating their association with CBS and the company they had tirelessly built up since 1946.

By 1969, CBS had been left with large overstocks of Electric XII parts. The model had not performed as well as expected and was being dropped from the line. As a result, piles of unwanted bodies, necks and pickups cluttered the factory. Simoni's bosses asked if something useful could be done with the unwanted parts and he came up with a plan. Once again, he took the bodies and sliced into them with a band saw to create a new shape. Similarly, he cut down the long 'hockey stick' headstocks to accept six machine keys instead of 12, covering over the damage done with thin slices of maple veneer. As the 12-string bridge was now surplus to requirements, he placed a Mustang Trem/bridge assembly in its place. The hole in the back of the body, which had accepted the guitar's string retainer, was filled in. To cover this eyesore, the guitar was finished with a sunburst front and solid black on the back. Hey presto, a new Fender guitar was born – the Custom!

Sure enough it had been customized, but from discarded parts and with little imagination. The Custom lacked the graceful curves of the little Swinger, and although it was a superior instrument with its high-end wide neck and split-coil pickups, what it gained in playability it lacked in looks and style. This sort of abomination would never have occurred under Leo's leadership and it was indicative of the direction in which the Fender company had gone in the four years since the CBS takeover.

The Custom was featured for one year in the 1970 full-line catalog. At $289.50, it was $20 more expensive than a standard Telecaster. Dealers and players alike were not fooled by the origins of the new guitar and the list price was lowered by 1971 in order to shift these odd instruments, many of which remained unsold in music shops for years. Customs also appeared under the 'Maverick' name with alternative headstock logos. Both versions are, not surprisingly, rare today.

It's unfair to lay the blame for the Custom on Simoni; he was simply doing his job and following instructions. Those instructions, however, came from people who cared little about guitars or the people who bought them – their main interest was profit. The Custom was the laughing stock of all who saw it, and it was blatantly obvious to most how, and why, it existed. Ironically, the tag line for the 1969 Fender full-line catalog read: 'Fender Lovin' Care.' The care, and the love, had all but vanished.

(facing page left, top to bottom) 1967, 1968 and 1969 full-line catalogs

(facing page right, top to bottom) 1970 full-line catalog, Custom ad from Fender Facts #17

(this page, right) 1969 Custom – Sunburst

end of a golden era

Since the CBS takeover, Don Randall had spent much of his time commuting between Columbia's corporate offices in New York and the Fender plant in Fullerton. His role was crucial to the new owners and he quickly rose from vice president of Fender Musical Instruments and Fender Sales to president of the newly incorporated CBS Musical Instruments Division. By 1967, this also included Rhodes keyboard instruments as well as Rogers drums. The new position was a far cry from the one he'd enjoyed while running Fender Sales and he felt removed from the product line he'd helped develop, name and nurture. Don had made good money from the sale of Fender in 1965 and he decided to opt out of corporate life in April 1969, when CBS allowed him an early unconditional release from his contract that was due to expire in 1970.

Leo Fender had remained distant and detached from the goings-on at the CBS plant through the late '60s and kept himself busy tinkering with new ideas and projects at his CLF research unit on East Elm Street, Fullerton. A new string-bending device for the guitar, called the 'Fender Bender,' was one of many ideas that CBS ignored, but perhaps the most remarkable was an invention that finally resolved the inherent problem of his bolt-on neck design. Leo came up with the 'bullet' truss rod which could be adjusted from the headstock of a guitar without removing the neck. A three-bolt neckplate, with micro-tilt adjustment of the neck, meant that

setting up a Fender guitar for better playability was easier than ever. It was a generous parting shot for the company he had sold five years earlier, but unfortunately, the invention would gain a bad reputation because its introduction coincided with a period of poor manufacturing standards at Fender. Having served out his consultancy contract, Leo would sever all ties with the CBS-owned Fender company during 1970.

In the space of five years, CBS had transformed Fender from a place where quality came first and musicians were treated with respect to a corner-cutting, cost-effective conglomerate cranking out pale imitations of what had gone before. Great instruments were still being produced, but how could they fail with such classic designs as the Stratocaster, Telecaster and Precision Bass? Fender guitars and amplifiers had been designed with mass production in mind, but the quality and care that had gone into the early production was now almost non-existent and that was beginning to show. It would be many years before Fender regained its former reputation and produce instruments that Leo, Don, Freddie and Forrest could be proud of. The instruments made by Fender during the '50s and '60s, under the supervision of the men who created them, will always remain the company's finest. They have stood the test of time and are today considered to be design classics and 20th-century works of art, a genuine testimony to the golden age of Fender.

Leo Fender
(1909–1991)

Leo's contract with CBS restricted his ability to compete with them until 1975, but he formed Tri-Sonics Inc with Forrest White and Tom Walker, a former Fender salesman, in March 1972. The name soon changed to Musitek, then Music Man, and Leo's silent partner status came to an end as his non-compete with CBS expired. Leo designed guitars, basses and amplifiers for Music Man from his CLF research unit, including the hugely successful Stingray bass launched in 1976. In late 1979, he formed a new company with George Fullerton, and former Fender sales rep Dale Hyatt, called G&L – which stood for George and Leo – to produce a new range of guitars and basses. Music Man was sold to Ernie Ball in 1984 and Leo continued to work at G&L until his death on 21 March 1991.

Don Randall
(1917–2008)

Randall started a new company in 1970 to produce a successful line of amplifiers under the Randall Instruments brand name. These were designed by Robert Rissi, formerly of Fender's amplifier R&D department. He sold the company in 1987. Don died on 23 December 2008.

Freddie Tavares
(1913–1990)

Tavares continued to work for Fender in the research and development department until 1985. He was heavily involved in Fender's vintage reissue series during the early '80s, which marked the company's first real attempt to revive the past glories of its golden age. Freddie died on 24 July 1990.

Forrest White
(1920–1994)

White abruptly quit Fender in December 1966 after allegedly refusing to sign off on the production of the solid state amplifier line, saying he had "too much respect for Leo to have any part in building something not worthy of his name." Forrest went on to work for Chicago Musical Instruments (CMI), who owned Gibson. After leaving CMI in late 1969, Forrest partnered with Leo in 1972 at Tri-Sonics, which would become Music Man. They worked together until the company was sold off in 1984. Forrest died on 22 November 1994.

George Fullerton
(1923–2009)

Fullerton continued to work at Fender after the CBS takeover but had difficulty finding a niche under the new management and bounced from position to position until leaving in March 1970. He moved to Ernie Ball's Earthwood guitar division as Production Manager until 1974, when he rejoined Leo Fender at CLF. He helped with designs for Music Man, eventually running production of these instruments from mid-1976. From 1979, George worked on G&L guitars and basses until his retirement when the company was sold to BBE in 1991. George died on 4 July 2009.

Bob Perine
(1922–2004)

Perine worked for Fender until 1969, when Don Randall left the company. Bob's ad agency, Perine/Jacoby, was dissolved in 1970. Not only was Perine a superb graphic designer but he was also a well-known fine artist whose watercolours are especially sought-after today. He designed Richard Smith's seminal book *Fender: The Sound Heard 'Round the World*, first published in 1995. Bob died on 6 November 2004.

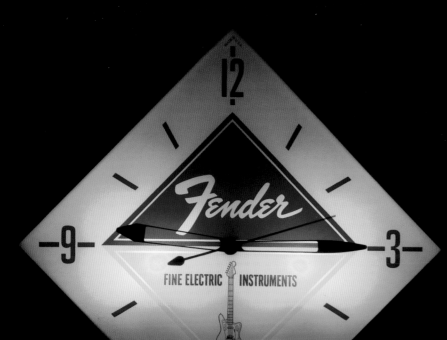

a collection of Fender artifacts from the 1950s and 1960s including clock, staff baseball team jersey, 'sunglasses' guitar case and dealer binders

index

index of fender equipment

Page Position	Year	Model	Color	Serial Number	Owner
002 left	1958	Jazzmaster	Blond (g/p)	32693	BF
002 centre	1956	Stratocaster	Blond	09443	BF
002 right	1956	Telecaster	Blond	11170	BF
008 full page	1945	K&F Lap Steel	Gray Crinkle	none	TF
012 page left	1943	1st prototype guitar	Black Crinkle	none	RAM
013 page right	1945	K&F Lap Steel & Amp	Gray Crinkle	none	AM
014 full page	1950	Champion	Copper	1346	TF
016 page left	1945	K&F Lap Steel	Gray Crinkle	none	TF
016 next	1946	K&F Lap Steel	Mahogany	402	TF
016 next	1946	K&F Lap Steel	Maple	831	TF
016 page right	1947	De Luxe	Walnut	B765	MK
017 bottom	1953	Deluxe	Blond	644	MK
018 page left	1951	Champion	Blue	2132	TF
018 centre	1950	Champion	Gray	1304	TF
018 page right	1954	Champion	Yellow	6973	TF
019 centre	1952	Champion	Green	3135	TF
019 page right	1950	Champion	Copper	1346	TF
020 page left	1956	Champ	Desert Sand	01259	TF
020 next	1960	Studio Deluxe	Desert Sand	6977	TF
020 next	1955	White	Pale Blue	HS10251	TF
020 page right	1956	White	Pale Blue	HS10998	MK
020 bottom	1955	White Amp	Pale Blue	AS00001	PT
022 top	1946	Model 26	Woddie	238	PT
022 middle	1946	Professional	Woddie	501	PT
022 bottom	1947	Dual Professional	Tweed	none	PT
023 left	1946	Princeton	Woodie	none	PT
023 centre	1946	Model 26	Woodie	none	PT
023 right	1946	Professional	Woodie	501	PT
024 full page & 25	1948	Dual 8 Professional	Dark	D405	SS
027 bottom	1955	Stringmaster	Blond	00480	BF
029 middle	1959	400	Desert Sand	00573	MK
030 bottom	1962	1000	Sunburst	00795	SS
032 full page	1952	Esquire	Blond	3454	BF
033 left	1950	Esquire (pine body)	Black	0129	CG
034 left	1949	1st prototype Esquire	White	none	JHL
036 left	1949	2nd prototype Esquire	Natural – Pine	none	GB
037 left & centre	1949	2nd prototype Esquire	Natural – Pine	none	GB
037 right	1950	Broadcaster	Blond	0653	J5
038 top	1950	Broadcaster	Blond	0239	JH
039 left	1950	Broadcaster	Blond	0661	MKS
039 centre	1950	Broadcaster	Blond	0573	PS
039 right	1950	Broadcaster	Blond	0239	JH
040 bottom	1952	Esquire	Blond	3454	BF
042 top two	1948	Champion 800	Green Tweed	659	PT
042 bottom two	1949	Champion 600	Two-Tone Leatherette	143	PT
043 left	1947	Pro-Amp	Tweed	none	PT
043 centre	1951	Princeton	Tweed	2099	PT
043 right	1950	Deluxe	Tweed	SL2705	PT
044 bottom	1952	Esquire	Blond	3454	BF
045 left	1952	Telecaster	Blond	4510	PS
045 next	1952	Esquire	Blond	1556	JH
045 next	1958	Telecaster	Blond	29830	PS
045 right	1955	Esquire	Blond	10586	MKS
045 bottom	1952	Esquire	Blond	3454	BF
047 right	1957	Telecaster	Sunburst	n/a	NH
048 full page	1962	Telecaster	Blond	n/a	VR
049 right	1963	Telecaster	Blond	L11285	AM
050 left	1959	Esquire (l/h)	Blond	38276	NG
050 right	1963	Telecaster Custom	Sunburst	97823	AM
051 right	1960	Telecaster	Fiesta Red	52846	BF
054 left	1964	Telecaster Custom	Sunburst	L52387	MD
054 right	1960	Telecaster Custom	Sunburst	50632	AM
055 left	1963	Telecaster Custom	Sunburst	97823	AM
055 right	1962	Esquire Custom	Sunburst	77833	JN
056 top left	1950	Broadcaster	Blond	0573	PS
056 top centre	1953	Telecaster	Blond	4902	VR
056 top right	1959	Esquire Custom	Sunburst	39734	AM

Page Position	Year	Model	Color	Serial Number	Owner
056 bottom left	1963	Telecaster Custom	Sunburst	97823	AM
056 bottom middle	1966	Telecaster	Candy Apple Red	159311	JS
056 bottom right	1970	Telecaster	Blond	346604	MW
057 right	1960	Telecaster	Fiesta Red	52846	BF
058 top & middle	1952	Deluxe	Tweed	6400	PT
059 left	1954	Pro-Amp	Tweed	5475	PT
059 middle	1952	Deluxe	Tweed	6400	PT
059 right	1954	Champ-Amp	Tweed	7493	PT
060 full page	1955	Precision Bass	Luar Green	7463	JM
061 right	1953	Precision Bass	Blond	0107	BF
062 left	1951	Precision Bass	Blond	0386	AM
065 left	1951	Precision Bass	Blond	0386	AM
065 right	1953	Precision Bass	Blond	0107	BF
066 left	1954	Precision Bass	Blond	1286	AM
066 right	1957	Precision Bass	Blond	19731	AM
067 left	1955	Precision Bass	Luar Green	7463	JM
067 right	1955	Precision Bass	Eggshell (g/h) (g/p)	7700	AM
068 left	1955	Precision Bass	Sunburst	8665	AM
069 left	1955	Precision Bass (l/h)	Sunburst	0653	AM
069 centre	1955	Precision Bass	Sunburst	8665	AM
069 right	1958	Precision Bass	Sunburst (g/p)	35213	AM
071 right	1958	Precision Bass	Sunburst (g/p)	35213	AM
072 right	1957	Precision Bass	Blond (g/p)	022938	AM
073 right	1959	Precision Bass	Blond (g/p)	41249	AM
074 left	1960	Precision Bass	Olympic White (g/h)	45735	AM
074 centre	1963	Precision Bass	Fiesta Red	94332	JL
074 right	1964	Precision Bass	Burgundy Mist	L16336	JL
075 left	1955	Precision Bass	Luar Green	7463	JM
075 centre	1957	Precision Bass	Blond	022938	AM
075 right	1963	Precision Bass	Daphne Blue	94888	AM
076 left	1960	Precision Bass	Sunburst	44266	AM
076 centre	1960	Precision Bass (l/h)	Sunburst	56023	EG
076 right	1960	Precision Bass	Black	54570	BF
077 left	1963	Precision Bass	Daphne Blue	94888	AM
077 right	1963	Precision Bass	Sonic Blue	L11718	AM
080 full page	1963	Stratocaster	Inca Silver	n/a	VR
082 bottom	1954	Stratocaster	Sunburst	0564	PS
083 right	1954	Stratocaster	Sunburst	0287	BF
086 right	1957	Stratocaster	Blond (bl/p)	-20271	JM
087 left	1954	Stratocaster	Blue	0656	JM
087 right	1955	Stratocaster	Beige	7016	JM
088 & 089	1956	Stratocaster	Gold (g/h)	15581	JM
090 & 091	1958	Stratocaster	Blond (g/h)	-21526	MKS
092 full page	1956	Stratocaster	Blond	09443	BF
098 left	1955	Stratocaster	Sunburst	8498	AM
099 left	1958	Stratocaster	Sunburst	027941	NG
099 centre	1958	Stratocaster (l/h)	Sunburst	32066	NG
099 right	1962	Stratocaster	Sunburst	75190	MK
100 right	1962	Stratocaster	Sonic Blue	84516	NG
102 left	1963	Stratocaster	Sunburst	L45130	MW
102 next	1962	Stratocaster	Sunburst	75190	MK
102 next	1961	Stratocaster	Sunburst	60092	MW
102 right	1962	Stratocaster	Foam Green	91248	PT
104 right	1962	Stratocaster	Fiesta Red	84102	MKS
105 right	1962	Stratocaster	Candy Apple Red (f/r)	69659	BF
106 left	1964	Stratocaster	Sonic Blue	L30428	MG
106 right	1964	Stratocaster	Olympic White	L34385	MKS
108 top	1960	Bassman	Tweed	BM04018	PT
109 left	1959	Vibrolux	Tweed	F02590	PT
109 centre	1960	Champ	Tweed	C13735	PT
109 right	1960	Bassman	Tweed	BM04018	PT
110 full page	1958	Musicmaster	Desert Sand (g/p)	027844	TF
113 bottom	1956	Musicmaster	Desert Sand (bl/p)	09208	TF
114 left	1958	Musicmaster	Desert Sand (g/p)	027844	TF
114 right	1958	Duo Sonic	Desert Sand (g/p)	-22940	TP
115 left	1960	Musicmaster	Tan	49807	TF
115 next	1960	Duo Sonic	Tan	46969	TP

index of fender equipment

Page Position	Year	Model	Color	Serial Number	Owner
115 next	1962	Musicmaster	Shaded Sunburst	88455	TF
115 right	1962	Duo Sonic	Shaded Sunburst	78593	TP
116 left	1963	Musicmaster	Olympic White (br/p)	L09188	TF
116 next	1963	Duo Sonic	Olympic White (br/p)	L07666	AM
116 next	1964	Musicmaster	Olympic White	L21670	TF
116 right	1964	Duo Sonic	Olympic White	L21498	TP
117 left	1963	Musicmaster	Red Mahogany	L21610	TF
117 right	1963	Duo Sonic	Red Mahogany	L16588	TP
120 left	1966	Musicmaster	Daphne Blue	193229	SC
120 right	1967	Duo Sonic	Daphne Blue	215176	MK
122 left	1965	Mandolin	Firemist Gold	1981	PS
122 centre	1956	Mandolin	Blond (g/p)	00721	JN
122 right	1957	Mandolin	Sunburst (g/p)	00518	SS
123 left	1969	Mandolin	Candy Apple Red	2650	DM
123 right	1970	Mandolin	Sunburst	1333	JN
124 full page	1964	Jazzmaster	Sunburst	L66410	MK
125 right	1959	Jazzmaster	Sunburst (g/p)	38856	JH
128 left	1958	Jazzmaster	Blond (g/p)	31734	BF
129 left	1958	Jazzmaster	Gold (g/p)	32693	BF
129 centre	1958	Jazzmaster	Red (g/p)	32908	BF
129 right	1958	Jazzmaster	Sunburst (g/p)	32256	JM
130 left	1962	Jazzmaster	Sunburst	71557	AM
132 top	1964	Jazzmaster	Sunburst	L66410	MK
134 left	1959	Jazzmaster	Sunburst	42052	TF
134 centre	1962	Jazzmaster	Black	86810	MK
134 right	1963	Jazzmaster	Lake Placid Blue	L37558	MK
135 right	1963	Jazzmaster	Shell Pink	L30403	BF
136 left	1961	Jazzmaster	Fiesta Red	70445	BF
136 centre	1961	Jazzmaster	Inca Silver	60167	BF
136 right	1959	Jazzmaster	Blond	38158	BF
137 left	1963	Jazzmaster	Candy Apple Red	L27095	BF
137 centre	1965	Jazzmaster	Olympic White	38862	BF
137 right	1963	Jazzmaster	Lake Placid Blue	L37558	MK
138 all 4 pictures	1964	Jazzmaster	Sunburst	L66410	MK
139 left & centre	1964	Jazzmaster	Candy Apple Red (g/h)	L44444	AM
139 right	1963	Jazzmaster	Dakota Red	L07489	BF
141 bottom	1962	Jazzmaster	Shoreline Gold	82357	MK
142 top	1960	Super-Amp	Brown Tolex	00121	PT
143 left	1961	Pro	Brown Tolex	03840	PT
144 right	1960	Super	Brown Tolex	00121	PT
144 full page	1965	Jazz Bass	Burgundy Mist (d/b)	128725	BF
146 left	1960	Jazz Bass	Blond	51038	JL
147 left	1960	Jazz Bass	Sunburst	55220	AM
147 right	1964	Jazz Bass	Sunburst	L22686	AM
149 left	1962	Jazz Bass	Fiesta Red	77950	JL
149 centre	1965	Jazz Bass	Firemist Gold	114050	PS
149 right	1965	Jazz Bass	Candy Apple Red	L41750	AM
150 right	1965	Jazz Bass	Foam Green	L80489	AM
151 left	1960	Jazz Bass	Blond	57392	NG
151 right	1962	Jazz Bass	Fiesta Red	77950	JL
152 & 153 left	1962	Showman	Blond Tolex	00702	PT
153 centre	1962	Reverb	Blond Tolex	R02183	PT
153 right	1962	Twin	Blond Tolex	00412	PT
154 full page	1966	Bass VI	Foam Green	149235	AM
156 left	1963	Bass VI	Fiesta Red	L04652	JL
157 left	1962	Bass VI	Sunburst	85489	MM
157 right	1962	Bass VI	Lake Placid Blue	90989	MW
158 left	1966	Bass VI	Foam Green	149235	AM
159 left	1962	Bass VI	Shoreline Gold	80510	PS
159 right	1961	Bass VI	Sherwood Green	71414	AM
160 left	1963	Bass VI	Champagne Sparkle	92125	AM
161 left	1963	Bass VI	Olympic White	L09966	AM
161 right	1963	Bass VI	Fiesta Red	L04652	JL
162 both	1961	Vibrasonic	Brown Tolex	00109	PT
163 left	1961	Concert	Brown Tolex	04375	PT
163 right	1961	Vibrasonic	Brown Tolex	00109	PT
164 full page	1969	Jaguar	Sunburst	271017	JS

Page Position	Year	Model	Color	Serial Number	Owner
167 centre	1962	Jaguar	Sunburst	86389	SS
167 right	1965	Jaguar	Black	L55086	BF
168 left	1965	Jaguar	Sherwood Green	L97087	BF
170 left	1965	Jaguar	Inca Silver	L95951	BF
171 left	1963	Jaguar	Blond	L13913	SS
171 centre	1965	Jaguar	Fiesta Red	L81834	BF
171 right	1964	Jaguar	Olympic White	L63107	BF
172 bottom	1964	Jaguar	Lake Placid Blue	L63207	BF
176 centre	1963	Vibroverb	Brown Tolex	A00128	PT
177 left	1961	Vibrolux	Brown Tolex	01622	PT
177 right	1961	Princeton	Brown Tolex	P00708	PT
178 full page	1968	Villager	Natural – Spruce Top	25495	MK
181 right	1964	Concert	Natural – Spruce Top	01006	JE
184 left	1965	Shenandoah	Natural – Spruce Top	11631	MG
184 right	1968	Villager	Natural – Spruce Top	25495	MK
185 right & 186	1967	Palomino	Natural – Spruce Top	21009	NK
190 bottom left	1962	Reverb	Brown Tolex	R01569	MK
190 bottom right	1962	Reverb	Blond Tolex	R02122	TF
191 top	1962	Reverb	Blond Tolex	R02122	TF
191 bottom left	1963	Reverb	Blond Tolex	R04254	BF
191 bottom right	1965	Reverb	Black Tolex	R06272	TF
192 left	1962	Musicmaster	Tangerine Sparkle	80437	SS
193 left	1958	Jazzmaster	Surfburst Sparkle	33719	VR
193 centre	1965	Jazzmaster	Blue Sparkle (d/b)	130480	VR
193 right	1965	Jaguar	Green Sparkle	L85970	PK
194 left	1964	Tremolux	Blond Tolex	A01882	BF
195 left	1963	BandMaster	Blond Tolex	57821	PT
195 right	1963	Tremolux	Blond Tolex	05438	PT
196 full page	1968	Mustang	Competition Burgundy	243642	BF
197 right	1966	Mustang	Daphne Blue	124837	AM
198 left	1968	Mustang	Dakota Red	247183	SS
198 right	1966	Mustang	Olympic White	139983	SS
199 left	1966	Mustang Bass	Daphne Blue	199932	AM
199 right	1967	Mustang Bass	Dakota Red	209288	SS
200 bottom	1968	Mustang	Competition Burgundy	243642	BF
201 left	1968	Mustang	Olympic White	248462	AM
201 centre	1968	Mustang	Competition Orange	237567	BF
201 right	1968	Mustang	Competition Burgundy	243642	BF
202 left	1969	Mustang Bass	Competition Burgundy	263261	BF
203 left bottom	1968	Mustang Bass	Competition Orange	257655	AM
203 centre	1969	Mustang Bass	Competition Red	294730	SS
207 left	1965	Bassman	Black Tolex	A10297	PT
207 centre	1965	Pro Reverb	Black Tolex	A02270	PT
207 right	1966	Deluxe Reverb	Black Tolex	A17144	PT
209 right	1966	Jaguar	Sunburst (d/b)	140182	MW
210 left	1966	Stratocaster	Sunburst	177255	AM
210 right	1966	Stratocaster	Candy Apple Red	125875	AM
211 right	1966	Telecaster	Candy Apple Red	159311	JS
214 left	1966	Marauder prototype	Lake Placid Blue	none	DR
215 right	1966	Marauder prototype	Sunburst	n/a	GG
216 full page	1966	Electric XII	Blue Ice	138140	MK
217 right	1965	Electric XII pre-production	Firemist Gold	L70888	PK
218 right	1965	Electric XII	Sunburst	106470	MW
219 left	1966	Electric XII	Olympic White	134554	MK
219 centre	1965	Electric XII	Sonic Blue	L48943	BF
219 right	1966	Electrix XII	Fiesta Red	137425	BF
221 left	1966	Electric XII	Candy Apple Red	130636	MK
221 centre	1965	Electric XII	Sunburst	106470	MW
221 right	1965	Electric XII	Lake Placid Blue	L83915	MK
222 left	1966	Electric XII	Olympic White	134554	MK
224 left	1966	Electric XII	Blue Ice	138140	MK
225 left	1966	Electric XII	Candy Apple Red	177895	JS
225 right	1966	Electric XII	Blue Ice (f/f)	137479	JS
226 left	1966	Slab-Body Precision Bass	Blond	131420	JH
228 full page	1967	Coronado XII	Sunburst	183060	MG

index of fender equipment

Page Position	Year	Model	Color	Serial Number	Owner
231 top left	1966	Coronado XII	Blue Ice	183363	BF
231 top centre	1966	Coronado XII	Cherry Red	181639	MW
231 top right	1967	Coronado XII	Firemist Gold	183424	PS
231 bottom	1967	Coronado XII	Sunburst	183060	MG
232 left	1966	Coronado II	Cherry Red	501580	VR
233 all but centre	1967	Coronado XII	Sunburst	183060	MG
233 centre	1967	Coronado Bass I	Sonic Blue (f/f)	207285	VR
234 right	1968	Coronado II	Antigua	235002	DR
235 left & right	1968	Coronado II	Wildwood II	217314	BF
236 left	1967	Coronado Bass I	Sonic Blue (f/f)	207285	VR
236 centre	1968	Coronado Bass II	Cherry Red	214376	AM
238 left	1965	Bass V	Candy Apple Red	600002	DM
239 detail	1965	Bass V	Candy Apple Red	600002	DM
239 left	1966	Bass V	Ocean Turquoise	600509	AMa
239 right	1967	Bass V	Sunburst	600959	BM
240 left	1966	Jazzmaster	Candy Apple Red	176779	DM
241 left	1968	Jaguar	Sonic Blue	248653	VR
241 right	1968	Jaguar	Lake Placid Blue	234616	MW
242 left	1968	Telecaster Custom	Candy Apple Red	236400	DM
242 next	1972	Precision Bass	Lake Placid Blue	395925	VR
242 next	1971	Precision Bass	Sunburst	320951	VR
242 right	1968	Precision Bass	Charcoal Frost	171274	AM
244 both pictures	1967	Jaguar prototype /custom	Sunburst	240568	BF
246 right	1969	Jazzmaster	Sunburst	252945	SS
247 left	1972	Jaguar	Blond	425761	SS
247 centre	1969	Stratocaster	Olympic White (f/f)	292949	SS
247 right	1972	Telecaster Custom	Candy Apple Red	378460	BF
248 left	1967	Jazz Bass	Lake Placid Blue	169946	AM
248 right	1972	Bass VI	Blond	546072	JS
250 left	1969	Stratocaster	Sunburst	280371	AM
252 left	1969	Rosewood Stratocaster	Rosewood	231697	SS
253 both pictures	1969	Rosewood Telecaster	Rosewood	284678	BF
255 left	1968	Super Reverb	Black Tolex	A27894	PT
255 centre	1968	Vibro Champ	Black Tolex	A19796	PT
255 right	1968	Twin Reverb	Black Tolex	A12468	PT
256 & 257 right	1967	Telecaster prototype	Natural – Spruce/Zebra	206032	AM
258 left	1968	Telecaster Thinline	Sunburst	230556	BF
259 left	1969	Telecaster Thinline	Natural – Ash	267149	AM
259 centre	1970	Telecaster Thinline	Yellow	304796	AM
259 right	1968	Telecaster Thinline	Candy Apple Red	225115	DM
260 left	1969	Telecaster Bass	Blond	298924	AM
262 left	1968	Telecaster Bass	Paisley Red	222248	JH
263 left	1968	Telecaster	Paisley Red	250076	JH
263 right	1968	Telecaster	Blue Flower	248410	DR
264 all pictures	1972	LTD	Sunburst (g/h)	33	BF
265 right	1969	Montego II	Sunburst	n/a	RB
267 right	1967	Bronco	Dakota Red	206453	BF
268 left	1969	Swinger	Daphne Blue	267695	MK
268 right	1969	Swinger	Black	271415	MK
269 left	1969	Swinger	Dakota Red	275146	BF
269 next	1969	Swinger	Olympic White (f/f)	269750	BF
269 next	1969	Swinger	Lake Placid Blue	264596	BF
269 right	1969	Swinger	Candy Apple Red	289481	BF
271 right	1969	Custom	Sunburst	226382	SN
272 bottom	1956	Stratocaster	Blond	09443	BF

All instruments are credited to the owner at the time of being photographed. The following abbreviations stand for: l/h – left-hand model, g/h – gold plated hardware, g/p – gold anodized aluminum pickguard, bl/p – black painted aluminum pickguard, br/p – brown plastic pickguard, d/b – dot and bound fingerboard, f/r – factory refinish, f/f – faded finish.

Fender owners: John 5 J5, Roy Acuff Museum RAM, Robin Baird RB, Greg Bayles GB, Sarah Cracknell SC, Mark Duncan MD, Jim Elyea JE, Brian Fischer BF, Terry Foster TF, Eli Gabrieloff EG, Nadav Galimidi NG, Cher Garriot CG, Gruhn Guitars, Nashville GG, Music Ground MG, Jan Hallquisth at Halkan's Rockhouse, Stockholm JH, Johnny Hanley JHL, Norman Harris at Norman's Rare Guitars, LA NH, Mikael Karlsson MKS, Martin Kelly MK, Noah Kelly NK, Paul Kelly PK, John Ludlow JL, Anthony Macari at Macari's Music, London AMa, Max Martin MM, Joe Menza JM, Dave Merlane DM, Albert Molinaro AM, Barry Moorhouse at the Bass Centre, London BM, Steven Najemian SN, John Nelson at Vintage Gear, Hollywood JN, Tim Pershing TP, Dave Rogers at Dave's Guitar Shop, La Crosse DR, Scott Silver at Chicago Music Exchange SS, James Stevenson at Angel Music, London JS, Hno3 Production AB PS, Perry Tate PT, Vintage & Rare Guitars, London and Bath VR, Mike Waiter MW

picture credits

All photography is by Paul Kelly unless otherwise stated.

All Fender ephemera came from the collections of Terry Foster and Martin Kelly.

The publishers would like to acknowledge and thank the following for kindly allowing their photographs to be part of this book.

Accent Records 218 above, **Balafon Image Bank, courtesy of Tony Bacon and Nigel Osborne** 215, 239 above right), 265, **Carl Dunn** 239 below left, **David Swartz for the book Norman's Rare Guitars** 47 right, **Flair Photography Bill Francis** 98 right, **fotobaron.com Baron Wolman** 224 below right, **Getty Images** Michael Ochs Archives 49 left, 93, 101, 251 above; Redferns/CA 169 right; Redferns/Chris Morphet 226 right; Redferns/GAB Archive 64; Redferns/Gilles Petard 40 above; Redferns/Ivan Keeman 183 below; Redferns/Jan Persson 160 above, 202 below right; Redferns/Val Wilmer 250 right, **Joe Menza** 66 above, **John Peden** 33, 34, **PoPsie courtesy and copyright Michael Randolph** 251 below left, **Rex Features, Daily Sketch** 252 right, **Richard Smith** 9, 11 all, 15, 35 above & below, 36 above right & centre right, 63 below, 83 left, 127 below, 128 right centre, **Robert Perine, used by permission of Blaze Newman, who retains copyright** 5, 26 below, 52 left & right, 53 below, 55 below left, 84 below left, 94-95, 112 above & below, 128 below, 140, 148 below, 166 above left & below, 181 left, 182 left, 183 above left & right, 186 above, 188, 193 below, 197 left, 198 left, 206 above, 212 left, 213 above & below, 220 left, 230 all, 237 all, 246 all left, 247 all below, 266, **Terry Foster Archive** 28 below, 41 all, 62 above right, 71 below left, 72 above left, **Tim Mullally courtesy of Dave's Guitar Shop, La Crosse** 214 left, 234 right, 263 right.

bibliography

Babiuk, Andy *The Story Of Paul Bigsby: Father Of The Modern Electric Solidybody Guitar* Hal Leonard Corporation 2009
Bacon, Tony and Paul Day *The Fender Book* Balafon Books 1992 and 1998 editions
Bacon, Tony and Barry Moorhouse *The Bass Book* Balafon Books 1995
Bacon, Tony *50 Years Of Fender* Balafon Books 2000
Bacon, Tony *Six Decades Of The Fender Telecaster* Backbeat Books 2005
Bacon, Tony *The Fender Electric Guitar Book* Backbeat Books 2007
Baños, Nachos *The Black Guard* Ignacio Baños, www.theblackguardbook.com 2005
Black, J.W. and Albert Molinaro *The Fender Bass* Hal Leonard Corporation 2001
Carson, Bill and Willie G. Moseley *My Life And Times With Fender Musical Instruments* Vintage Guitar Books 1998
Duchossoir, Andre *The Fender Stratocaster* Hal Leonard Corporation 1989
Duchossoir, Andre *The Fender Telecaster* Hal Leonard Corporation 1991
Fullerton, George *Guitar Legends: The Evolution Of The Guitar From Fender To G&L* Centerstream Publishing 1993
Gruhn, George and Walter Carter *Gruhn's Guide To Vintage Guitars* Miller Freeman Books 1991 and 1999 editions
Gruhn, George and Walter Carter *Electric Guitars and Basses* Miller Freeman Books 1994
Harris, Norman and David Swartz *Norman's Rare Guitars* Swartz Inc 1999
Iwanade, Yasuhiko *The Galaxy Of Strats* Rittor Music Inc 1998
Matthews, Barry *Fender Bass For Britain* Authorhouse 2009
Morrish, John *The Fender Amp Book* Balafon Books 1995
Pittman, Aspen *The Tube Amp Book* Groove Tubes 1991 and Backbeat Books 2003 editions
Roberts, Jim *How The Fender Bass Changed The World* Backbeat Books 2001
Smith, Richard *Fender: The Sound Heard 'Round The World* Garfish Publishing/Hal Leonard Corporation 1995
Teagle, John and John Sprung *Fender Amps: The First Fifty Years* Hal Leonard Corporation 1995
Werner, James D. *Werner's List: Volume Twenty Two* James D. Werner private press 1998
Wheeler, Tom *American Guitars: An Illustrated History* Harper & Row Publishers 1982
Wheeler, Tom *The Stratocaster Chronicles* Hal Leonard Corporation 2004
Wheeler, Tom *The Soul Of Tone* Hal Leonard Corporation 2007
White, Forrest *Fender: The Inside Story* Miller Freeman Books 1994

acknowledgments

Thank you friends...

Firstly and most importantly we would like to thank the owners of all the fine Fender instruments featured within these pages. Every single person that generously gave their time, trust and belief to this project, without you this book simply would not exist.

In no particular order: Brian Fischer, Albert Molinaro, Peter Svensson, Joe Menza, Scot Silver, Perry Tate, John Ludlow, Tim Pershing, Nadav Galimidi, Jan Hallquisth, Mikael Karlsson, Dave Merlane, Vintage & Rare, James Stevenson, Mike Waiter, Dave Rogers, John 5, Greg Bayles, Jim Elyea, John Nelson, Max Martin, Sarah Cracknell, Noah Kelly, Anthony Macari, Roy Acuff Museum, Cher Garriot, Mark Duncan, Johnny Hanley, Barry Moorhouse, Steven Najemian, Gruhn Guitars and Norman Harris.

Louise Chandler – editor
Lora Findlay – typsetting
Ann Harrision – legal advice and support
Mathew Clayton – commisioning editor
Ian Mitchell – for getting the ball rolling

Special thanks to Jim and Pam Elyea at History for Hire in LA for the loan of their remarkable space, their patience, hospitality and knack of smoothing the path.
Brian and Stephanie Fischer, the perfect hosts, generous to a fault.
Albert Molinaro for the loan of his fantastic guitars and Andy Jackson and Mike Roberts for helping Albert deliver them.
Sage Kobayashi – for making sure all the guitars in LA were in top top shape.
Joe Menza and family – we hope we didn't outstay our welcome.
Scott Silver – for offering us access to his fantastic collection at incredibly short notice.
Perry Tate – it was worth two speeding tickets to see your collection.
We would also like to thank Tony Bacon, Paul Day and Nigel Osborne for their encouragement and support from the off – thanks for believing!

Richard Smith – for information, advice and encouragement.
Blaze Newman – for opening up her fantastic archive to us.
John Peden – for supplying the "missing" pictures.
David Swartz – 1957 two-tone Sunburst Telecaster picture.
Tim Mullally – LPB Marauder, Antigua Coronado and Blue Flower Telecaster pictures.

Andy Hackett, James Stevenson and Noah Kelly at Angel Music. Danny Boucher at Premier Music Services. Richard Henry at Richard Henry Guitars Ltd. Chris Trigg, Adam 'Flea' Newman, Andy Lewis, Joe Light, 'Little' Barrie Cadogan, Martin Brown and Simone Butler at Vintage and Rare in London. Anthony Macari at Macari's Musical Instruments. Justin Harrison, Rick Harrison and Crispin Weir at Music Ground. Eliot Michael at Rumble Seat Music. Jeff Barrett, Robin Turner, Andrew Walsh and all at Heavenly. Nick Dewey, John Niven, Ryland Fitchett, Robb Lawrence, Phil Kubicki, Gene Fields, Steve Soest, Zeke Zimgiebel, Andy Lewis, Ian Thompson, Paddy Lowe, Celeste Kelly, Joe Mee, Pete Kaperonis, Alan Rogan, Clive Brown, Wunjo Guitars, Jeff Baker, Bob Hewitt, Michael Bayley Huges, Dave Hunter, Naoko Doi, Adam Landry, Peter G. Merritt, The Brozeski Family of Oil City PA, Dani Kaplan, Jeremy Boyd, Dave Brolan and Phil King. Jason Farrell, Kristy Swanson and everyone at the Fender Musical Instruments Corporation – still the greatest electric guitar maker in the world. Denise Bates, Laura Price, Tracey Smith, Georgina Atsiaris, Caroline Alberti, Pene Parker, Gary Almond, Leanne Bryan, Karen Baker and all at Octopus – Cassell Illustrated.

Plus a special thanks from Paul to Debsey, Sadie and Donovan.

Some credit must also go to the good people at Ebay, without whom the Fender ephemera collections of messrs Terry Foster and Martin Kelly would not be imaginable.

Finally, thanks to Leo Fender, Don Randall, Doc Kauffman, Freddie Tavares, Forrest White, George Fullerton, Roger Rossmeisel, Bob Perine and everyone who ever worked at Fender during the Golden Age – your work lives on!

www.vintageguitarbooks.com